HIGHLIGHT 7

Mittelschule Bayern

für R-Klassen

Cornelsen

HIGH**LIGHT**

Mittelschule Bayern
Band 7
für R-Klassen

Konzepterarbeitung von
Susan Abbey, Nenagh, Irland
Wolfgang Biederstädt, Köln
Frank Donoghue, Nenagh, Irland

Erarbeitet von
Sydney Thorne, York
Susan Abbey, Nenagh, Irland
Frank Donoghue, Nenagh, Irland

in Zusammenarbeit mit der Englischredaktion
Klaus Unger (Projektleitung);
Silvia Wiedemann (koordinierende Redakteurin);
Karin Wedepohl

Vokabelanhang
Ingrid und Georg Raspe, Düsseldorf

Beratende Mitwirkung
Matthias Fischer, Aschaffenburg
Barbara Gehlhaar, München
Sabine Schaffer, Würzburg
Dr. Christoph Vatter, Donaustauf

Umschlaggestaltung
Cornelsen Verlag GmbH, Berlin, unter
Verwendung der Entwürfe von Klein & Halm
Grafikdesign, Berlin

Layoutkonzept
finedesign – Büro für Text & Gestaltung, Berlin;
designcollective, Team für Mediengestaltung,
Berlin

Layout + technische Umsetzung
designcollective, Team für Mediengestaltung,
Berlin

www.cornelsen.de

1. Auflage, 1. Druck 2019

Alle Drucke dieser Auflage sind inhaltlich
unverändert und können im Unterricht nebeneinander
verwendet werden.

© 2019 Cornelsen Verlag GmbH, Berlin

Das Werk und seine Teile sind urheberrechtlich geschützt. Jede Nutzung in anderen als den gesetzlich zugelassenen Fällen bedarf der vorherigen schriftlichen Einwilligung des Verlages. Hinweis zu §§ 60 a, 60 b UrhG: Weder das Werk noch seine Teile dürfen ohne eine solche Einwilligung an Schulen oder in Unterrichts- und Lehrmedien (§ 60 b Abs. 3 UrhG) vervielfältigt, insbesondere kopiert oder eingescannt, verbreitet oder in ein Netzwerk eingestellt oder sonst öffentlich zugänglich gemacht oder wiedergegeben werden. Dies gilt auch für Intranets von Schulen.

Soweit in diesem Lehrwerk Personen fotografisch abgebildet sind und ihnen von der Redaktion fiktive Namen, Berufe, Dialoge und Ähnliches zugeordnet werden oder diese Personen in bestimmte Kontexte gesetzt werden, dienen diese Zuordnungen und Darstellungen ausschließlich der Veranschaulichung und dem besseren Verständnis des Buchinhalts.

Im Lernmittel wird in Form von Symbolen auf eine CD bzw. DVD verwiesen; diese enthalten – bis auf die Hör- bzw. Hörsehverstehensübungen – ausschließlich optionale Unterrichtsmaterialien. Die CD und die DVD unterliegen nicht dem staatlichen Zulassungsverfahren.

Die Mediencodes enthalten zusätzliche Unterrichts- materialien, die der Verlag in eigener Verantwortung zur Verfügung stellt.

Druck: Firmengruppe APPL, aprinta Druck, Wemding

ISBN 978-3-06-033393-6 (Schülerbuch)
ISBN 978-3-06-033832-0 (E-Book)

PEFC zertifiziert
Dieses Produkt stammt aus nachhaltig bewirtschafteten Wäldern und kontrollierten Quellen.
www.pefc.de

Dein Englischbuch enthält folgende Teile:

Unit 1 bis 4	Die vier Kapitel des Buches
Diff-Bank	Weitere Aufgaben – unterschiedlich schwer
Wordbank	Zusätzliche Wörter zu bestimmten Themen
Text file TF	Weitere Lesetexte, passend zu den Units
Skills file SF	Beschreibung wichtiger Lern- und Arbeitstechniken
Language file LF	Zusammenfassung wichtiger Sprachregeln
Vocabulary	Wörterverzeichnis zum Lernen der neuen Wörter
Dictionary	Alphabetisches Wörterverzeichnis zum Nachschlagen (*English-German* und *German-English*)

Die Units bestehen aus diesen Teilen:

Lead-in	Einstieg in die neue Unit
Theme 1 / Theme 2	Neue Themen mit vielen Aktivitäten und Übungen
Story	Eine Geschichte zum Lesen
Focus on language	Texte und Aufgaben zum Entdecken von Regeln und Üben wichtiger Strukturen
Skills training	Hören / Listening (L) – Lesen / Reading (R) – Sprechen / Speaking (S) – Schreiben / Writing (W) – Sprachmittlung / Mediation (M) – Hörsehverstehen / Viewing (V)
Test / Your task	Üben, Vertiefen, Lernfortschritt feststellen

In den Units findest du diese Symbole:

🎧	Hörtexte / Buchtexte auf CD
▶	Filme auf der DVD
⊙	Leichtere Übungen
●	Schwierigere Übungen
Parallel exercise → p.102	Bei dieser Aufgabe gibt es eine leichtere oder schwierigere Variante in der Diff-Bank.
More help → p.98	Hilfen zu einer Aufgabe in der Diff-Bank
More practice 1 → p.97	Weitere Übungen in der Diff-Bank
⊕	www.cornelsen.de/webcodes

Für deine Arbeit mit den Units ist außerdem wichtig:

- Am Anfang jeder Unit findest du eine Liste der angestrebten Kompetenzen. So weißt du, was du nach dieser Unit auf Englisch kannst.
- Unten auf den Unit-Seiten findest du Sätze mit einem grünen Häkchen (✓). Sie zeigen dir, was du nach der Erarbeitung dieser Seite kannst.

INHALT

Unit 1 · I love London

Lerninhalte	*Your task (Lernaufgabe)	Texte
- über Sehenswürdigkeiten in London sprechen - London aus der Sicht von vier Teenagern kennenlernen - einen U-Bahnplan lesen - von seinem Wohnviertel erzählen - sich beim Einkaufen verständigen - im Café bestellen	**Tips for a great day in London** Einen Tag in London planen und die Ideen in einer Präsentation vorstellen (S.26–27) 	**Quiz** *What do you know about London?* (S.8) **Magazine** *Why do we love London?* (S.10) **Advert** *London for teenage visitors* (S.12) **Tube map** *On the Tube* (S.13) **Graphic novel** *Clever Sherlock!* (S.14–16)

*REVISION 1: The simple present

Unit 2 · In Ireland

Lerninhalte	*Your task (Lernaufgabe)	Texte
- Aspekte des Lebens in Irland kennenlernen - über das Leben auf dem Land sprechen - sagen, dass man etwas schon einmal oder noch nie gemacht hat - Ratschläge geben - sich verabreden	**An interview for a chat show** Ein Interview für eine Talkshow vorbereiten und durchführen (S.48–49) 	**Chat** *A new life* (S.32) **Picture story** *This isn't a park!* (S.33) **Newspaper article** *Well done, Molly!* (S.34) **Story** *The country detectives* (S.36–37) **Advert** *Adverts in Clonmel* (S.45)

*REVISION 2: The simple past

Unit 3 · Scotland is different

Lerninhalte	*Your task (Lernaufgabe)	Texte
- Fakten zu Schottland erfahren - sich mit dem Thema „Arbeitslosigkeit" auseinandersetzen - eine Unterkunft telefonisch buchen - höflich sein - sagen, wem etwas gehört - über unbestimmte Mengen sprechen	**An English website for a German B&B** Eine Website für eine Pension erstellen und ein Buchungsformular entwerfen (S.70–71) 	**Article** *Another Inverness shop closes* (S.54) **Dialogue** *An idea in hard times* (S.55) *A phone call* (S.57) **Website** *Lochside Bed and Breakfast* (S.56) **Jigsaw** *Ghosts don't exist!* (S.58–60) **Festival programme** *Belladrum Tartan Heart Festival* (S.67)

*REVISION 3: The *will*-future

Kompetenzen	Sprache	Seite
**Listening and speaking	Hören und Sprechen:** nach dem Weg fragen und Wegeerklärungen verstehen (S.13); sich am Fahrkartenschalter verständigen (S.23) **Reading	Lesen:** Informationen erfassen (S.8–10, 12); eine Graphic Novel verstehen (S.14–16) **Writing	Schreiben:** Notizen anfertigen (S.11, 21); Vorlagen für eigene Texte nutzen (S.21) **Study skills	Methodentraining:** Wörter nach Themenfeldern sammeln (S.17); mithilfe von Wortbildungsregeln neue Wörter verstehen (S.22) **Mediation	Sprachmittlung:** englische Schilder auf Deutsch erklären (S.17) **Viewing	Hörsehverstehen:** *A London tour* (S.8); *The funny ringtone* (S.24)	**Wortschatz** *London sights, travel in London, clothes, food, my neighbourhood, word building, propword 'one'* **Strukturen** *some/any* und ihre Zusammensetzungen **Aussprache** Doppellaut [aʊ] *****Test and Check!** Wiederholen Lernfortschritt überprüfen	8 28

Kompetenzen	Sprache	Seite
**Listening and speaking	Hören und Sprechen:** Einzelheiten entnehmen (S.31); eine Bildgeschichte verstehen (S.33); Nachrichten am Telefon entgegennehmen und weitergeben (S.35) **Reading	Lesen:** Informationen erfassen (S.32, 34); einen Lesetext verstehen (S.36–38); Kurztexte und Anzeigen verstehen (S.45) **Writing	Schreiben:** Notizen anfertigen (S.35); Sätze verbinden (S.44) **Mediation	Sprachmittlung:** Fragen zu englischen Anzeigen auf Deutsch beantworten (S.45) **Viewing	Hörsehverstehen:** *Welcome to Dublin* (S.31); *Chill in the country* (S.46)	**Wortschatz** *Telephoning, country words, should/shouldn't* **Strukturen** *present perfect, word order* **Aussprache** Wortgruppen bilden, flüssig sprechen *****Test and Check!** Wiederholen Lernfortschritt überprüfen	30 50

Kompetenzen	Sprache	Seite
**Listening and speaking	Hören und Sprechen:** Einzelheiten entnehmen (S.54, 57, 66); eine höfliche Konversation führen (S.57); Zahlen verstehen (S.64); einen Song bewerten; (S.66) seine Lieblingsmusik vorstellen (S.66) **Reading	Lesen:** Informationen erfassen (S.54, 56, 67); eine Geschichte erschließen und Informationen auswerten (S.58–61) **Writing	Schreiben:** ein Formular ausfüllen (S.65); Essgewohnheiten beschreiben (S.63) **Study skills	Methodentraining:** Wörter erschließen (S.65, 67); mit dem Wörterbuch arbeiten (S.65); Skimming (S.67) **Mediation	Sprachmittlung:** Fragen zu einer englischen Webseite auf Deutsch beantworten (S.56) **Viewing	Hörsehverstehen:** *Welcome to Scotland* (S.53); *Tally's video diary* (S.68)	**Wortschatz** *useful words for tourists, being polite, food, music, reflexive pronouns, relative pronouns, numbers over 1000* **Strukturen** *possessive pronouns, much/many* **Aussprache** freundliche Intonation *****Test and Check!** Wiederholen Lernfortschritt überprüfen	52 72

INHALT

USA – here we come

Lerninhalte	*Your task (Lernaufgabe)	Texte
- einen Überblick über die USA gewinnen		

Unit 4 • In the heart of the USA

Lerninhalte	*Your task (Lernaufgabe)	Texte
- über Sehenswürdigkeiten in Memphis, Tennessee sprechen - das Schulleben in den USA kennenlernen - über Essgewohnheiten sprechen - über Feiertage in Deutschland berichten - Vergleiche anstellen - über Kunst sprechen - über das Wetter sprechen - sich beschweren	**A business plan** Einen Businessplan erarbeiten und mithilfe eines Posters vorstellen (S. 94–95)	**Factual text** Burkle Middle School (S. 78) **Official writing** Formal letter (S. 79) Formal email (S. 91) **Leaflet** Memphis middle schools' business competition (S. 81) **Story** Something special (S. 82–84) **DVD cover** Elva and Elvis (S. 90)

Anhänge

PARTNER B-SEITE	96

DIFF-BANK	
Unit 1	97
Unit 2	101
Unit 3	107
Unit 4	112

*TEXT FILE	
London for tourists (Unit 1)	118
A German student in Ireland (Unit 2)	120
Scotland (Unit 3)	122
A year of special days in the USA (Unit 4)	124

*SKILLS FILE	
Vokabeln lernen	126
Unbekannte Wörter verstehen	127
Im Wörterbuch nachschlagen	128
Aus Fehlern lernen	129
Proben und Prüfungen	130
Texte besser verstehen	132
Hören und Notizen machen	133
Eigene Texte schreiben	134
Bilder beschreiben	137
Einen Kurzvortrag halten	138
Mediation	139

Kompetenzen	Sprache	Seite
**Reading and speaking	Lesen und Sprechen:** Bilder und Orte auf einer Karte zuordnen (S.74)		74

Kompetenzen	Sprache	Seite
**Listening and speaking	Hören und Sprechen:** Fotos beschreiben (S.77); Durchsagen verstehen (S.79); einen Dialog auswerten (S. 80); Zustimmung und Ablehnung ausdrücken (S.87); Wettervorhersagen verstehen (S.89) **Reading	Lesen:** eine Geschichte interpretieren (S.82–85); den Aufbau eines DVD-Covers erkennen (S.90); sachliche Schreiben erfassen (S.91) **Writing	Schreiben:** amerikanische und deutsche Schulen vergleichen (S.78); eine formelle Email verfassen (S.91) **Study skills	Methodentraining:** Wortschatz in Listen strukturieren (S.79) **Viewing	Hörsehverstehen:** *Mo's bow ties* (S.92)	**Wortschatz** *school, food, British and American English, weather* **Strukturen** Steigerung mit *more/most* und *less/least* **Aussprache** *British and American English* ***Test and Check!** Wiederholen Lernfortschritt überprüfen	76

LANGUAGE FILE	
Simple present	140
Present progressive	141
Simple past	142
Present perfect	143
Future tenses	144
Wortstellung	145
Mengenangaben *(much/many)*	145
Some/any und ihre Zusammensetzungen	146
Vergleiche	147
Personalpronomen	148
Possessivpronomen	148
Der Plural von Nomen	149
Der Genitiv mit *of*	149

*WORDBANK	
My neighbourhood	150
City and country	151
Music	152
Food	153

VOCABULARY	154
DICTIONARY (English-German)	172
DICTIONARY (German-English)	190
SOUNDS/ALPHABET	205
GRAMMATICAL TERMS	206
LIST OF NAMES	207
LÖSUNGEN DER TEST AND CHECK!-SEITEN	208
QUELLEN	212
IRREGULAR VERBS	214
ENGLISH NUMBERS	215
CLASSROOM ENGLISH	216

*Fakultativ / Nicht verpflichtend

Unit 1
I love London

1 Here are the Houses of Parliament in London. The name of the bell in the clock tower is …
A Big Tom. **B** Big Bill. **C** Big Ben.

2 In books and films Sherlock Holmes is a famous London …
A detective. **B** film star.
C singer.

3 Who lives at Buckingham Palace?
A The King. **B** The Queen.
C The President.

1 What do you know about London?
Do the quiz with a partner. Pick A, B or C. If you don't know the answer, just guess. Then check your answers on page 96.

2 A London tour
a Watch the film and put the names of these famous places together.
1b: Tower Bridge, 2 …

1	Tower	a	Eye
2	The Tower of	b	Bridge
3	St James's	c	Parliament
4	Buckingham	d	Palace
5	The London	e	London
6	The Houses of	f	Park

In dieser Unit lernst du …
- Londons wichtigste Sehenswürdigkeiten kennen.
- Techniken zum Erschließen von neuem Wortschatz anzuwenden.
- Texte im Buch als Vorlage zu nutzen.
- nach dem Weg zu fragen und Wegbeschreibungen zu verstehen.

➜ Am Ende der Unit wirst du in einer Präsentation Ideen für einen spannenden Tag in London vorstellen.

4 On the Tube you can travel by …
A bus. **B** train. **C** car.

6 What's the name of this famous football stadium?
A Westminster. **B** Wimbledon. **C** Wembley.

The London Quiz

5 Tourists are on the London Eye for …
A five minutes. **B** thirty minutes. **C** two hours.

7 In London, buses are red and taxis are … **A** red. **B** yellow. **C** black.

b Now check your answers with a partner.

c Watch the film again. What's the right information?
1. Buses are free for London people under 14/16.
2. The best bus for tourists is bus number 11/21.
3. Tower Bridge can open for big boats/buses.
4. St James's Park is a great place for a break/game.
5. Buckingham Palace has 775 windows/rooms.
6. The London Eye is 35/135 metres high.

More practice 1 → p. 97   Workbook 1–2 → p. 3

➜ Ich kann über Sehenswürdigkeiten in London sprechen. ✓

THEME 1

Young Londoners

buzz — A magazine for Fulham and Hammersmith

Why do we ♥ London?

By our young reporter, Sam Holmes.

What do young Londoners really think of their city?

I've lived in London all my life and I love it here! There are so many things to do here! But what's good about London? And what is not so good? I asked some of my friends.

Sam Holmes

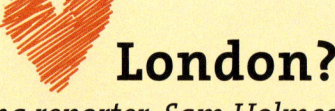

Ruby Patel

I love fashion. In London you can see the new fashions before they're in the magazines. And London's shopping centres and markets are great for clothes. The markets are cheaper – and really cool. I think Camden Market is best.

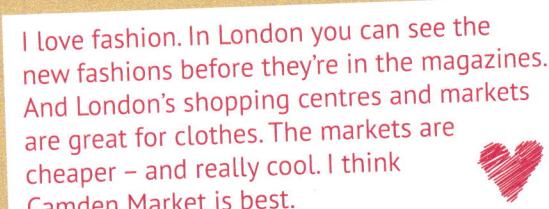

Tally O'Connor

I love the different cultures in London. My mum is Greek (my real name is Talia – that's Greek.) My dad is half Irish and half Scottish. With so many different cultures in London, the food, the music and the concerts are great. But I'm not allowed to go to any concerts without mum or dad.

Alfie Harper

What's good? The people here are very friendly. I came to London two years ago, and I soon found good friends. And we have two big football clubs near where I live – Chelsea and Fulham. I'm a Chelsea fan. (My friend Tally is a Fulham fan, but nobody is perfect!) What's not so good? London is noisy. And very expensive.

Ich kann Zeitschriftentexte verstehen.

1 A text about London

a 👥 Answer with a partner: Who wrote the text? Who will read it? Does the text have …
1 a title?
2 an introduction?

b Look at your answers in **1a** and decide: Is this text …
A a blog?
B an article for a magazine?

2 Sam, Ruby, Tally and Alfie

a 🔵 Match sentences A–D with Sam, Ruby, Tally and Alfie.

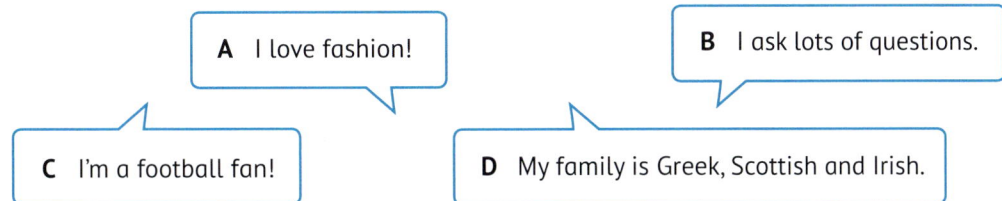

A I love fashion!
B I ask lots of questions.
C I'm a football fan!
D My family is Greek, Scottish and Irish.

b True (✔) or false (✘)?
1 Sam is a reporter for BUZZ.
2 Ruby is interested in clothes.
3 She doesn't like markets.
4 Tally likes the food from different countries.
5 She goes to concerts alone.
6 Alfie only sees good things in London.

c 👥 Who would you like to meet? Why? Talk to a partner.
Partner A Who would you like to meet?
Partner B I'd like to meet Ruby. She likes clothes, and I like clothes too. What about you?
Partner A I'd like to meet … because …

3 Four cool places in London 🎧 1.01

a Four young people talk about cool places in London: Piccadilly Circus, Abbey Road, The Tate Modern and the V&A. Listen and say if sentences 1–6 are true or false.
1 In Piccadilly Circus you can see acrobats and animals.
2 It's a busy place.
3 Beatles fans like to go to Abbey Road.
4 The Tate Modern is a theatre.
5 V&A is short for Victoria and Anthony.
6 The V&A is a museum of fashion.

b Listen again. Why are the four places cool? Make notes in English or in German.

More practice 2 → p. 97

1 Verwende Symbole und Abkürzungen, z.B. + für „und".
2 Mache nur Stichwörter, schreibe keine ganzen Sätze.

Workbook 3–4 → p. 4

➡ Ich lerne London aus der Sicht von vier Teenagern kennen. ✓   eleven   **11**

THEME 2

London for teenage visitors

A

The London Dungeon

Fun, exciting – and scary!

History without the boring bits!

Tube: *Waterloo*

B

Chelsea stadium tours – Stamford Bridge

See the dressing rooms and walk through the players' tunnel. Book a tour and visit the museum.

Tube: *Fulham Broadway*

C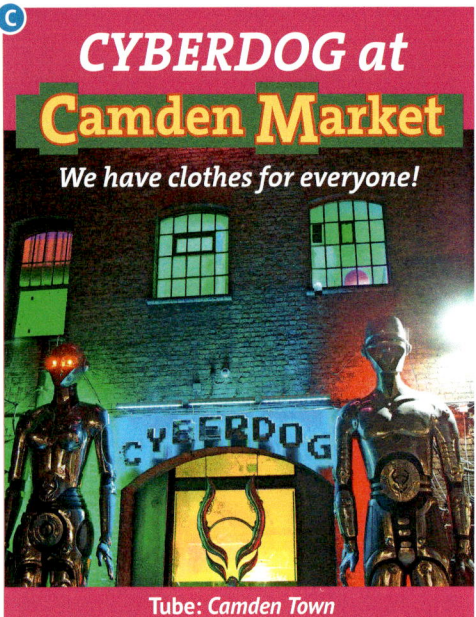

CYBERDOG at Camden Market

We have clothes for everyone!

Tube: *Camden Town*

D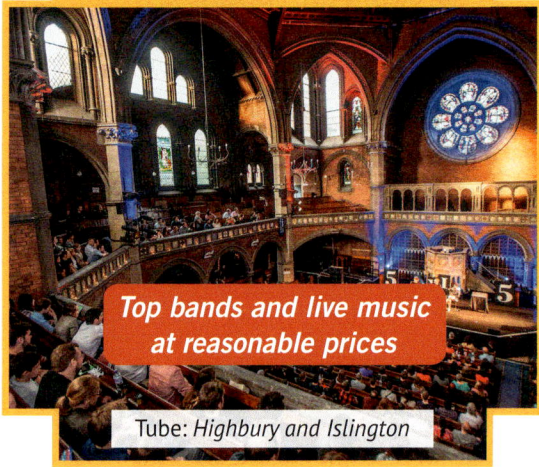

UNION CHAPEL

Top bands and live music at reasonable prices

Tube: *Highbury and Islington*

E

Oyster Card

It's cheaper and easier to travel on the Tube or by bus if you buy an **Oyster Card**.

F **OXFORD STREET**

- Britain's favourite high street.
- More than 300 shops.
- One of the busiest streets in Europe.

1 London adverts
Match the adverts A–F with these four topics: music, shopping, sport, transport.
Which advert doesn't fit?

More practice 3 → p. 97

2 On the Tube
a Look at the Tube map. Find Victoria Station. What lines is it on? *It's on the Circle Line, the …*

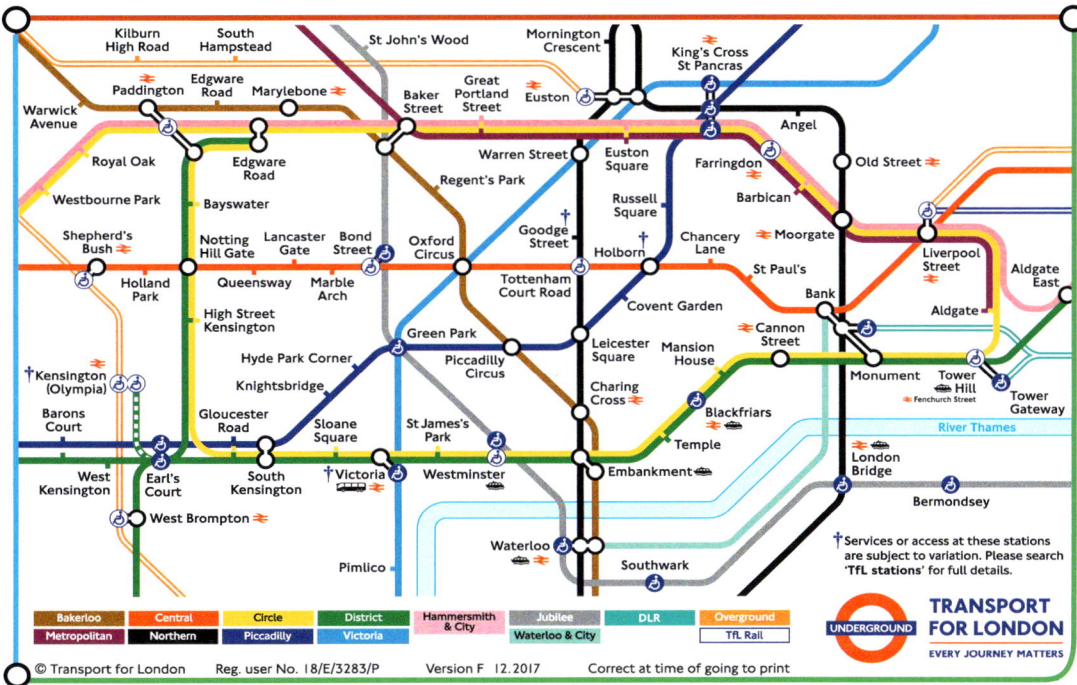

b Two journeys by Tube
1. You're at Victoria. You want to go to Piccadilly Circus.
   Which tube lines do you take? Where do you have to change?
   I take the … Line and the … I change at …
2. Now you want to go from Victoria to Tottenham Court Road.

3 AND YOU? Using the Tube
a You're at Victoria. Listen to the dialogue and practise it with a partner.
Partner A Excuse me, please. Which line should I take for Queensway?
Partner B You need the Victoria Line.
Partner A Do I have to change?
Partner B Yes, change at Oxford Circus and take the Central Line for Queensway.
Partner A Thanks very much.
Partner B No worries.

b Now you want to go to the London Dungeon. Look at advert A on p.12. What's the Tube station? Ask your partner how to get there. Start at Victoria Tube Station. Use the dialogue in 3a, but change the words in blue. Swap roles.

Workbook 5 → p. 5

➡ Ich kann U-Bahnpläne lesen und nach dem Weg fragen. ✓   thirteen **13**

STORY

1 **Before you read**

Look at the pictures. Where do the friends go? What do they do?

> They get on the Tube.

> They go to a …

> They play …

Clever Sherlock!

1.03 **About me**

My name is Sam Holmes.

5 But everybody calls me 'Sherlock'. Like Sherlock Holmes – the great detective!

My friends call me a geek because I like things like books, history, museums.
10 My friends like shopping, music, football. But I don't like these normal things. They're too – normal!

what my friends like

what I like

1.04 **Saturday plans**

15 So when I met my friends Ruby, Alfie and Tally last Saturday, I wanted to go to the …

I love the dinosaurs
20 there. But of course my friends laughed.

They said:

Ruby wanted to go shopping.

I said: **BORING!** 25

But the others said "OK".
And Tally said, "Oh, come on, Sherlock. It'll be fun."
So I said, "OK."

Disaster on the Tube **1.05** 30

We went to the Tube station in Fulham.

We ran down to our train, but Alfie was too slow. The train left and Alfie was still on the platform.

Poor Alfie! We tried to text him, but our 35
phones didn't work on the Tube.

Then I had an idea.
"We'll get off at the next station and wait for the next train."
And that's what we did. Five minutes later 40
the next train came and Alfie was on it.

He was happy to see us.
"That was very clever, Sherlock," Tally said.
So I was happy too.

Shopping Disaster

So we all went shopping.
But we didn't go to a normal department store. No, we went to …

– the most famous one in London! It is very expensive.

When we went through the door, Ruby said, "We have to go in quickly. They don't like groups of kids here."

Alfie had a rucksack with a football in it. And that was the next disaster.

A security man came and said,

"You aren't allowed to have a rucksack in Harrods. And if you're under 15, you aren't allowed in the shop without an adult."

Then I had an idea. I saw a woman in the shop and I shouted, "MUM, we're here!"
The woman looked surprised.
The security man looked surprised too.

And we left the shop very quickly.
"Very clever, Sherlock," Tally said to me.

Disaster in Hyde Park

So next we went to Hyde Park.

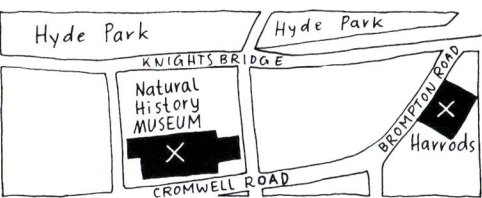

We played football, but we didn't see the teenagers behind a tree.
They had cans of drink with them – and Alfie kicked the football into their picnic!

"Hey, you idiot!" a big boy shouted. "We're keeping your football!"

Then I had an idea.
I went behind a tree and took out my phone.
A LOUD noise came from it – like the noise of a police car.

The teenagers heard it, ran away – and left the football!

"Very clever again, Sherlock," Tally said.
I felt like a million dollars!

1 STORY

In the museum

So we were in Hyde Park with NO money and NO more ideas.

"Erm …" I said. "The Natural History Museum is near here – and it's free."

So we went there.
First we went to see the dinosaurs – and my friends loved them!

And they all loved the earthquake room too. It's great because you can really feel the earthquake there! Everybody loved it.

And now everyone loves the museum – especially Tally.

So I think that I am a clever Sherlock!

2 You choose Do a or b.

a What places are important in the story?
1 a Tube station
2 a hospital
3 a shop
4 a park
5 a post office
6 a museum

b Who thought this in the story? Alfie, Tally, Ruby, Sherlock – or all of them?
1 I want to see the dinosaurs. (p.14)
2 I want to go shopping. (p.14)
3 I can get the next train! (p.14)
4 Sherlock was very clever in *Harrods*. (p.15)
5 Oh thanks, Sherlock. I have my football back. (p.15)
6 The earthquake room is great. (p.16)

More practice 4 → p. 98

3 Why and what? More help → p.98

Copy and complete the sentences.
1 Sam's friends call him *a geek* because …
2 His friends said "BORING!" when …
3 Alfie didn't get on the Tube train because …
4 They had a problem at Harrods because …
5 The teens in the park ran away when …
6 The friends went to the museum because …

More practice 5 → p. 98   More practice 6 → p. 99   Workbook 6–7 → p. 6

Ich kann eine Graphic Novel verstehen.

4 🔊 WORDS Things in the story
Write the words. They are all in the story.

1 b...
2 m...
3 d...
4 p...
5 c...
6 t...

5 WORDS Travel in London
a Copy this table.

transport	people	places
...	...	...

b 🔊 The words in the box are from the story. Write them in your table.
You can put some words in more than one column.

> boy • car • everybody • friends • museum • park • platform • security man • shop • teenager • train • Tube station • woman

c 👥 Write more words for each category in your table – as many as you can.

6 Signs
a Match sentences 1–5 with signs A–D.
You won't need one sentence.
1 Go this way please to try on new clothes.
2 Please take all your rubbish home.
3 Our products are from farms near here.
4 Please only sit at these tables if you buy something here.
5 Adults only. You have to be over 18 to have a drink here.

A IF YOU ARE LUCKY ENOUGH to look under **25** WE WILL ASK YOU FOR ID **TO PROVE** that you are over **18**

B **All our** fruit & vegetables are *locally* grown

b MEDIATION
Erkläre auf Deutsch, was die Schilder bedeuten.

> Übersetze nicht wörtlich.
> Erkläre in deinen eigenen Worten, was die Schilder bedeuten, z.B. bei Schild A: „Hier musst du vielleicht ... zeigen."

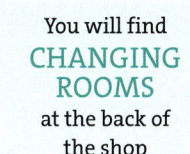

C PLEASE NOTE: These tables are reserved for customers.

D You will find CHANGING ROOMS at the back of the shop

Skills file 11 → p. 139

➡ Ich kann Wörter nach Themenfeldern sammeln. ✓

FOCUS ON LANGUAGE

1 In a department store

a Read or listen to the dialogue. Tally and Ruby are in a department store. What's the problem for Ruby?

Tally   What are you looking for, Ruby?
Ruby   Well, I have some money for a new top. I know markets are cheaper, but I just want to look.
Tally   Look, here are some tops. They're nice.
Ruby   Yes, but this one is really expensive – and there aren't any tops in my size.
Tally   There's a sales assistant over there. You could ask her.
Ruby   Excuse me, do you have any cheaper tops?
Assistant   Yes, there are some cheaper tops over there, next to the changing rooms. They're in our sale.
Ruby   Ah, that sounds better. Thank you. Come on, Tally – let's go and see.

b Copy and complete the sentences from the dialogue.
1 I have … money.
2 Look, here are … tops.
3 There aren't … tops in my size.
4 Do you have … cheaper tops?
5 There are … cheaper tops over there.

> **FOCUS**
>
> **Some und any**
> 1 *Some* bedeutet „etwas" *(some cheese)* oder „einige/ein paar" *(some books)*.
> 2 In verneinten Sätzen verwendest du …
> 3 In Fragen verwendest du …
>
> Language file 9 → p. 146

c Read and complete the rule.

d Choose the right word: some or any.
Tally   Look, these tops are nice.
Ruby   And look, there are some/any really nice jackets here.
Tally   Yes, but they don't have some/any jackets in the sale.
Ruby   That's true, they're all really expensive. But do they have some/any trousers in the sale?
Tally   Yes, some/any trousers are half price.
Ruby   Yes, but they're not my colour.
Tally   Oh, Ruby! You don't want to buy some/any clothes here, remember?

Workbook 8 → p. 7   More practice 7 → p. 99

Ich kann mich beim Einkaufen verständigen.

2 In the department store cafe

a Listen to four dialogues in the cafe. What does the customer eat and drink? Note your answers.

b 🔘 👥 Practise the dialogue with a partner.
Partner A   Can I help you?
Partner B   Yes, I'd like some soup, please.
Partner A   I'm sorry. We don't have any soup.
Partner B   Do you have any fish and chips?
Partner A   Yes, we do.
Partner B   Then I'd like some fish and chips, please.

c 👥 Change the words in orange and practise more dialogues.

3 In other parts of the department store

a Look at the cartoon. What's the problem?

Excuse me. Does anybody here speak German? My dad only speaks German.

I'm sorry, we don't have anybody in this department. Nobody speaks German here. But I know somebody who can help.

b Study the FOCUS-box.

FOCUS

Jemand, niemand, etwas, nichts

1 In Aussagesätzen:
   I saw somebody.   → jemand
   I saw nobody.   → niemand
   I saw something.   → etwas
   I saw nothing.   → nichts
2 In verneinten Sätzen:
   I didn't see anybody. → niemand
   I didn't see anything. → nichts
3 In Fragen:
   Did you see anybody?   → jemand
   Did you see anything? → etwas

c You're in the women's clothes department. Choose the right word.
A   I'm looking for something/nothing (1) for my dad. And do you have nobody/anything (2) for my brother?
B   I'm sorry, we have nothing/anybody (3) for men and we don't have anything/something (4) for boys.
A   Do you have anything/nobody (5) for me then? I need something/anything (6) for the beach.
B   Yes, we have some/any (7) nice bikinis over there.

More practice 8 → p. 99   Language file 9 → p. 146   Workbook 9–10 → pp. 7–8

➡ Ich kann im Café bestellen.   ✓

FOCUS ON LANGUAGE

4 Cycling clothes

Look at the page of an online cycling shop.
Copy and complete the list on the right.
Use the adjective + *one/ones*.

Object	What you prefer
1 helmet	I prefer the green one.

1 Pick your helmet
2 Pick your trousers
3 Pick your shoes
4 Pick your shirt
5 Pick your socks
6 Pick your gloves

FOCUS

Das Stützwort *one*

Im Deutschen kannst du sagen: „Der Kleine, die Große, die Blauen."

Im Englischen brauchst du das Wort *one* (Singular) oder *ones* (Plural) nach dem Adjektiv.

Which helmets do you like?

The white *one*?

Or the red *ones*?

5 PRONUNCIATION Speak good English!

 1.11

a The sound of the red letters in the words below is [aʊ] as in allowed and house.
Listen and repeat the words.
1 allowed, towel, cow, down
2 house, mouse, around, without

b Now say the following words.
Find the odd one out in each line.
1 about, trousers, proud, young
2 town, slow, tower, brown
3 loud, shout, should, pound

Der englische Doppellaut [aʊ] wie in pr<u>ou</u>d und t<u>ow</u>n wird meistens wie das deutsche „au" in „Haus" gesprochen.
Es gibt aber Ausnahmen, z.B. y<u>oung</u> [jʌŋ].

 1.12

c Listen and check.

Workbook 11–14 → pp. 8–10

SKILLS TRAINING Writing

1 Ruby's post about her neighbourhood

a Read Ruby's post.

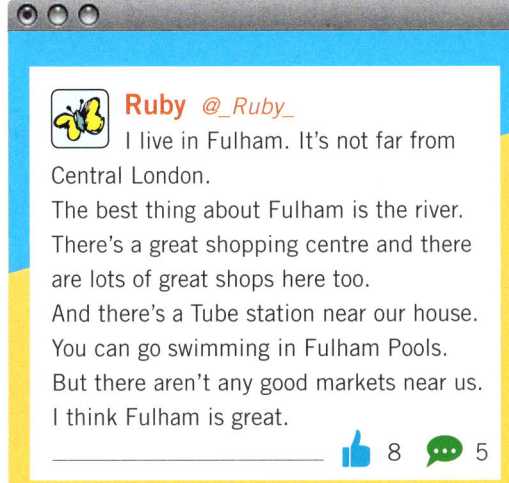

Ruby @_Ruby_
I live in Fulham. It's not far from Central London.
The best thing about Fulham is the river.
There's a great shopping centre and there are lots of great shops here too.
And there's a Tube station near our house.
You can go swimming in Fulham Pools.
But there aren't any good markets near us.
I think Fulham is great.

👍 8   💬 5

b Now make notes for Ruby's post.

1 Place   *Fulham*
2 Best thing
3 There's / There are …
4 You can …
5 What's not so good
6 Final comment

2 Alfie's post about his neighbourhood

Copy and complete Alfie's post. Ruby's post will help you!

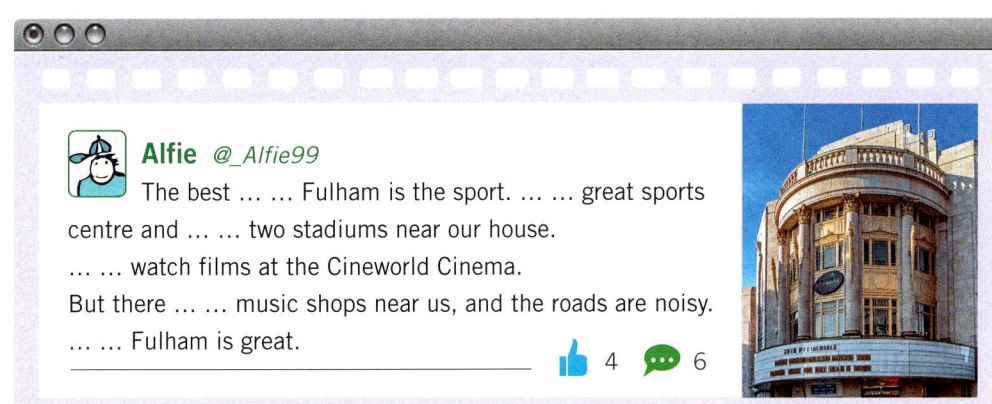

Alfie @_Alfie99
The best … … Fulham is the sport. … … great sports centre and … … two stadiums near our house.
… … watch films at the Cineworld Cinema.
But there … … music shops near us, and the roads are noisy.
… … Fulham is great.

👍 4   💬 6

3 You only have five minutes! `More help` → p.100

How many words can you find in five minutes to complete these sentences?
1 The best thing about our neighbourhood is the river / the sport / …
2 There's a skate park / bus stop / … and there are lots of cafes / two stadiums near our house.
3 You can go shopping / watch films / …
4 But there aren't any parks / music shops / … near us.

`Wordbank 1` → p.150

4 AND YOU?

Write a post about your neighbourhood.
Write at least 40 words.
I live in Augsburg. It's not far from Munich.
The best thing about Augsburg is …

Übernimm die Sätze aus Rubys Blog und ändere sie für deinen Text.

`Skills file 8` → p.134–136   `Workbook 15–16` → p.11

Ich kann Vorlagen für meine eigenen Texte nutzen. ✓

1 SKILLS TRAINING Understanding new words

> Words that you know can help you to understand new words.
> For example you know work.
> So a worker = work + er is someone who works (Arbeiter/in). That's easy!

1 Words with -er

a Match the words 1–4 with the pictures A–D.
1 singer   2 footballer   3 runner   4 diver

 A
 B
 C
 D

b 👥 Decide with a partner what these words in are in German. Then check in a dictionary.
1 driver
2 reader
3 walker
4 writer
5 dancer
6 talker

> Driver comes from *drive*.

> So in German it's …

2 Adjectives with -y

What are the red words in German?

> It will be sunny in the south-east, but rainy and cloudy in the north and west.

> I went hiking in hilly country, and on the way home I felt very sleepy.

1 sun	= *Sonne*	→ sunny	= sonnig
2 rain	= *Regen*	→ rainy	= …
3 cloud	= *Wolke*	→ cloudy	= …
4 hill	= *Hügel*	→ hilly	= …
5 sleep	= *Schlaf*	→ sleepy	= …

3 Opposites with un-

Lauren is the opposite of Natasha. Complete her sentences.

sure – unsure   fit – unfit

1 Natasha is happy.
2 Natasha is friendly.
3 She eats healthy food.
4 She tells interesting stories.
5 But her room is untidy!

1 Lauren is often unhappy.
2 Lauren is …
3 She eats …
4 She tells …
5 But her room is …

Workbook 17 → p.12

More practice 9 → p.101   Skills file 2 → p.127

 Ich kann mit Wortbildungsregeln neue Wörter verstehen. ✓

SKILLS TRAINING Speaking

1 🔘 **Tickets to London**

a Read or listen to the dialogue.
What's the bad news?

Andy Good morning. A ticket to London Euston, please.
Assistant Single or return?
Andy Return, please.
Assistant A return ticket to London is £39. Your next train is at 9.23 on platform 3.
Andy Do I have to change?
Assistant No, it's a direct train to London Euston.
Andy Thank you. Oh, is the train on time?
Assistant Let me see … Oh, I'm sorry. It's an hour late.

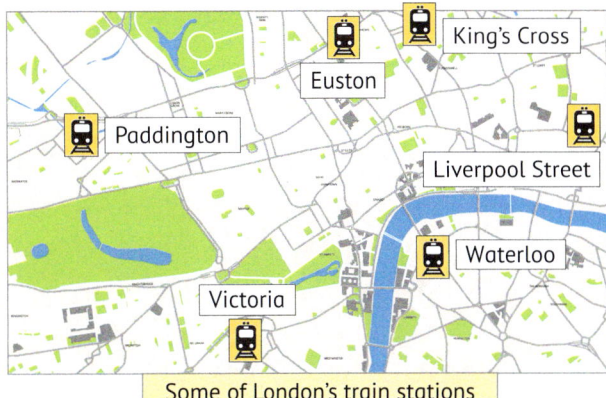

Some of London's train stations

b 👥 Read the dialogue twice with a partner. Try to read fluently.
Not: Is | the | train | on | time? But: Is‿the‿train‿on‿time?

2 **More tickets**

👥 Practise the dialogue with a partner.
Choose your ticket.

Tourist Good morning. A … to London …, please.
Assistant Single or …?
Tourist …, please.
Assistant A … to London … is £… Your next train is at … on platform …
Tourist Do I have to change?
Assistant No, it's a … / Yes, you have to change in …
Tourist Thank you. Oh, is it on time?
Assistant Let me see … Yes, it's … / No, it's about …

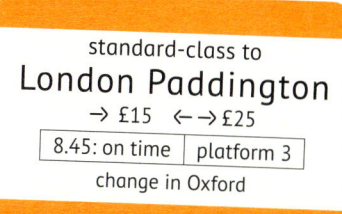

standard-class to
London Paddington
→ £15 ←→ £25
8.45: on time | platform 3
change in Oxford

standard-class to
London Victoria
→ £8.25 ←→ £15
10.10: 10 min late | platform 5
DIRECT

3 👥 **ROLE-PLAY Buying tickets**

Partner A Stay on this page.
Partner B Go to page 96.

a You want a single ticket to Plymouth.
Your partner works at the station.
Act out a role-play.
Note the price and time of your train. Is it on time?
You start: *Good morning. A …*

b Now you're the sales assistant.
Look at the information.
Act out a role-play.

standard-class to
Manchester
→ £11.50 ←→ £20
8.32: 4 min late | platform 5
change in Leeds

Workbook 18–19 → p. 13

➡ Ich kann mich am Fahrkartenschalter verständigen. ✓   twenty-three 23

SKILLS TRAINING Viewing

The kids from London SW6

1 Before you watch

a Look at the film stills.

b **Think** about the three questions:
1 Are the kids in Plymouth or London? How do you know?
2 Who is in the film?
3 Where do the people go in the film: to a shop, a cafe, a park, a stadium, …?

> I think the film is in London because there's a Tube station.

> Yes, I agree. And I can see …

c **Pair** Talk about the questions with a partner. Does he/she agree?

> We think that the film is in …

d **Share** Tell the class what you both think.

2 The funny ringtone

a Watch the film. Then put the photos in the right order.

b Now answer these questions:
What do the friends drink in the cafe?
Where do they go then?
Who has a problem?

c Now watch the film again and check your answers.

3 What can you remember?
Ask your partner three questions about the film.
Can he/she answer them?

Who
- lives in London SW6?
- gives Ruby her phone?
- has a smoothie / some tea?
- buys clothes at Camden Market?
- puts on a hat?
- loses something?

24 twenty-four   ➡ Ich kann eine Filmepisode in London verstehen. ✓

➡ TEST AND CHECK!

> First test yourself.
> Then check your answers on page 208.

1

1 WORDS London words
Copy and complete the sentences with words from the box.

> dinosaurs • earthquake • Eye • minutes • Houses • King • Palace • Queen

1 A trip on the London ... takes thirty ...
2 Big Ben is part of the ... of Parliament.
3 Buckingham ... is the home of the ... or ...
4 See ... or feel an ... in this museum.

2 SPEAKING On the Tube
Jonas is at Victoria and wants to go to Baker Street. He asks for help. Write a dialogue.

Jonas	Excuse me, please. ... line ... for ...?
Woman	... need ...
Jonas	... change?
Woman	Yes, ... and take the Jubilee Line ...
Jonas	...
Woman	...

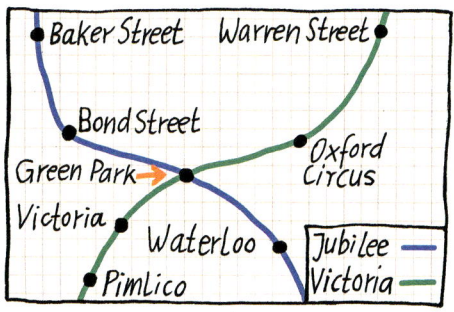

3 LANGUAGE Back home
Choose the correct word.

Noah	Hi there. Is anybody/somebody (1) at home?
Mum	Hello Noah. I'm in the kitchen.
Noah	Hi Mum. Do you know where Lilly is? I need her for my homework.
Mum	She's in town. Can I do anything/something (2) to help?
Noah	I need to write anything/something (3) about ponies.
Mum	Oh, I'm sorry. I know anybody/nothing (4) about ponies. You'll have to wait until Lilly's back home. Are you hungry? I don't have any/some (5) biscuits. But there's any/some (6) cheesecake. Here you are.

Workbook → p.14

➡ Ich kann meinen Lernfortschritt überprüfen. ✓

YOUR TASK

Tips for a great day in London

You are going to give a presentation with tips for a great day in London. Follow steps 1–7.

→ **STEP 1 Find ideas.**
Think of great things to do for young people in London.
You'll find ideas on pages 8–12.
Write at least four ideas.
You can visit …
You should see …
And … is an interesting place.

→ **STEP 2 Share your ideas with a partner.**
Agree on four or more things to do. Write them down.

> I think they should see the shops in Oxford Street. That's fun.

> OK. But the shops in Oxford Street are expensive. They could also take the number 11 bus. That isn't expensive.

> Yes, that's a good idea! And they could also go and see …

→ **STEP 3 Make a plan for the day.**
Make a plan for one full day in London. Decide who will talk about which activities.

In the morning: bus number 11
For lunch …
In the afternoon …
In the evening …

> I'll talk about the morning and lunch, if you like.

> OK. And I'll talk about the afternoon and evening.

→ Ich kann einen Tag in London planen. ✓

STEP 4 Find out more.

- Go to 🌐 (see page 3) and put in: suciqo.
- Find more information about your places or activities, for example:
  - Name of place
  - What can you see or do?
  - When does it open/start?
  - How much does it cost?
  - What's the Tube station?

Look. The concert is in the evening.

Great. So they can go to Oxford Street before the concert.

STEP 5 Make notes.

- Use a system that works for you, for example:
  1. Make notes and learn your talk from your notes.
  2. Write important words on cards and look at the cards when you talk.
  3. Make a wordweb with the important information.
  4. Write the text of your talk and learn it.
- Write a first sentence:
  Hi. I'm going to give you tips for a super day in London.
- Look on the internet and find photos or pictures for your talk.

STEP 6 Practise your presentation.

- Practise your talk out loud.
- Record your presentation and then listen to it.
- Does your presentation sound good?
- 👥 Practise in groups of four. Listen to the others in your group and make a comment.

👥 STEP 7 Give your presentation.

When you talk:
- Look at your class.
- Don't just read from your notes.
- Talk slowly and clearly.
- Explain new words.
- Ask: Do you have any questions?

Do you have any questions?

Skills file 10 → p. 138

→ Ich kann eine Präsentation vorbereiten und vorstellen. ✓

REVISION 1: The simple present

1 Angelo's email

You met a nice boy last week. His name is Angelo and he's Italian.
Angelo doesn't speak German and you don't speak Italian – so you write in English.

a Read Angelo's email.
Does Angelo write about **1** his parents? **2** his pets? **3** his school?

> Hi!
> Thanks for your email and the photos. Your house looks nice!
> I don't live in a house – we live in a flat in Bologna. My dad works five days a week in a home for old people. My mum works from home. I have an older brother, Luigi. He doesn't have a job, but he sometimes helps in a garden centre.
>
> My school is OK, but we get homework every day. Does your school give you lots of homework too?
>
> After school my friends and I usually chat in town. We often listen to music. Do you have a favourite singer? That's all for now. Please write soon!
>
> Angelo

b The simple present
1 Verben nach *I, you, we, they*
Copy four verbs in the simple present: *we … I …*
2 Verben nach *he, she, it* enden auf *-s*.
Copy three examples from the email:
My dad … My mum … He …
3 Verneinungen bildest du mit *don't* oder *doesn't*.
Copy two examples from Angelos's email: *I … He …*
4 Fragen beginnen mit *Do …?* oder *Does …?*
Copy two examples from the email: *Does …? Do …?*

c Now copy and complete these typical time phrases.
1 five days a w___
2 somet___
3 every d___
4 us___y
5 of___

2 Angelo's second email

Language file 1 → p.140

Read the email. Pick the right form of the verb.

> Hi,
> I want/wants (1) to send you a photo of our dog, Mona. She's so cute! She like/likes (2) running in our park. Luigi take/takes (3) her there every morning and I go/goes (4) with her in the evening. Mona often go/goes (5) into the water there because she love/loves (6) swimming.
> We all love/loves (7) Mona.
>
> Angelo

Mona sleeps in the kitchen.

3 Angelo and his family

Read the following sentences. They're all wrong! Look again at Angelo's email.
Then write correct sentences with *don't* and *doesn't*.
1 Angelo and his parents live in a house.
    No, they don't live in a house. They live in a flat.
2 Angelo's parents work in a hospital.
3 Angelo's brother Luigi has a job.
4 Angelo gets homework once a week.
5 Angelo and his friends always go home after school.
6 Mona, Angelo's dog, sleeps in his room.

4 A video chat with Angelo

You have some questions for Angelo.
What are the missing words?

> How • What • When • Where • Who • Why

> Bei Interviews brauchst du meist Fragewörter und das *simple present*. Achtung:
>
> | Where? | = Wo? |
> |---|---|
> | Who? | = Wer? |

You:
1 … does your school begin?
2 … do you go to school?
3 … is your favourite subject?
4 … do you like this subject?
5 … do you have lunch?
6 … are your best friends at school?

Angelo:
At 8.30 am.
I walk.
Art.
Because the teacher is nice.
I have lunch at school.
My best friends are Luciano and Carlo. They're fun!

5 AND YOU?

a Look again at the email in exercise **1**.
Then write an email to Angelo.
Answer his questions.
Write about your family, school and hobbies.
Write as many sentences as you can.

> Use some sentences in ex. 1, 2, and 3 and change them for your text. For example:
>
> We live in a flat.
> → *We live in a flat too.*
> I have an older brother.
> → *I don't have an older brother.*

> *Hi Angelo!*
> *Thanks for your two emails and for the photo of Mona. She's cute!*
> *I have … brothers and sisters.*
> *My dad works in … and my mum …*
> *I go to school in …*
> *We get lots of homework too!*
> *After school …*
> *I like music too. My favourite singer is …*
> *That's all for now. Please …*

b **Partner check:** Show your email to a partner and check your partner's email. Did your partner answer Angelo's questions? Did he/she write about family, school and hobbies?

twenty-nine

Unit 2 In Ireland

Ireland is a country; its capital city is Dublin. **Northern Ireland** is part of the United Kingdom.

1. One third of all Irish people live in the country.

2. Green is the colour of Ireland. Many people wear green on St Patrick's Day, Ireland's national day (17th March).

3. You are never far from the sea in Ireland.

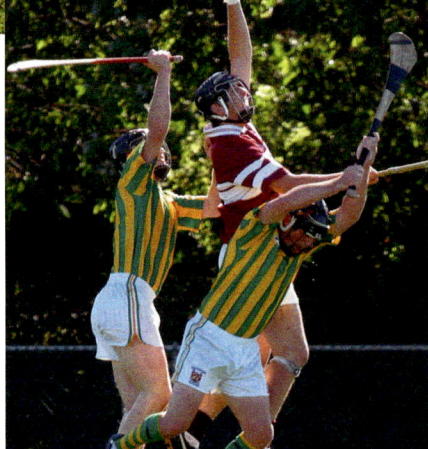

Gaelic football and hurling are popular Irish team games. Hurling is a bit like hockey, but faster!

1 A first look

Look at the pictures here and the map at the beginning of the book. Then read the sentences below. Are they true or false?

1. Most Irish people live in the country.
2. Hurling is an Irish sport.
3. The 17th March is an important day in Ireland.
4. The Atlantic Ocean is west of Ireland.
5. Northern Ireland is part of the country of Ireland.

More practice 1 → p. 101

Busy streets and tall buildings in the centre of Dublin, the capital of Ireland.

In dieser Unit lernst du …
- Aspekte des Lebens in Irland kennen,
- am Telefon etwas auszurichten,
- zu sagen, was du schon einmal oder nie gemacht hast,
- dich zu verabreden.

➡ Am Ende der Unit wirst du ein Interview durchführen.

2 Welcome to Dublin

a **WORDS** What do you think you will see on a tour of Dublin? Write 5–6 ideas.

> big shops • a bridge • busy streets •
> a harbour • a hospital • a market •
> a park • a river • tall buildings

b Watch the film. Tick the things on your list if you see them.

c Read the sentences. Are they true or false?
1 People relax in St Stephen's Green.
2 Grafton Street is great for skating.
3 *Molly Malone* is a song.
4 A shop in Temple Bar has Dublin's best bread.
5 People buy fruit and vegetables in Moore Street.
6 The Jeanie Johnston is an old car.

d Watch the film again and check your answers. Correct the wrong answers.

Molly Taylor lives near Ballypatrick, 145 kilometres south of Dublin.

Ireland uses kilometres, not miles.

3 Meet Molly Taylor

Molly Taylor lives in the country in Ireland.

a Listen to Molly. Does she talk about:
A her family?   B her village?
C places in town?

b Listen again and pick **A** or **B**.
1 Molly lives **A** on a farm. **B** in a town.
2 Molly has a **A** cat. **B** dog.
3 Molly has some new
   A neighbours. **B** pets.
4 Lessons at school are in
   A English. **B** Irish.
5 In Clonmel there's a
   A cinema. **B** swimming pool.

c Check your answers with your partner.

Workbook 1 → p. 16

➡ Ich kann Informationen über Irland verstehen. ✓

THEME 1

In the country

1 A new life

a 🔊 Rob Blake moved from Dublin to the country two weeks ago. Now he is chatting with a friend in Dublin. Read the dialogue. Who is in the photos?

Rob Hey Sean. How are things in Dublin?
Sean Hi Rob. All's good here. And you?
Rob Not so good … There's nothing to do here! But we've bought a dog. His name is Wally. He's great.
Sean Cool!
Rob Dad has already started a new CCTV business. And he has bought a new van. So he's happy.
Sean That's cool.
Rob Mum has found a job in a tennis club. And she has met nice people there. But the village is really small. There's just one shop, one pub, … and that's all!
Sean And have you met some nice girls?
Rob Well, there's a girl on the next farm. I've seen her, but I haven't spoken to her yet. But sorry, Sean, I have to go and cut the grass now. That's life in the country!

A

B

C

D

Sean is an Irish boy's name. You say [ʃɔːn].

b Read the dialogue again and finish these sentences.
1 Sean lives in …
2 Wally is Rob's new …
3 Rob's … has a CCTV business.
4 Rob's village is really …
5 A girl lives on the next …
6 Rob now has to cut the …

More practice 2 → p. 101

c What's new for Rob and his parents? Copy and complete the sentences. *Parallel exercise* → p. 102

> has seen • has found • has bought

1 Rob's dad has started a new business and he … a new van.
2 Rob's mum … a job in a tennis club and she has met nice people there.
3 Rob … a girl on the school bus, but he hasn't spoken to her yet.

2 This isn't a park!

a 🎧 1.16 Look at pictures A–E.
Then listen to **part 1** of the story and put the pictures in the right order.

b 🎧 1.16 Listen again to **part 1** of the story.
Choose the correct answer.
1 Rob and Wally are
   A in a garden. **B** on a track.
2 Wally is running after **A** a sheep. **B** a rabbit.
3 Rob didn't close **A** a gate. **B** a door.

c 🎧 1.17 Now listen to **part 2**.
What's true: **A** or **B** ?
A The girl becomes less angry and tells Rob her name.
B The girl is angry and will tell the police about Rob.

d 🎧 1.17 Listen to **part 2** again.
Choose the correct answer.
1 The girl is
   A 14 **B** 17 years old.
2 She can drive
   A on the farm. **B** in the village.
3 They'll meet again
   A on the farm. **B** on the bus.

Workbook 2–3 → p. 17

➡ Ich kann einem Dialog Informationen entnehmen. ✓   thirty-three **33**

THEME 2

Molly and the sheep

1 Molly is in the newspaper

a Before you read: Look at pictures A–F. What could be the right order? Then read the newspaper article. Were you right?

The police in Ireland are the Garda. Police officers are gardai.

Clonmel Post

Well done Molly!

Last Wednesday Molly Taylor, 14, from the village of Ballypatrick, found three of her family's sheep in the river.
5 First she phoned home, then she walked into the water to help the sheep.
Later Molly said, "It was OK for me because the water wasn't deep. But it was dangerous for the sheep. So I had to work
10 hard." Farmer John Taylor, Molly's father, spoke about his daughter.
"Molly did so well," he said. "I'm proud of her. She saved the sheep. We've never had an accident like this before." Garda
15 Dave Butler said: "We think that dogs ran after the sheep. Dogs mustn't run in fields where there are animals. Please tell us if you have seen dogs near the Taylors' farm."

b You saw a dog in the fields near Ballypatrick. Pick dog A or B. Tell the garda about the dog. Your partner takes the role of the garda.

Garda	What's your name?
You	(give your name)
Garda	Can you spell that, please?
You	(spell your name)
Garda	Thanks. Can you describe the dog, please?
You	Yes. The dog was … It had …

black/white/brown • long/short • legs/tail/ears

More practice 3 → p. 102
Workbook 4–5 → p. 18

2 Can I take a message?

a Read and listen to the dialogue. Can Rob speak to Molly?

Mr Taylor	Hello?
Rob	Oh hello. Is that Mr Taylor?
Mr Taylor	Yes, it is. Who's speaking?
Rob	This is Rob Blake.
Mr Taylor	Sorry, can you say that again, please?
Rob	It's Rob! Can I speak to Molly, please?
Mr Taylor	Ah, Rob! I'm sorry, Molly isn't here. Can I take a message?
Rob	Oh yes, yes please. I read about Molly and the sheep, and I wanted to say 'Well done.'
Mr Taylor	That's very kind of you, Rob. I'll give her your message.
Rob	Great. Thank you. Goodbye.
Mr Taylor	You're welcome. Bye.

b Listen again. Then copy and complete Mr Taylor's notes.

Messages

Who phoned? ....

Wanted to speak to ....

Message *Well done!*

c How can you say these things? Write your answers.
1 Du sprichst am Telefon. Frage, mit wem du redest.
2 Sage, wer du bist.
3 Sage, dass du mit Adam sprechen möchtest.
4 Frage, ob du etwas ausrichten kannst.
5 Sage, dass du die Nachricht weitergeben wirst.

d Now Molly is phoning the Blakes. Act out the dialogue with a partner.

Workbook 6 → p. 19

➡ Ich kann Notizen machen und Nachrichten weitergeben. ✓

thirty-five **35**

2 STORY

 1 Before you read
Listen to the phone call.
Are these sentences true or false?
1 Molly says she needs help.
2 Molly's dad is feeling well.
3 Rob can come now.
4 Rob is unhappy.

The country detectives

 1 The country girl
Rob, Molly and Wally drove along the track. They came to a field with lots of sheep.

Rob opened the gate and the sheep ran into
5 the next field. Molly and her dog Missy came behind them. Then Rob closed the gate.

"You're very good with the sheep, Molly," Rob said. Molly smiled. And Rob smiled too.

He really liked her.

 10 **2 Bags in the bushes**
Suddenly Wally found something in the bushes.

"What is it, Wally?" Rob asked.

Then he saw lots of big bags in the bushes –
15 bags with lots of rubbish in them.

"Molly, look at this," Rob shouted.

"Lots of people leave their rubbish here," she said angrily. "And the Garda can't catch them, because they do it at night."

"I have an idea," 20
Rob answered.
"Dad could put CCTV cameras on your farm. Then you could catch 25
the people!"

3 Lights at night
Rob's dad was interested. He came to the farm on Saturday and put CCTV cameras in different places and a monitor in the farm 30 office.

In the evening Molly's dad still wasn't well, so he had to stay in bed. Molly and Rob watched a film, and then they checked the CCTV monitor. 35

First they saw nothing, but suddenly they saw a fox.
"It has one of our chickens!" Molly shouted. "Come on!"

36   thirty-six

40 They ran quickly to the chickens – but then they suddenly saw car lights!

1.23

4 A clever trick

"Rob," Molly said, "you drive my car. Park at the end of the track, in front of the gate, so
45 they can't drive away. I'll stay here and take a photo of the car number."

"Er, Molly," said Rob. "Last week I told you I can drive …, but I can't really drive!"

"Oh Rob!" she said. "OK, I'll park the car.
50 You stay here and take a photo of the number. Do you have your mobile?"

Rob went to the big black car and took a photo of its number. Then he went back to the farm and waited for Molly.

1.24
55 ### 5 Not so clever really

Later two gardai were at the Taylors' door. They spoke with Molly's mother.

"Good evening. Do you have a car, number 05 TS ▓▓ ▓▓▓ ?"

60 "That's my daughter's car," Mrs Taylor said.

"Is there a problem?"

"Well, yes. We're trying to catch people who leave rubbish on your farm. She parked her car at the end of the track, and we can't go
65 home."

That week there was an article in the Tipperary Post:

New business helps farmers

A new business in Ballypatrick has put CCTV cameras on a farm to
70 catch people who leave their rubbish there. Now lots of other farmers are interested in putting up cameras. "It's a good idea," Garda Butler said.

And Rob messaged Sean: 75

Rob
Molly and I are good friends now.

Sean
Only good friends?

Rob
Well, …

Sean
And what about life in the country?

Rob
It's great! I really like it now 🙂.

STORY

2 **You choose** Do a or b

a Put the pictures in the right order.

b Who was it?
Copy the sentences and put in the missing names.
1 … wasn't well and had to stay in bed.
2 … and … ran along the track to Molly's farm.
3 … found bags of rubbish in the bushes.
4 … put up CCTV cameras on the Taylors' farm.
5 … and … saw a fox and then they saw lights of a car.
6 … wrote down the number of the car and … parked her car at the end of the track.
7 Later two … spoke with …
8 The … couldn't go home because …'s car was in front of the gate.

Look back at the story and check your answers.

> Molly (3x) • Molly's father •
> Molly's mother • Wally (2x) •
> Rob (3x) • Rob's father •
> police officers (2x)

3 **What happened when …?**
Pick the correct endings and write the four sentences.

1 Rob closed the gate		police officers were at her door.
2 Molly was angry	when	they checked the monitor.
3 Rob and Molly saw the fox		the sheep went into the new field.
4 Mrs Taylor was surprised		she saw the rubbish in the bushes.

Workbook 7 → p.20

More practice 4 → p.103

4 **What do *you* think?**

a   Read the sentences. Pick Ⓐ or Ⓑ.
1   Molly phoned Rob because Ⓐ she needed help. Ⓑ she wanted to see Rob again.
2   Molly's idea to park the car at the end of the track was Ⓐ brave. Ⓑ stupid.
3   Rob now likes life in the country because Ⓐ he has a dog. Ⓑ he likes Molly.

b   Compare with other students in your class. Did you have the same answers?

5 **WORDS** **Words in the story**

a   Write the words.

b   Copy and complete the sentences with words from a.
1   You take a photo on your …
2   You can open and close a …
3   A … can film people.
4   You walk along a …
5   … is stuff that you don't need.
6   A car uses its … when it's dark.
7   A … is like a small tree.
8   A … is an animal like a wild dog.

6 **WORDS** **Words in the country**

Can you write a word for something in the country with each letter of the alphabet? You can use the dictionary (pages 172–189).
A – **a**nimal
B – **b**ridge
C – **c**hicken
…
…
Q – **q**uiet places
…
X – **X**-ray fish
Y – **y**ellow (bushes)
Z – **z**ebra

The X-ray fish lives in the Amazon River.

More practice 5 → p. 103

➜ Ich kann Wörter zu einem Thema sammeln. ✓

2 FOCUS ON LANGUAGE

1 The questionnaire

Molly has a questionnaire for the other students in her class.

a First she answers the questions about herself. Has she ever been in hospital?

	Have you ever played hurling?	Have you ever watched a 3D film?	Have you ever seen a fox?	Have you ever been in hospital?
Molly Taylor	Yes, I have.	Yes, I have.	Yes, I have.	No, I've never been in hospital.

b Molly asks Hana, Ali and Noah the same questions. Copy the table below. Then listen to the interview and note the students' answers.

	played hurling	watched a 3D film	seen a fox	been in hospital
Molly	✓	✓	✓	✗
Hana	✗			
Ali				
Noah				

c Now read Molly's report. Find three mistakes in it.

Three students have played hurling.
Three students have watched a 3D film.
Two people have seen a fox.
Only one person has been in hospital – me!

2 The present perfect

Copy and complete rules 1–6.

FOCUS

1 Das *present perfect* besteht aus … Teilen:

I You	have	watched	a 3D film.
He She It	has	played	hurling.
We They	have	never been	in hospital.

2 Nach *I / you / we / they* kommt have + verb
Nach *he / she / it* kommt … + verb

3 Regelmäßige Verben erhalten die Endung …

4 Die Formen von unregelmäßigen Verben musst du lernen:
She *has s…* a fox.
They *have b…* in hospital.
Eine Liste findest du auf Seite 214–215.

5 Mit dem *present perfect* sagst du nicht wann, sondern *ob* bzw. *wie oft* etwas gemacht wurde. Signalwörter sind *ever, never* und *already*.

6 Statt … kann die Kurzform *'ve* stehen.

Language file 4 → p. 143   More practice 6 → p. 103

Ich kann sprachliche Regeln erkennen. ✓

3 **Molly and Rob**
Read the sentences and pick the right form of the verb.
1 I know that Rob has/have seen a fox.
2 And I know that he has/have never learned to drive a car.
3 Molly and Rob has/have travelled to Dublin lots of times.
4 Molly and her family has/have always lived on a farm.
5 Rob has/have lived in Dublin, but Molly has/have never lived in Dublin.

> Do you remember?
> I have
> You have
> He/She/It has
> We have
> They have

More practice 7 → p. 104

4 **AND YOU?**

a Read the sentences. Are they true or false **for you**?
1 I've lived in my house all my life.
2 I've always liked animals.
3 I've never lived on an island.
4 I've never climbed a tree.

b Write six sentences about yourself. *I've never …* or *I've …*   Parallel exercise → p. 104

1 I … looked after a baby.

2 I … spoken to a star.

3 I … been to a beach.

4 I … had a disaster.

5 I … found money in the street.

6 I … worked on a farm.

c • Now write four more sentences about yourself.

I've	(never)	(play) (watch) (live) (find)	hurling. an Irish film. in the country. …

I've never played hurling. But I've watched …

Workbook 8–12 → pp. 21–23

Ich kann sagen, was ich schon einmal gemacht habe.

FOCUS ON LANGUAGE

5 You should ...

a Make sentences and give good advice for German visitors to Ireland.

You should You shouldn't	take coats and rain trousers, even in summer. say "Dublin is one of the nicest towns in England." try to visit Dublin. It's a great city! have a problem with miles, because Ireland uses kilometres. say *please* and *thank you* in a shop. remember that cars drive on the left.

b **Here and there**

Copy and complete these tips for Irish visitors to Bavaria. Use *should* or *shouldn't*.

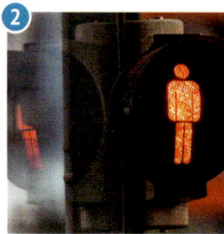

1. When you cross the road, you ... look left and then you ... look right.
2. You ... cross the road when the man is red.
3. *Weißwurst* is popular – you ... try it!
4. You ... walk on the cycle track.

More practice 8 → p. 105

6 WORD ORDER

a Read about Ashling's holiday in Spain. What did she do in Spain?

> We went to Spain two years ago. We stayed in a holiday flat for a week. We went to the sea every day. And we had a picnic on the beach most days.

b Work with a partner. Look again at what Ashling said, then read the FOCUS-box.

c Write the sentences with the parts in blue in the right order.
1. Molly and Rob went to a concert in Dublin / yesterday evening.
2. They met at 10 am / at the bus stop in Clonmel.
3. The bus to Dublin arrived on time / at the bus stop.
4. The two friends arrived in Dublin / at 12.45.
5. Rob's dad met them after the concert / in Dublin.
6. They arrived at 9 pm / back in Clonmel.

Workbook 13–15 → pp. 23–24

FOCUS

Die Wortstellung

Im Englischen – wie im Alphabet:

	Ort	vor	Zeit
They went	to town		at 8 pm.
Sie fuhren	um 8 Uhr		in die Stadt.

Im Deutschen ist es umgekehrt.

Language file 7 → p. 145

SKILLS TRAINING Speaking

Arranging a meeting

1 **PRONUNCIATION** A visit to the cinema

a Listen to the dialogue.
   When and where can Molly meet Rob?

b Read the tip, then listen again.
   Listen for the chunks.

c Now read the dialogue with a partner.
   Try to make pauses only between the chunks.

> **TIPP**
>
> Beim Sprechen bildet man Wortgruppen, die zusammengehören. Diese heißen *chunks*. Sie sind im Dialog **1c** farblich markiert.

Molly	Hi, Rob. Would you like to see the new Aidan Turner film on Saturday?
Rob	Hey, great idea. When is it on?
Molly	On Saturday, at 5.15. When shall we meet?
Rob	Can we meet at the cinema at 4 pm?
Molly	OK. See you at the cinema at 4 o'clock.
Rob	OK. Nice idea, Molly. Bye.
Molly	Bye, Rob.

2 Chunks
   Now listen to the beginnings of two dialogues.
   Which dialogue sounds better: 1 or 2?

3 Four dialogues
   Young people are making plans to meet. Copy the table.
   Then listen to four dialogues and complete the table.

meet where?	meet when?
…	…

4 👥 **AND YOU?** More help → *p. 105*

You're in Dublin. Organize a meeting with a friend.

activity	go – concert in Dublin – Sunday
on	Sunday – 2 pm
meet	bus stop in Clonmel – 9.45 am

Write the dialogue with a partner.
Then read it aloud. Think of the chunks.
(Look at ex. **1c** for help.)

➡ Ich kann mich verabreden. ✓

forty-three 43

SKILLS TRAINING Writing

Linking words and time phrases

1 Sean's blog

a Read the text. What does Sean like in Dublin?

City life

I came to Dublin two years ago. At first I didn't like it. But now I think it's great. The town centre is cool because there's life in the streets. Also I really like my neighbourhood. It's easy to walk to my friends' houses, so we usually meet every evening. And we occasionally go to a concert together. Dublin is great for sport, and I often watch rugby at the weekend. Dublin has great festivals, like the St Patrick's parade on 17th March. I love city life. What about you? Do you prefer living in the city or in the country?

b Copy the table.
Write the red and green words from the text in the table.

TIME PHRASES	LINKING WORDS
two years ago	but
…	…

2 Rob's comment

Rob wrote a comment on Sean's blog. Copy and complete it with time phrases and linking words from the box.

Rob @RobBlake

I moved to the country … (1).
… (2) I didn't like it here, … (3) now I think it's cool. The people help you if you have a problem. … (4) I like walking in fields with my dog. Clonmel is a nice town near us. My friends and I go there … (5) … (6) there are good shops there. We … (7) go to the cinema too. So we have the best of town and country!

- last April
- every Saturday
- at first
- occasionally
- because
- but • also

3 AND YOU? More help → p. 106

What do you prefer: Living in the city or in the country? Write your comment on the blog.
Write about
• the people • what you like • what you can do.

Write as many sentences as you can.

I prefer living in the country. I like it because it's quiet and I can …

Workbook 16–17 → p. 25   Wordbank 2 → p. 151   Skills file 8 → pp. 134–136

Ich kann Sätze verbinden.

SKILLS TRAINING Reading

1 Adverts in Clonmel

You're a tourist in Clonmel. Read texts A–E and pick a text for each sentence 1–4.
You won't need one text.
1 You need a place to stay.
2 You want to see a show or performance.
3 You're interested in new sports.
4 You want to see an Irish film.

A

Coming soon to screens all over Ireland:
Uncle Paddy
From one of Ireland's leading directors comes the beautiful story of modern life on Achill Island.
At a cinema near you from 20th July!

Classification: PG (Parental guidance)

B

LOST

MY **HULALI 3000** SMARTPHONE

I lost it in or near the Westgate car park. Please help if you can – I desperately need it for work. Reward for return of the phone €25.

Call David

C

The Clonmel Tea Rooms

We have Clonmel's best home-made cakes, biscuits, scones, and toast all day (10 am–5 pm). Gluten free available.

At lunchtime we serve home-made soup and sandwiches. We also have a variety of teas, coffees and hot chocolate, and soft drinks, including local apple juices.

In summer months, sit in our garden and enjoy a sandwich or a slice of cake.

We also have rooms and can offer bed and breakfast accommodation. Please ask for details.

D

CLONMEL Camogie Club

Come and try camogie, a team sport for women, very much like hurling.
We train at 7 pm every Thursday at our club in Waterford Road. Phone or text Shelagh on 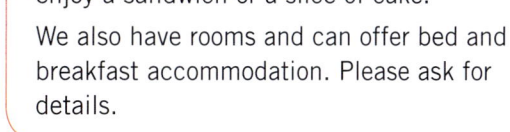.

Players must be 14 or over

E

CLONMEL ORMONDE FESTIVAL 3–9 AUGUST

Our most exciting programme ever includes
Music: The Houseboaters, Jonny Holbek, etc.
Sculpture: Natural forms in wood and stone
Dance: Finalists from County Tipperary
Green Cow Barbecue, every day at 4 pm

2 MEDIATION

a Your friend Alex doesn't understand much English. Answer Alex's questions in German about advert C.
1 Wann haben die *Tea Rooms* geöffnet?
2 Gibt es noch andere Getränke außer Tee?
3 Was gibt es außer Kuchen noch zu essen?
4 Können wir draußen sitzen?

b Alex has found a phone. Is it maybe the phone from advert B? Tell him the most important information about the lost phone – in German.

More help → p.106

More practice 9 → p.106   *Skills file 11* → p.139   *Workbook 18* → p.26

→ Ich kann Kurztexte und Anzeigen verstehen. ✓

2 SKILLS TRAINING Viewing

The kids from London SW6

1 **A visit to grandad's farm**

In this film, our four friends from Unit 1 visit a farm.

Before you watch: Look at the film stills, then think about these three questions.

1 What are the names of the four friends?
2 Where do the friends live? What will be new for them on the farm? Collect ideas.
3 Do you think they will like life on the farm? Why (not)?

Scene 1: The four friends plan a visit to …

Scene 2: The friends arrive at … and they meet …

Scene 3: The kids have …

Scene 4: But first they have to …

Scene 5: In the evening they …

Scene 6: The next morning they …

2 **Chill in the country**

Now watch the film. Then work with a partner and copy and complete the sentences for the film stills. Write as much as you can.

3 **AND YOU?** **What do you think?**

Read the five sentences below. Then talk about the sentences with a partner.
Do you agree?

1 The kids had a good time in the country.
2 They enjoyed the work on the farm.
3 Alfie's grandad wasn't very nice.
4 The kids had lots of fun in the evening.
5 They'll all come back again next weekend.

● Also say why: *I agree / disagree because …*

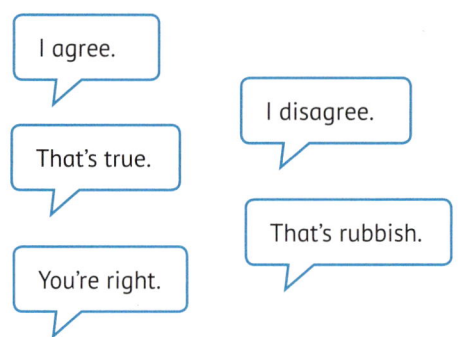

I agree.

That's true.

You're right.

I disagree.

That's rubbish.

Ich kann eine Filmepisode über das Landleben verstehen.

→ TEST AND CHECK!

First test yourself. Then check your answers on page 209.

2

1 WORDS Town and country words

Copy the diagram. Then put the words from the green box into your diagram.

bridge • department store • farm • farm gate • field • hairdresser's • hill • park • post office • pub • river • sheep • shop • stadium • station • swimming pool • tall buildings • track • underground trains • village

2 LANGUAGE A visit to a farm park

What's the missing word: *has* or *have*?

Rob's younger sisters Jodie and Evie … (1) visited a farm park and seen lots of things. Now they're in the cafe, and their teacher Mr O'Brien … (2) just walked in.

Teacher   Hi! … (3) you had a good time so far? What … (4) you seen?
Evie   We … (5) already visited the rabbits. They're cool!
Jodie   And I … (6) sat on a tractor. That was great!
Teacher   Sounds good. Go and see the donkeys. They're cute.

3 WRITING A picture story

Copy and complete the story. Use time phrases and linking words.

time phrases: ~~One day~~ • Suddenly • On Friday morning • That night
linking words: but • because • and • So

One day (1) Mr Jones was really angry … (2) his dog found rubbish in a field. … (3) Mr Jones talked with his family about the problem. Mr Jones phoned Rob's dad, Mr Blake. "I'm busy," said Mr Blake, "… (4) I can come on Friday." … (5) Mr Blake came with his cameras … (6) Mr and Mrs Jones put CCTV cameras in the fields. … (7) Mr and Mrs Jones watched the monitors. … (8) they saw two people and a car.

Workbook → p.27

→ Ich kann meinen Lernfortschritt überprüfen.   ✓   forty-seven   **47**

2 ➡ YOUR TASK

An interview for a chat show

The story of Molly Taylor and the sheep was a hit on the social media. It got 2,259,491 likes 😉. So Molly is now famous.

You work for a TV company in Bavaria. You hear about Molly and you interview her for a chat show.

➡ **STEP 1 Prepare questions.**
What information will be interesting for TV viewers in Bavaria? You'll find ideas on page 34. Write at least four questions.
How long have you lived in …?
When did you see the sheep in …?
Were you scared …?
Do you have a boyfriend, Molly?

➡ **STEP 2 Share your ideas with a partner.**
Agree on six questions for Molly.

My first question is: How long have you lived in Ballypatrick?

That's good! My first question is: Can you speak Irish?

Hey, good idea! So we have two good questions. My next question is …

➡ **STEP 3 Decide a scenario.**
- Is the interview shortly after Molly saved the sheep?
- Or is it 20 years later, Molly and Rob are married and have problems with their children?
- Or is Molly now the third woman president of Ireland?
- Or …?
You decide!

My name is Molly Taylor and I'm 80 years old.

48 forty-eight

STEP 4 Prepare Molly's answers.

Now write your answers. They can be funny, interesting, …

Interviewer	Do you have a boyfriend?
Molly	Oh, I've had many boyfriends!
	My first boyfriend was called Roy, I think.
Interviewer	Where were the sheep?
Molly	In the river. The water was deep, I had to swim a bit.

STEP 5 Practise your interview.

Decide with your partner who will be Molly and who will ask the questions.

Then practise your interview. You can make notes.
Use a system that works for **you,** for example:

| Make notes and learn you sentences from your notes. | or | Write keywords on cards and hold the cards when you talk. | or | Write the full sentences and learn them by heart. |

STEP 6 Act out your interview.

Do this
- in a group
- or in front of your class
- or film your interviews and exchange them with a parallel class.

TIP
- Don't speak too fast.
- Try not to read your questions and answers.
- Look as often as possible at the person you are talking to.

Ich kann ein Interview vorbereiten und durchführen.

REVISION 2: The simple past

1 Emily's postcard from Belfast
Emily is staying with her cousin Mara in Belfast.

a Read Emily's postcard. What did Emily do in Belfast (two things)?

> Hi Sarah!
> I arrived here in Belfast three days ago. Mara met me at the airport and we drove to her house. We chatted and then we watched a film.
>
> On the first day Mara and I visited Titanic Belfast. I didn't know it before, but Belfast people made the Titanic here in 1912.
> We saw so much! So we didn't do very much in the evening.
>
> On the second day I went into Belfast city centre. I liked it! I bought some cool presents (one for you – surprise!). And yesterday Mara's parents took me to the sea. We sat in the sun and ate ice cream.
> What did you do? Did you go bowling?
> See you soon!
> Emily

b The simple past

1 Regelmäßige Verben enden auf *-ed*.

Copy five examples from Emily's postcard: *I arrived   we ...*

2 Unregelmäßige Verben enden nicht auf *-ed*.

Find and copy the simple past forms of *meet, drive, make, see, go, buy, take, sit, eat*:
Mara met   we ...

3 Verneinungen verwenden das Wort *didn't*.

Copy two examples from Emily's postcard: *I didn't ...   we ...*

4 Fragen beginnen mit dem Wort *Did ...?*

Copy two examples from Emily's postcard: *What did ...?   Did ...?*

c Copy and complete these typical time phrases for the simple past from Emily's postcard.

1 three days a__
2 and th__
3 on the f____ day
4 in the e_____
5 on the se____ day
6 yest_____

Language file 3 → p.142

50   fifty

2 Emily's photos

Now Emily is showing photos of her visit to Belfast.
Copy and complete the sentences. Use the right form of the verbs.

1 *We didn't drive into Belfast because it was quicker by bus.*

1 We ... (not drive) into Belfast because it was quicker by bus.

2 We saw the City Hall, but we ... (not do) the tour for tourists.

3 We went to Belfast Zoo, but we ... (not see) the tigers.

4 We visited the Botanic Gardens and we ... (not pay) – because they're free.

5 I tried an Irish breakfast. It was so big that I ... (not finish) it.

6 We ... (not go) on a boat trip around the harbour because we ... (not have) time.

3 AND YOU?

a Write an email to Emily about a visit to a city. Write as many sentences as you can.

> Hi!
> I hope you're OK.
> Last week I was in Munich / Nuremberg / ...
> I stayed with a friend / in a hotel / ...
> On the first day ...   On the second day ...   On the last day ...

You can use some sentences from exercises 1 and 2 and change them:

On the second day I went into Belfast.
→ On the second day we went bowling.

b **Partner check:** Show your email to a partner and check your partner's email – especially the verbs in the simple past.

4 An elephant's trip to Belfast

a Copy and complete the rhyme.
Elephant, elephant, where did you go?
I went to Belfast two hours ago.
Elephant, elephant, what ... you ...? (see)
I ... lots of people, but they ... me! (saw, not like)
Elephant, elephant, then what ... you ...? (do)
I ... the wrong bus and ... back at the zoo! (take, arrive)

b Now say the rhyme with a partner.

Unit 3 Scotland is different

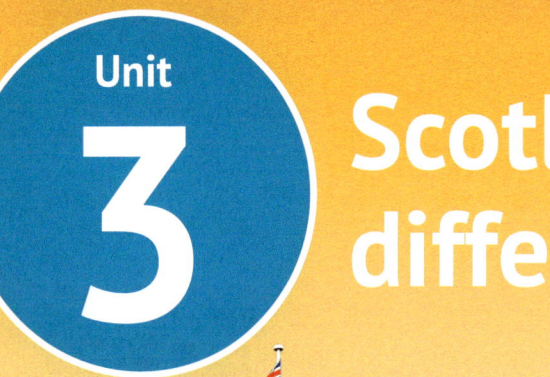

1 Find out about Scotland

Match sentences 1–8 with photos A–H.

1 Scotland's flag is blue and white.
2 Here is Loch Ness. *Loch* is the Scottish word for *lake*.
3 This is a bridge in Glasgow, which is Scotland's biggest city.
4 This is Edinburgh Castle. Scotland is famous for its castles.
5 Scotland is in the north of Europe. In the Shetland Islands you have 19 hours of daylight in June – from 3.30 until 22.30.
6 In Scottish dancing, men wear kilts and people play music on bagpipes.
7 Many road signs are in two languages.
8 You can see on the map that Scotland has lots of islands.

More practice 1 → p. 107

52 fifty-two

In dieser Unit lernst du ...
- das Leben in Schottland kennen,
- eine Unterkunft zu suchen und zu buchen,
- ein Formular auszufüllen,
- durch den Gebrauch von Pronomen Doppelungen zu vermeiden.

➡ Am Ende der Unit wirst du eine Webseite für eine Pension erstellen.

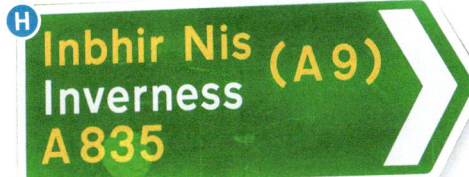

2 Welcome to Scotland

a Look at the words in the box. Then watch the film. Which things do you see in the film?

b Read the sentences. Are they true or false?
 1 Mehdy starts his trip in Inverness.
 2 In the kilt shop Mehdy puts a knife in his sock.
 3 Mehdy's Scottish clothes cost more than £500.
 4 Mehdy goes to see the Highland Games.

c Now watch the film again. Check your answers.

> bagpipes •
> a castle •
> Scottish dancing •
> kilts •
> Scottish food •
> a famous lake •
> a Scottish sport

Workbook 1–2 → p. 29

➡ Ich kann Informationen über Schottland verstehen.

3 THEME 1

A new life

1 **News for the MacDonalds**
2.01
The MacDonald family lives in Dores, a village near Inverness, Scotland.

a Listen to the dialogue.
Is the family happy?

b Now listen again and find out:
1 What are the names of the people A–D?
 Alec Kara Kate Jamie
2 Does Alec have a job?
3 Does Kate have a job?

c Listen again. Alec says he'll maybe be *unemployed*. Does *unemployed* mean:
A in trouble with the police?
B without a job?
C in a better job?

> Du kannst die Bedeutung aus dem Zusammenhang erschließen:
> Worum geht es in dem Gespräch?

2 **More news**

a Read the title. What do you think: Is it good or bad news for the MacDonalds? Then read the article and check your answer.

b Read the article again and take notes:
1 What's the name of the shop?
2 What can you buy there?
3 Why is the shop closing?
4 How many people worked there?

c **WORDS**
Find the five right words in the box.

> clothes • customers • doors •
> equipment • hairdresser • unemployed

1 you open them when you go into shops
2 you wear them every day
3 people who buy things in a shop
4 when somebody has no work
5 a person who cuts your hair

Inverness NEWS

Another Inverness shop closes

Macbean's, the town's number one shop for sports clothes and equipment, closed its doors for the last time today.

"Our customers go shopping online," said Alec MacDonald, the manager of Macbean's. "Or they go to big shopping centres. They don't want smaller shops like ours."

"Now I've lost my job," said Alec, "and seven other people have lost theirs too. We're all unemployed now."

Two shops closed in Inverness centre last month – a hairdresser's and a toy shop. So this is more bad news for the town centre.

Workbook 3 → p. 30

More practice 2 → p. 107

3 An idea in hard times

a The next evening, the MacDonalds were in the kitchen. Read the dialogue. What was the new idea?

Jamie Please don't go to Glasgow, Dad. It's too far.
Kara We need you here.
Mum Well, your dad and I talked about things. And I had an idea …
Kara What's your idea, Mum?
Mum Well, we live in a beautiful place. And lots of tourists visit Loch Ness and the Highlands. And they need places to stay … bed and breakfast places.
Kara Yes … and …?
Mum Well, we have a big old house which has lots of rooms. We can start a B&B!
Jamie But we don't know anything about B&Bs!
Kara We can teach ourselves. Great idea, Mum!
Dad Well, we can think about it. Come on! Let's eat. Help yourselves.

b Who …
1 is in the kitchen?
2 thinks dad shouldn't go to Glasgow?
3 had an idea?
4 says that the family could open a B&B?
5 thinks it's a good idea?   More practice 3 → p.108

4 You choose Do A or B.

A WORDS

a Find the opposites in the text:
1 ugly   2 not many   3 go away
4 new   5 can't   6 terrible

b Now find a word in your answers in **a**. Write:
– the sixth letter in word 1.
– the first letter in word 3.
– the first letter in word 2.
– the fourth letter in word 6.
– the third letter in word 5.
– the third letter in word 4.

What is the word? Give an example.

B SPEAKING   More help → p.108

a Why should tourists visit Scotland? Make notes – as many as you can.
… because the Highlands are beautiful.

b 👥 Now tell your partner why he/she should visit Scotland. Talk for as long as you can!
A You should visit Scotland!
B Why?
A Because … beautiful! And you could go to … Or you visit …

c 👥 Then swap roles.

Lochside Bed and Breakfast

1 The new website

a Look at the home page for the new B&B. What do you click if you want …

1 the phone number or email address?
2 more pictures?
3 more information about tourist activities?
4 to know if each room has its own bathroom?

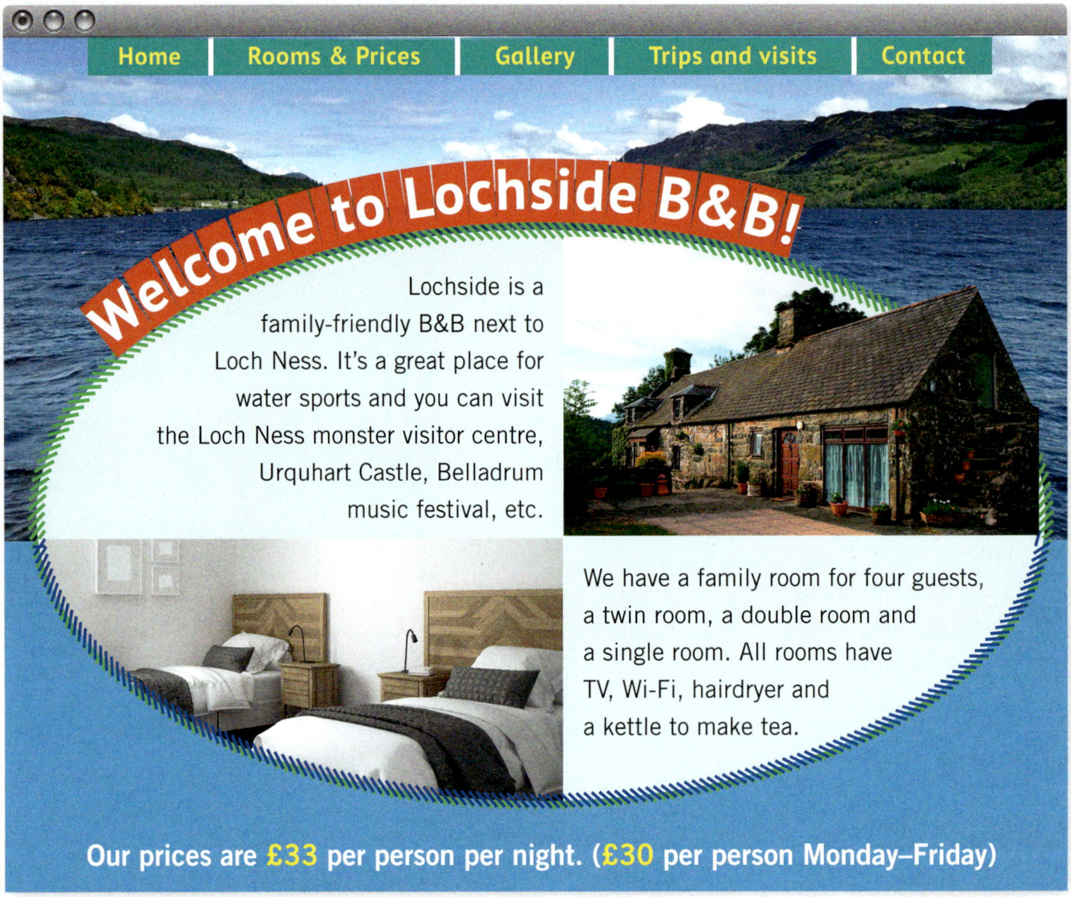

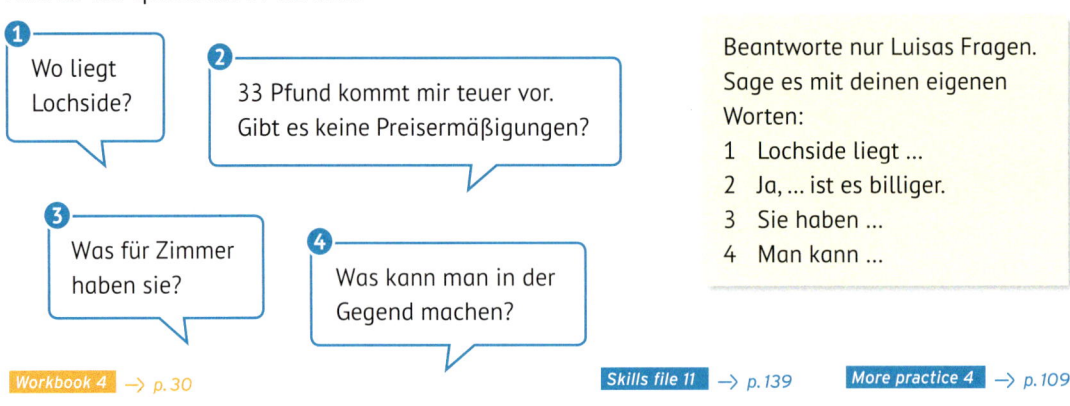

Home
Rooms & Prices
Gallery
Trips and visits
Contact
Welcome to Lochside B&B!
Lochside is a family-friendly B&B next to Loch Ness. It's a great place for water sports and you can visit the Loch Ness monster visitor centre, Urquhart Castle, Belladrum music festival, etc.
We have a family room for four guests, a twin room, a double room and a single room. All rooms have TV, Wi-Fi, hairdryer and a kettle to make tea.
Our prices are £33 per person per night. (£30 per person Monday–Friday)

b MEDIATION Your friend Luisa has found Lochside's website. Answer her questions in German.

1 Wo liegt Lochside?

2 33 Pfund kommt mir teuer vor. Gibt es keine Preisermäßigungen?

3 Was für Zimmer haben sie?

4 Was kann man in der Gegend machen?

Beantworte nur Luisas Fragen. Sage es mit deinen eigenen Worten:
1 Lochside liegt …
2 Ja, … ist es billiger.
3 Sie haben …
4 Man kann …

Workbook 4 → p. 30 Skills file 11 → p. 139 More practice 4 → p. 109

Ich kann Fragen zu einer englischen Website auf Deutsch beantworten. ✓

2 Guests from Canada

a Listen to the Grants, a family from Canada. How many people are there in the family?

b Listen again. Are the sentences true or false?
1 The Grants like Lochside because it has a family room and it's not too expensive.
2 They want a room for one night from tomorrow.
3 They decide not to send an email.
4 Abi is happy to phone the B&B.

3 A phone call

a Read the dialogue. How will the Grants find their B&B?

Jamie	Lochside B&B. This is Jamie MacDonald.
Mrs Grant	Hi. This is Michelle Grant. I'd like to book a room for two nights from tomorrow.
Jamie	And what sort of room would you like, Mrs Grant?
Mrs Grant	We'd like the family room, please, for four people.
Jamie	No problem. What time will you arrive?
Mrs Grant	Ah …, at about seven o'clock, I think.
Jamie	Sorry, can you repeat that, please?
Mrs Grant	We'll arrive at about 7 pm.
Jamie	No worries. Phone us if you can't find us.
Mrs Grant	Oh, we'll be OK. We have GPS.
Jamie	OK. See you tomorrow evening then.
Mrs Grant	Thank you. Goodbye.

b What does Jamie say when he doesn't understand?

More practice 5 → p. 109

4 Booking a room by phone

a Copy and complete the dialogue with your name and words from the box.

about • book • for • single • sort • tomorrow • what

You	I'd like to … a room … two nights from tomorrow.
Jamie	What … of room would you like?
You	A … room.
Jamie	That's fine. … time will you arrive?
You	At … 7 o'clock.
Jamie	Can I have your name?
You	Yes, my name is …
Jamie	We'll see you … then.

b The dialogue in **a** isn't very polite. Follow the rules below and make it better. Then practise the dialogue with a partner.

> Sei höflich!
> • Sage „hello" am Beginn des Gesprächs und nenne deinen Namen.
> • Sage ganz oft „please" und „thank you".
> • Bedanke dich am Ende und verabschiede dich.

Workbook 5–7 → pp. 31–32

➔ Ich kann eine Unterkunft telefonisch buchen. ✓

3 STORY

1 👥 **JIGSAW** **A story in four parts**
Before you start: Form groups of four. Each student chooses **one** part of the story A, B, C or D on pages 58–60. Note: The parts of the story are **not** in the right order.

2 **Your part of the story**
Read **your** part of the story (A, B, C or D) and **don't** tell the others about it.
Then copy the table and take notes.

My part of the story is part …

1 Who was in it?	2 When did it happen?	3 Where did it happen?
…	…	…

Ghosts don't exist! (Careful! Parts A, B, C, D are not in the right order!)

A The Grants left their car in the car park and all the family came into the big old house.
The old man took them upstairs to a room with four very old beds.

Duncan and Abi were very excited.
"This is a real Scottish castle," Duncan said.
"Maybe there are ghosts!" Abi said and laughed.
"Ghosts don't exist," her mum answered.

Late in the evening the family sat in a big kitchen. There was a fire and a big table with lots of good food on it. Musicians played music, and some people danced. The Grants chatted, enjoyed the food and danced too.
"My family has always lived in Scotland," the old man said. "What about yours?"
"Mine left Scotland more than 200 years ago," Mr Grant said. "Then you're welcome home," the old man said.

But the next morning the Grants saw nobody in the castle. Then, when they went outside to their car, they saw the old man on the walls of the castle. He was alone, playing the bagpipes. The Grants shouted "Thanks!" But the old man just played his bagpipes.

B This time the Grants found the narrow road to Dores and arrived at Lochside Bed and Breakfast at about 11 am. They went in and told the MacDonalds about the old man and the castle.

"Do you have a map?" Mrs Grant asked. "Mine is in our missing bag. Maybe we can find the castle on yours." Kate MacDonald brought a map. They looked at it and Mrs Grant pointed at Urquhart castle. "I think that's where we were last night," she said.

"It can't be – it's a ruin!" Kate MacDonald said. "But, ... well, the last family that lived at Urquhart Castle was the Grant family!" The Grants from Canada were very excited. "Let's go and see Urquhart Castle – now!" Abi said. So they went. Soon the Grants parked at Urquhart castle. Was it the car park from the night before? They weren't sure.

Then they walked around the ruins. It really was a beautiful old castle – about 800 years old. "Maybe our family came from here a long time ago," Mr Grant said. "Yes, the ghosts of the Grants are here," Mrs Grant said.
"But ghosts don't exist," the others answered and laughed.

C It started to rain at about 7 pm. It was very dark now. The road was narrow and Mr Grant drove very slowly. But they couldn't find Dores, the village with their B&B. They only saw woods and fields.

"I'm trying to phone the MacDonalds," Mrs Grant said. "But my phone doesn't work. Can you try yours, Abi?" "Hey! That's stupid! Mine has no signal," said Abi. "It must be the mountains," Duncan said.

It was now after 9 o'clock, and everybody was tired and fed up. "I'll stop at this car park," Mr Grant said. "Maybe somebody can help us." Suddenly Mrs Grant said, "Look! There's a light over there!"

She and Mr Grant ran in the rain to the end of the car park and came to a big building. An old man was at the door. The Grants told him about their problems.
"Och, come in. You can stay here for the night," he said.

3 STORY

D It was the Grant family's first day in Scotland. They landed at Inverness in the early evening – but then one of their bags was missing. And when they wanted to hire a car, Mrs Grant couldn't find her driving licence.
"It's OK," Mr Grant said. "I have mine."

Then, when Mr Grant began to drive, the kids shouted "Dad, you have to drive on the left!" And Mr Grant quickly went to the other side of the road.

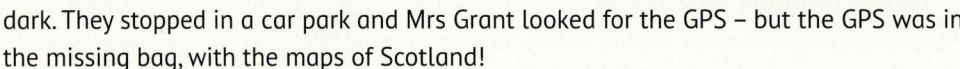

The Grants drove to Inverness. Then they looked for the road to the village of Dores, where their B&B was. But they couldn't find it because it was dark. They stopped in a car park and Mrs Grant looked for the GPS – but the GPS was in the missing bag, with the maps of Scotland!

"It isn't a problem," Duncan said. "Dores is near Loch Ness. So let's find the road that goes to the lake."

They soon found a narrow road with a sign to Loch Ness. "Ah! Things are looking better," Mr Grant said.

3 Your second group

Make a **new group** with three different students who have read the same text as you. Compare your tables from exercise 2. Did you forget anything?

My part of the story is part …

1 Who was in it?	2 When did it happen?	3 Where did it happen?
The Grants	At about … pm.	…

In part … there were only the Grants.

Yes, only the Grants.

Only the Grants?

OK. And when did your part happen?

60   sixty   → Ich kann eine Geschichte erschließen. ✓

4 👥 **Back in your first group**
Now go back to your first group.

a Look at the pictures below. Which two pictures are right for your part of the story?
Tell your partners.
My part is part … . The pictures for part … are … and …

b Tell the students in your group about your part of the story.
Listen to the others.

c Now decide together: What is the right order of parts A, B, C and D?

d Then close your books and listen to the whole story. Enjoy it!

More practice 6 → p. 110

Workbook 8 → p. 33

Ich kann Informationen auswerten.

3 FOCUS ON LANGUAGE

1 Abi Grant's blog

a Read the sentences from Abi's blog about her visit to Urquhart Castle. Who lost a hat?

Abi's BLOG

At Urquhart Castle today we saw a hat on the ground. "It's not ours," I said. "But I'll ask those people over there. Maybe it's theirs?"
I went to a man and a woman. I showed them the hat and asked, "Is this yours?"
"No, it isn't," said the man. "I have a hat like that, but mine is red and green."
Then I asked the woman. "No, it's not hers!" the man answered. "It's a man's hat."
So I went back to Duncan and mom and dad, and suddenly Duncan said, "I know! The old man in the castle, on our first evening … It's his! I remember!"
But was the old man a ghost? And can a ghost lose his hat?

b Copy the FOCUS-box. Then find the missing words in the text and complete the box.

FOCUS

Mit Possessivpronomen kannst du Wiederholungen vermeiden:

1 my hat → mine
2 your hat → ...
3 his hat → ...
4 her hat → ...
5 our hat → ...
6 their hat → ...

Language file 12 → p. 148

c Now read the two comments on Abi's blog. Copy them. Choose the right words.

@ **Harry:** We have a hat like that!
… (Yours / Ours) is blue and green.

@ **Wiseguy:** OK, you found a hat and you asked some people if it was … (his / theirs). But you never asked your mom if it was … (hers / his). And you never asked your dad if it was … (his / ours). My dad likes jokes, and I think maybe … (yours / mine) likes jokes too. Ask him, and I think he'll say, "Yes, OK, it was … (mine / hers)."

2 Different sorts of pets

Replace the blue words with possessive pronouns.

1 … (my pet) is a rabbit.
2 … (our pet) is a dog.
3 … (her pet) is a bird.

4 … (his pet) is a rat.
5 … (their pet) is a cat.
6 And what is … (your pet)?

Ich kann sagen, wem etwas gehört.

3 Buying food for the B&B

a Mrs MacDonald and Jamie are ordering food online.
What do they need to buy?

Jamie   OK, Mum. How much bacon do we need?
And how many tomatoes?
Mum   We need lots of bacon and lots of tomatoes!
Jamie   OK. And how many sausages? And how much tea?
Mum   We don't need many sausages. We bought lots of sausages last week. And we don't need much tea. Lots of customers prefer coffee.

b Copy and complete the FOCUS-box.

FOCUS

Mengenangaben
Bei Mengenangaben musst du aufpassen:
1. Um welche Art von Satz geht es? 2. Ist das Nomen zählbar oder nicht?

Zählbare Nomen *(countable nouns)* haben eine Pluralform: *two tomatoes, three sausages.*
Nicht-zählbare Nomen *(uncountable nouns)* kannst du nicht in den Plural setzen: *bread, butter, tea.*

	countable nouns	uncountable nouns
positive sentences	We need *lots of* tomatoes.	We need … bacon.
questions	How *many* sausages?	How … tea?
negative sentences	We don't need *many* sausages.	We don't need … tea.

c Write the words from boxes A and B in the right lists.

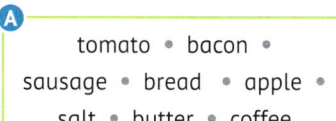

A: tomato • bacon • sausage • bread • apple • salt • butter • coffee

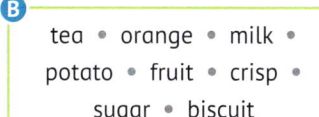

B: tea • orange • milk • potato • fruit • crisp • sugar • biscuit

countable nouns	uncountable nouns
tomato	bacon
…	…

Language file 8 → p. 145

d The MacDonalds need lots of the food from box A and not much of the food from box B.
Copy and complete the sentences. Write countable nouns in the plural.
1 The MacDonalds need lots of …   2 They don't need much …

4 AND YOU?

Write at least eight sentences about what you (don't) eat and drink.
Use words from the table or your own words.

| I eat
I drink
I don't eat
I don't drink | lots of
many
much | oranges • apples • fruit • vegetables •
chocolate • sweets • crisps • nuts •
meat • chicken • cheese • water •
tea • coffee • juice |

Example: *I don't eat much meat.*

More practice 9 → p. 112   *Wordbank 4* → p. 153   *Workbook 11–12* → p. 35

Ich kann über unbestimmte Mengen sprechen.

3 FOCUS ON LANGUAGE

5 PRONUNCIATION

a Read and listen to these useful sentences.
1. Sorry, I don't understand.
2. Can you repeat that, please?
3. Can you help me, please?
4. Where's the toilet, please?
5. One student ticket, please.
6. Thank you for your help.

Mit der richtigen Intonation klingst du viel freundlicher. Und wenn du freundlich klingst, helfen die meisten Menschen gerne. 😉

b Listen again and repeat the sentences.

c Now say the sentences to a partner. Do you sound friendly?

6 Numbers at Lochside B&B

a Where do the guests at Lochside B&B come from? Listen to the dialogue and take notes. You won't need all the places in the box.

> Canada • Germany • Spain •
> Ireland • London • Glasgow

1. Our fortieth guest came from ...
2. Our fiftieth guest came from ...
3. Our sixtieth guest came from ...
4. Our sixty-fifth and sixty-sixth guests came from ...

b Alec talks about the money that the guests pay to Lochside B&B.
Listen and look at the numbers in red. They are wrong! Write the correct numbers.

1	120 guests		£4300
2	175 guests	pay	£5125
3	225 guests		£7895
4	300 guests		£10,700

7 Scotland in numbers

Read the texts to your partner.

1. The Kelpies are 30-metre high sculptures. One year after opening they welcomed their millionth visitor.

2. In 2017 Scotland had 566,000 visitors from the USA, 372,000 from Germany, 206,000 from France and 115,000 from Canada.
Many North Americans are interested in their Scottish family history.

3. Scotland has its own football team. It was 67th in the world in 2016. But Scotland had a good year in 2017 and climbed to 32nd in the world by the end of 2017.

4. More than 100,000 babies were born in Scotland in 1948, but only 52,861 babies were born in Scotland in 2017.

Workbook 13–14 → p. 36

Numbers → p. 215

Ich kann Zahlen verstehen. ✓

SKILLS TRAINING Writing

Filling in forms

1 A week in a Bavarian family

Jamie MacDonald wants to travel with his school to Augsburg, Inverness's twin town in Bavaria. He wants to spend a week with a family there. But first he has to fill in a form.

a WORDS

With a partner, read the black words on the form. Can you guess what they mean in German?

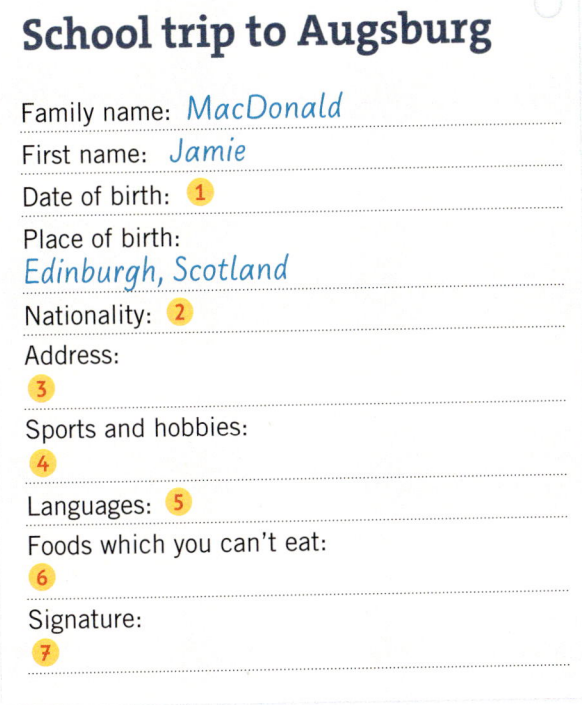

School trip to Augsburg

Family name: MacDonald
First name: Jamie
Date of birth: ①
Place of birth: Edinburgh, Scotland
Nationality: ②
Address:
③
Sports and hobbies:
④
Languages: ⑤
Foods which you can't eat:
⑥
Signature:
⑦

TIPP

Wenn du ein Wort nicht kennst oder vergessen hast, kannst du die Bedeutung oft erschließen.

1 Vielleicht sieht es wie ein deutsches Wort aus:
address → ?
nationality → ?

2 Oder du kennst schon ein ähnliches englisches Wort:
birthday → Geburtstag
date of birth → ?

3 Oder du nutzt deine Erfahrung aus: Du weißt z. B., dass man auf Formularen unten unterschreibt. Was könnte also *signature* heißen?

Skills file 2 → p. 127

b Match ① – ⑥ on the form with Jamie's answers A–F.
 A I'm allergic to nuts.
 B Lochside, Dores, Inverness
 C Scottish
 D 26th March 2007
 E rugby, swimming, games, cooking
 F English, school French, school German

c ● You're a student in Augsburg and you're going to spend a week with a family in Inverness. Copy and complete the form for yourself.

Workbook 15 → p. 37

TIPP

Benutze ein Wörterbuch, wenn du ein neues Wort brauchst. Bist du z. B. allergisch gegen Sojabohnen?
1 Suche das englische Wort für Sojabohne → soya bean
2 Achte auf die richtige Anwendung im Satz:
I'm allergic *to* soya beans.

Skills file 3 → p. 128

→ Ich kann ein Formular ausfüllen. ✓

3 SKILLS TRAINING Listening and speaking

Talking about music

1 Scottish *Musician of the Year*?
A radio programme is trying to choose *Scotland's Musician of the Year*. First read the sentences below. Then listen to the programme and pick **A**, **B** or **C**.

1 Calvin Harris's real name is Adam
   A Whiles. **B** Whyles. **C** Wiles.
2 When he was at school he found it hard to
   A learn maths. **B** use a guitar. **C** make friends.
3 After school he needed money for
   A his first car. **B** music equipment. **C** nice clothes.
4 So Calvin worked
   A as a DJ. **B** in a fish factory. **C** in a post office.

2 A great song
Jamie and Kara are listening to Calvin Harris's song *My Way*.

a Listen to the song and read the dialogue. What's great about this song? What isn't great?
   Jamie I really like this song.
   Kara   Yes, it sounds great! Who sings it?
   Jamie Calvin Harris. I like his voice. And the electronic drums are great.
   Kara   Yes, the song has a good beat. I don't know about the words …
   Jamie Oh, it's about finding your way when there's a problem. Have you seen the video? It's fantastic!
   Kara   Yeah, the video is amazing. But it makes me feel sad.

b Now read the dialogue with a partner. Then swap roles.

c What do you think about the song? *I think it's great / OK / boring / terrible / …*

3 AND YOU?
Play one of your favourite songs to a group of students. Tell the students why you like it. Listen to their songs.

Talk about the song:	It has a great beat. It's full of energy. The words are great/funny.
Talk about the instruments:	I like the guitar and the drums. The drums are great!
Talk about the singer:	I really like … I think he/she has a great voice.
Talk about your feelings:	The song makes me feel happy/great/sad/angry/…

Wordbank 3 → p.152

Ich kann über Musik sprechen.

SKILLS TRAINING Reading

A festival programme

1 ⊙ **Skim the programme**
Is it a film or a music festival? When is it?

> **TIP**
> When you skim a text, don't read every word. You just want to know what the text is about.

Belladrum — TARTAN HEART FESTIVAL

"Maybe the most popular music festival in the Highlands"

at Belladrum, near Inverness   No age limit*

THURSDAY 3rd AUGUST
Sister Sledge . First Aid Kit . Louis Berry *and many more!*

FRIDAY 4th AUGUST
The Pretenders . Feeder . Tigerstyle *and many more!*

SATURDAY 5th AUGUST
Franz Ferdinand . K T Tunstall . Birdy *and many more!*

TICKETS: £82 FOR ONE DAY, £143 FOR THREE DAYS

- ♥ A great list of amazing Scottish and international artists
- ♥ Wide choice of music, including rock, Celtic rock, dance, indie, blues and folk
- ♥ Beautiful setting in a park with hills all around
- ♥ A great programme, free events, e.g. street theatre, arts and crafts workshops
- ♥ Family-friendly festival: food and drink available, on-site camping with quiet night hours.
- ♥ Note: glass isn't allowed at the festival.
- ♥ Regular bus service to and from Inverness

*Under 18s must be accompanied by an adult

2 Information about a festival
Read the information. Which words tell you …
1 Musicians come from different countries.
2 You can buy things to eat at the festival.
3 You don't need a car to get to the festival.
4 The festival isn't far from Inverness.
5 Lots of people like this festival.
6 You can sleep in a tent.

Workbook 16–17 → pp. 38–39

3 ⊙ **WORDS**
a Which words mean
   1 perhaps 2 very nice to look at
   3 small mountains 4 you don't pay
   Check your answers in a dictionary.

b Find the opposites in the text:
   1 terrible 2 noisy 3 day 4 over

Skills file 6 → p. 132

→ Ich kann ein Veranstaltungsprogramm verstehen.   sixty-seven   67

3 SKILLS TRAINING Viewing

The kids from London SW6

Do you remember Sherlock, Tally, Ruby and Alfie from London SW6?
In this episode Tally has a visitor from Scotland, her cousin Hamish.

1 Tally's video diary

a Look at the four pictures from Tally's video diary and read the questions.
Can you guess the answers?

1 Is Tally making breakfast or lunch?
2 Does she use salt or sugar?

3 Is Ruby puzzled or fed up?
4 Does the Scottish word *wee* mean big or small?

5 Does Alfie want to buy fish and chips or a pizza?
6 Is Alfie surprised at the Scottish money or the price?

7 Does Hamish dance or play the bagpipes?
8 Who dances best: Tally, Ruby, Alfie or Sam?

b Now watch the film and answer the questions.

c Watch the film again and check your answers.

2 AND YOU? Video diaries

With a partner make a video diary like Tally's.

a Collect ideas. What can you make your diary about?
– Your day/evening/weekend/…
– Something funny in class/at home/…
What do you need for your video diary? (equipment, people, …) Where can you film the diary?

b Write a script for your diary. Use a dictionary.

c Film your diary. Then present it in class.

Ich kann ein Video erstellen.

TEST AND CHECK!

First test yourself. Then check your answers on page 210.

1 LANGUAGE The phone on the beach

Write sentences 1–6. Replace the red words with the possessive pronouns *mine, yours, his,* etc.

1 A phone! Maybe it's his phone?   2 Is this your phone?   3 No. Maybe it's their phone.

4 Thanks, but it isn't our phone.   5 Maybe it's her phone.   6 Yes, it's my phone. Thank you!

2 SPEAKING Booking a B&B

You and your family want a room, so you phone a B&B.
Write your sentences.

You   Hi. / Simon Koch. / This is / for tomorrow night. / to book / I'd like / two double rooms
B&B   Yes, no worries. The price is 110 pounds.
You   that / breakfast? / Is / with
B&B   Yes, it is. What time will you arrive?
You   arrive / evening. / We'll / the / in
B&B   In the evening is fine.
You   very / you / Thank / much.
B&B   No problem. Have a good journey! Bye.

3 READING A train trip in Scotland

Read the advert. Are the sentences below true or false?

1 You can see this train in the Harry Potter films.
2 The trip is 84 kilometres long.
3 Mallaig is a place with boats.
4 The train stops and you can walk over the bridge in Glenfinnan.
5 You can buy food on the train.
6 The price is £35 for a single ticket.

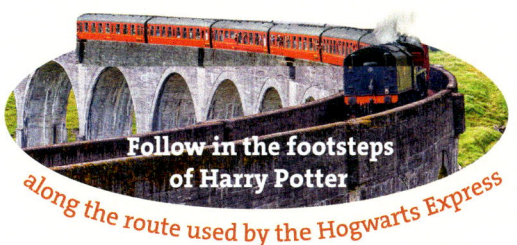

The Jacobite Steam Train

Follow in the footsteps of Harry Potter along the route used by the Hogwarts Express

- Travel in the train that Harry Potter uses in the films.
- Start in Fort William, near Ben Nevis, Britain's highest mountain. Travel 84 miles to Mallaig, a small harbour that is great for fish and chips.
- The train crosses the famous bridge in Glenfinnan, and you can take great photos from the train.
- We sell tea with scones and cream on the train.
- £35 for an adult return ticket

Workbook → p. 40

Ich kann meinen Lernfortschritt überprüfen.

3 YOUR TASK

An English website for a German B&B

You are going to write English texts for a website for a B&B in Bavaria.

Follow steps 1–5.

STEP 1 Find ideas.
Copy and complete the wordweb. Make notes.
You don't have to write full sentences.

Where is your B&B?
- in your town or village?
- in/near the mountains?
- in/near a big city?

Find a name for your B&B.

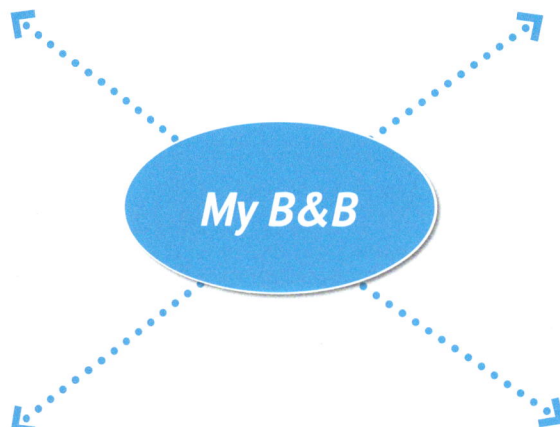

The rooms in your B&B
How many?
Double, or …?
What do they cost?
What is there in the rooms: Wi-Fi, …?

Information for your guests
- What can your guests visit near your B&B?
- What activities can they do?
- What events are there near your B&B?

→ **STEP 2 Write the texts for your home page.**

1. Write a welcome text and some information about your B&B.
   Welcome to … B&B
   … is a family-friendly B&B next to …
   Then look online and find a photo for your B&B.

   You need more help?
   Go to  (see page 3) and put in: dahico.

2. Write about your rooms and prices.
   We have … rooms:
   … double rooms and … single rooms.
   All rooms have Wi-Fi, TV, …
   Prices are from … to … euros per night.

3. Write about trips and events.
   Our B&B is in … about … km from …
   You can go …ing, enjoy …
   Or you visit …
   What about a trip to …?

4. Write about your breakfast.
   Breakfast is served from … to … o'clock.
   We offer tea, coffee, juice, bread, …

→ **STEP 3 Compare with a partner.**
Check your partner's texts.
- Do you have any more ideas?
- Did your partner use the right words?
- Do you understand the texts?
- Can you find any grammar or spelling mistakes?

→ **STEP 4 Write a booking form.**
Work with a partner again.
a Decide what information you need from the guests:
Name, email, phone number,
date of arrival, date of departure,
number of guests, …

b Write the form.

→ **STEP 5 Look at all the websites.**
Look at all the websites in your class.
Then decide in your class:
- which is the best B&B?
- which is the best website?

→ Ich kann eine Website entwerfen und realisieren. ✓

REVISION 3: The *will*-future

1 Plans

a Read this email from your Scottish friend Andy.
What does he want to do in August?

Dear Burak

Hooray! We have a week's holiday!

Today I'll stay at home. But tomorrow I'll go into town with some friends, and tomorrow evening we'll watch the new Sherlock Holmes film. I hope it won't be too American!

And next Thursday I'll start my new job. I'll do my first paper round – I hope it won't rain!

I'd like to come and see you in Germany this week, but I won't have the money. But I'll have more money in summer, so maybe I could visit you in August. When will your summer holidays begin?

Do you have plans for this weekend? Will you stay at home? Or will you visit your grandparents again?

All the best
Andy

Andy will do his first paper round next Thursday.

b The future

1 Die Zukunftsform bildest du mit *will* oder *'ll*.

Copy six examples from Andy's email: *I'll stay* …

2 Verneinungen bildest du mit dem Wort *won't*.

Copy three examples from Andy's email: *It won't be* …

3 In Fragen brauchst du das Wort *will*.

Copy three examples from Andy's email: *When will …?* …

c Copy four time phrases for the future from Andy's email: *Today, tomorrow, …*

Language file 5 → p.144

2 Your weekend plans

Write ten sentences with the words in the table.

Maybe I'll I think I'll I won't	buy chill go make meet play do chat with visit watch	to Munich. my grandparents. some new clothes. into town. my favourite games. a special meal. a film. my friends. my homework. at home.

72 seventy-two

3 More weekend activities

a **Think** Look again at exercise **2**. Write sentences with the same verbs, but with different endings. Write as many as you can!

1 *Maybe I'll buy a new laptop, tickets for a concert, …*
2 *I think I'll make a cake, a birthday card, …*
3 *I'm sure we'll go to the water park, …*

b **Pair** Compare with a partner. Copy his/her ideas.

c **Share** Write your ideas on the board.

4 The weather next weekend

Look at the weather forecast for Glasgow. What will the weather be like next week?

Monday	Tuesday	Wednesday	Thursday	Friday	Saturday
	23°C	15°C			24°C

Fill in *will* or *won't*.

1 It … be cloudy on Monday, but it … rain. It … be very windy.
2 On Tuesday it … be sunny and warm.
3 On Wednesday it … be cloudy again and colder.
4 On Thursday it … be rainy and a bit windy.
5 On Friday it … be rainy again. It … be a bit sunny and it … be windy.
6 On Saturday it … be warm again. But it … be sunny.

5 AND YOU?

a Look again at Andy's email in exercise **1**. Then write to Andy and answer his four questions. Write at least six sentences.

*Hi Andy
Thanks for your email.
I hope we'll meet in summer. My holidays …
Next weekend I'll …
On Saturday …   And maybe we'll also …
On Sunday …   And I hope we'll … too.
…*

Say what you **will do** and also what you **won't do**.
You'll find ideas in Andy's letter and in exercise 2.

● Maybe you can also write what you did yesterday (1–2 sentences). Then you'll need the simple past. Look at pages 50/51 for help. For example:
I didn't answer your email yesterday because I went to a party. It was good fun, but it was late when I got home.

b **Partner check:** Show your email to a partner and check your partner's email. Check especially the verbs with *will* or *won't*.

USA – here we come

1 👥 **The USA and you**
Make a wordweb with all the things that you know about the USA. Think about famous people, places, sport, music and food.

2 **Famous places**
👥 Work with a partner.
Match photos 1–6 with places A–F on the map.

3 **In the USA**
Watch the film and pick Ⓐ or Ⓑ.
1 The USA is the Ⓐ third Ⓑ fourth biggest country in the world.
2 The USA has Ⓐ 15 Ⓑ 50 states.
3 The USA has Ⓐ two Ⓑ four time zones.
4 The two biggest cities are New York and Ⓐ San Francisco. Ⓑ Los Angeles.
5 The capital of the USA is
   Ⓐ New York. Ⓑ Washington DC.

The Niagara Falls, in the USA and Canada

The Grand Canyon, Arizona

Manhattan, New York

Mardi Gras in New Orleans

Universal Studios, Hollywood, California

The Golden Gate Bridge, San Francisco, California

4 AND YOU?

a THINK Where would you like to go in the USA? Make notes. 🔵 Say why:
… because it's famous / I know it from films / it's fun / there's so much to do there / …

b 👥 PAIR Talk to a partner. Tell him/her about where you want to go. Say why. Ask where he/she wants to go. Agree on one place.

c SHARE Tell the class what place you've picked.
🔵 Say why.

Workbook 1 → p. 42

Unit 4
In the heart of the USA

In dieser Unit lernst du …
- das Schulleben in den USA kennen,
- Vergleiche anzustellen,
- Wettervorhersagen zu verstehen,
- dich zu beschweren.

➔ Am Ende der Unit wirst du eine Geschäftsidee vorstellen.

1 Welcome to Memphis, Tennessee

a 🔅 Look at photos A–F. Then find a caption for each photo.

> art • by the river • music • a building • transport • a famous person

b Now match a text 1–6 with each photo.

1 One of the most interesting buildings is the Memphis Pyramid. Why a pyramid? Because Memphis got its name from Memphis, Egypt. Of course, the pyramid there is a lot older!

2 The city's most famous son is Elvis Presley, the King of rock and roll. You can visit his house and see his clothes, his cars and his planes.

3 The suspension railway goes from the city center to the entertainment park on Mud Island.

4 Memphis is the city of music. Justin Timberlake was born here, and B. B. King, the King of blues, lived here. And you still often hear live music in Beale Street today.

5 Memphis has some great murals. This one by artist Marcellous Lovelace next to the Civil Rights Museum shows a protest march of black workers in 1968.

6 Memphis is on the Mississippi River, the longest river in the USA. It is famous for its three very long bridges.

2 Talk about the photos

Pick two photos and ask your partner. Then change roles.

> What can you see in photo A?

> There is … / There are …

a bridge • big buildings • cars •
an old house • musicians • people •
a river • a blue sky • a city street •
a train • a pyramid •
a work of art • a singer • …

Workbook 2 → p. 42

Ich kann Fotos beschreiben.

THEME 1

Ben Chung

Burkle Middle School

1 School life

a Here's Ben's presentation about life in his school. Look at the photos. What's different from your school?

I'm in 7th grade at Burkle Middle School. We're 25 students in my class, and most of us come to school by bus (our school buses are for students only). Many of us have breakfast at school.

We're at school all day. At 7.45 we listen to the day's announcements. We then have classes from 8.15 to 3.00 pm. Most of us have lunch in the school canteen.

Most students stay at school after 3.00 pm for activities like art club, music club and lots of different sports clubs. Our school football, baseball and basketball teams are really good!

Our school is very strict about food. The canteen only sells healthy food – no junk food like chips or candy.

2.15

b Now read and listen to Ben's presentation. What's important at his school (two things)?

c `Here and there` **School life**
Write about three differences between Ben's school and your school.

Ben's school	my school
most students come …	most students …
…	

`Workbook 3` → p. 43

`More practice 1` → p. 112

78 seventy-eight   ➡ Ich kann das Schulleben in den USA mit meinem vergleichen. ✓

2 Monday's announcements *Parallel exercise* → p. 113

a 🎧 Listen to today's announcements. Who speaks in the announcements?

Many US students say the *Pledge of Allegiance* every morning.

b Listen again. Are sentences 1–5 true or false?
1. The baseball team won on Saturday.
2. The basketball team came first in their competition.
3. This is *A New Start* week.
4. There's news of a new competition in art club.
5. Ben has to go to the principal's office.

3 A letter to Ben's dad

a Read the principal's letter. Is it good or bad news for Ben?

b Now complete the sentences.
1. The school only sells …
2. Ben is in trouble because he …
3. The principal asks Ben's dad to …

c Find the words or phrases in the letter:
1. food that is good for you
2. opposite of *more*
3. the word for sweets, crisps, burgers, etc.
4. opposite of *bought*
5. these say what you must do at school
6. best wishes

BURKLE MIDDLE SCHOOL

Monday, May 10th

Dear Mr Chung

We only sell healthy food here at school.
This is very important because we think young people should eat more healthy food and less junk food.

Today Ben brought junk food to school and sold it to other students. Students aren't allowed to sell things at school. This is against our school rules. I took the food and I have it in my office.

Please talk to Ben about this. And please come to the school so that we can give you Ben's junk food.

Yours sincerely
Roger Bell (Principal)

4 WORDS Food

a Make lists of food words. Write as many words as you can.

fruit/vegetables	meat	other	drinks
apples	ham	cheese	

Wordbank 4 → p. 153

b Ask your partner about what he/she eats and drinks. Then change roles.
- A What do you eat for breakfast?
- B I have bread, butter and jam.
- A And for lunch?
- B For lunch I usually eat …
- A … in the evening?
- B I often eat …
- A … between meals?
- B …

Skills file 1 → p. 126   *Workbook 4–5* → p. 44

→ Ich kann über meine Essgewohnheiten sprechen. ✓

THEME 2

A new start

1 Trouble at home

a ⊙ Ben's dad talked to Ben about the principal's letter.
Do you think Mr Chung was
– happy?
– sad?
– angry?
– surprised?

b Read what Ben's dad said. Then put Ben's answers in the right order.

Dad:	Ben:
Ben, what happened at school?	– Chips, candy.
What sort of food?	– OK, Dad. I'll make a new start.
Why did you sell junk food?	– I sold some food at school.
But it's against the school rules!	– I wanted to make some money.
You must never do this again, Ben!	– I know! I'm really sorry, Dad.

c 👥 Now act the dialogue.
Use the tone that you chose in part **a**.

2 WORDS

a Match the pictures with the words in the box.
Example: *A – chocolate bars   B – …*

- candy *(AE)*
- ~~chocolate bars~~
- cookies *(AE)*
- French fries *(AE)*
- fruit
- hot dogs

More practice 2 → p. 113

b Match the British and American words.

candy	biscuits
French fries	sweets
cookies	chips

TIP

Most words in British English *(BE)* and American English *(AE)* are the same – but some words are different.

→ Ich kann englische und amerikanische Wörter unterscheiden. ✓

3 A new idea

a Mrs Fox, the business studies teacher, is talking to Ben. Is she angry with him?

Mrs Fox	Ben, you've been less interested in class in the last few weeks. What's wrong?
Ben	Oh, I don't know. I'm not good at anything.
Mrs Fox	I hear you're good at selling junk food.
Ben	Ha, ha, ha. Very funny.
Mrs Fox	Well, I think you could be good at business, Ben.
Ben	Good at business?
Mrs Fox	Yes. And I have an idea. Can you come to business club today? The new business competition is perfect for you. I can give you more information about it.
Ben	I don't know … Oh, OK, then. I'll come. Thank you.

b Read the dialogue again and finish these sentences:
1 Mrs Fox teaches …
2 She knows that Ben tried to sell …
3 She thinks that Ben could be good at …
4 Ben should come to …
5 Mrs Fox thinks that … is perfect for Ben.
6 She wants to give Ben more …

4 The competition

a Read about the competition.
When and where will the Memphis school teams sell their things?

b ⊙ Read the brochure again, then pick **A** or **B** in sentences 1–6.
1 You take part **A** in teams. **B** alone.
2 You try to make
   A $100. **B** as much money as you can.
3 Teams who make the biggest
   A cakes **B** profit   win the competition.
4 All teams get tickets to a
   A movie theater. **B** swimming pool.
5 The winners in Memphis will go to a competition in **A** New York. **B** Nashville.
6 The Nashville winners will get
   A a hundred dollars.
   B a thousand dollars.

Memphis middle schools' business competition

- Work in teams and sell things.
- Try to make a lot of money.
- Teams who make the biggest profit win.
- All teams – from the most successful to the least successful – win free tickets to a movie theater.
- The Memphis teams will sell their things at Memphis Farmers Market on July 4th, Independence Day.
- The winners in Memphis will take part in the competition in Nashville. The winners in Nashville will win $100.

Workbook 6–7 → p. 45

Ich kann Informationen erfassen.

4 STORY

1 🔊 **Before you read**

Match the captions with pictures 1–6.
- A Not many people want to buy cakes.
- B At the market
- C Hey, this isn't bad!
- D A messy kitchen
- E Thinking about the past
- F Friends again?

Something special

2.18

Ben looked around the kitchen. It was very, very messy. "This looks bad," Ben thought. "I must clean the kitchen before dad comes home, or he'll go crazy."

5 Then the door opened, and Ben's dad came in.

"What has happened to this kitchen?" he asked. He looked angry.
"I just made some cupcakes with my
10 friends," Ben said. "It's for a business competition at school."

But Ben's father wasn't interested. "Forget about the competition," he said. "You have to work hard at school.
15 That's how you'll get a good job."

"But Dad, I don't like school. I want to work in the shop with you," Ben answered.
"Sit down, Ben," his father said. "I'll tell you a story."

2.19

"Your grandfather left China when he was 20
a boy," said Mr Chung. "He came to the USA.

He didn't have much money but he worked hard. And me? I left school when I was 16. Now I work seven days a week in the shop. I have little time for myself – and for you." 25

"Dad," Ben said. "I've heard these stories many times!"
"But you can learn from them!" his dad answered. He was angry now. "You're going to work hard at school and get a good job! 30

My son shouldn't be the least successful student at school!" Ben and his dad didn't talk again that evening.

🎧 2.20 The next day Ben and his friends brought their cupcakes to school. But in one hour they sold only six cakes. It was a disaster!

Ben was fed up at home that evening. His dad felt it.
"I'm sorry that I was angry last night," he said. "I said some silly things."
"Thanks, Dad," Ben said.

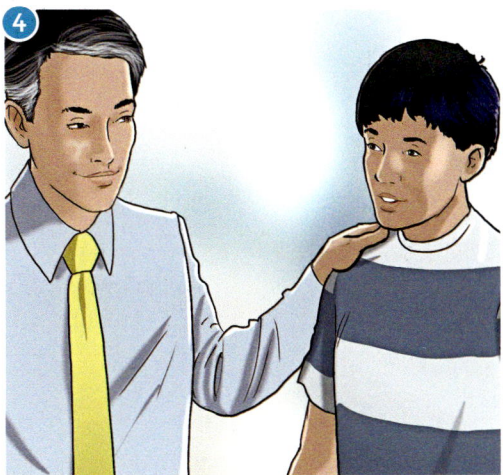

Then he told his father about the disaster.
"Please try a cupcake, Dad," he said. "Eat as many as you like. I have 44 cakes here!"
Ben's dad laughed.
Then he took one of the cakes and tried it.
"Hmmm, it's a good cupcake," Ben's dad said. "But it isn't good enough!"
"What do you mean, Dad?" Ben asked.
"Ben, if you want to win your competition, your cakes must look special – more special than this."
"You're right, Dad. I'll think about it," Ben said.

🎧 2.21 The next day Ben waited at the bus stop to catch the school bus. He remembered his father's words. How could the cupcakes look 'more special'?

Then Ben saw a poster about Graceland, the home of Elvis Presley, one of the most famous Americans of all time. The poster had a picture of Elvis …
"Maybe this is an idea for our business," he thought, and he took a photo.

When Ben showed his photo to the other kids in his team, they were very excited.
"We can do something with this," they all agreed.

eighty-three   83

STORY

2.22
70 On July 4th, Independence Day, twelve schools sent a team to Farmers Market for the Memphis competition. They all wanted to sell as much as they could.
   The team from Blackstone Middle
75 School sold milkshakes and made a profit of 102 dollars. Germantown Middle School sold second-hand books and made 85 dollars. Ben's team sold their cupcakes – and this
80 time they sold lots and lots of them.

They made a profit of 155 dollars and won the competition!

2 The special ideas
Look at picture 6. What were the Burkle students' special ideas? Finish the sentences.
1 Ben and his friends looked like …
2 All the cupcakes had a picture …

3 What's the right answer?   *Parallel exercise* → p. 113
Copy the sentences and pick the right ending – **A** or **B**.
1 Ben's dad was unhappy at first because **A** the kitchen was messy. **B** the cakes were bad.
2 Ben's dad thinks school is **A** important. **B** a waste of time.
3 Ben's dad thought the cakes were **A** better than the cakes in his shop.
   B OK, but could be better.
4 Ben got his new idea from **A** a poster. **B** a text message.

More practice 3 → p. 114

4 What do *you* think?
a What do you think Ben and his dad learned in this story?
   Pick the most important answer(s).

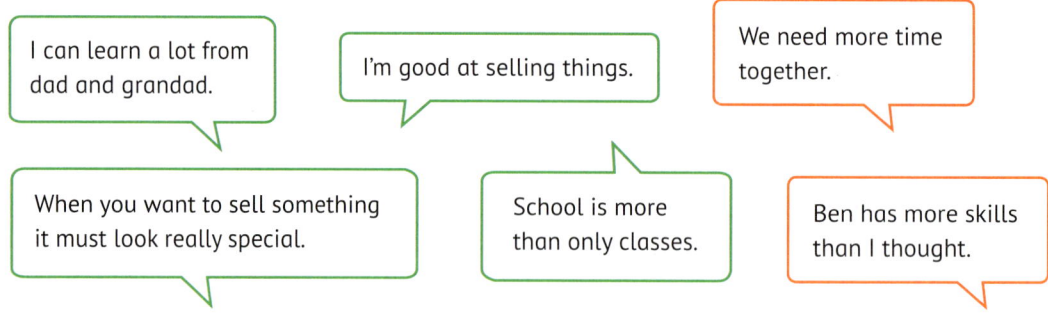

b Compare with other students in your class.
   Did you have the same answers?

Ich kann eine Geschichte interpretieren.

5 Dad's surprise for Ben

a Listen to the end of the story. Put pictures A–F in the right order.

b Listen again and answer the questions.
1. Where did Ben get the Elvis Presley clothes?
2. Where did Ben get the idea for the Elvis photos on the cakes?
3. What can you buy to eat at the stadium?
4. When does the baseball game begin?
5. What's the score in the baseball game?
6. What will Ben and his dad do now?

6 Here and there — Public holidays

Many Americans celebrate Independence Day together on 4th July.

a Discuss with a partner: when do people in Germany often celebrate together?

| Christmas | Eid al-Fitr, the end of Ramadan | 3rd October | Fasching | Family birthdays |

b Now choose a day when people in Germany celebrate together.
Make notes:
- the date/name of the day,
- what many people eat, sing, buy, do,
- what you do on that day.

More help → p. 114

c WALK AROUND
Tell a partner about at least four things about your special day. When your teacher gives a signal, move on to a different partner.

> I want to talk about Fasching. Lots of people wear funny clothes. They meet their friends in town. And often they eat … / drink … / give … In my family we don't do these things. We watch the parades on TV. We often eat … / visit … / invite …

Workbook 8–9 → p. 46

Ich kann von einem Fest erzählen. ✓

eighty-five 85

FOCUS ON LANGUAGE

1 Three games

In business club, Ben and his team compared three games: N2, Gilmen and Darkuz.

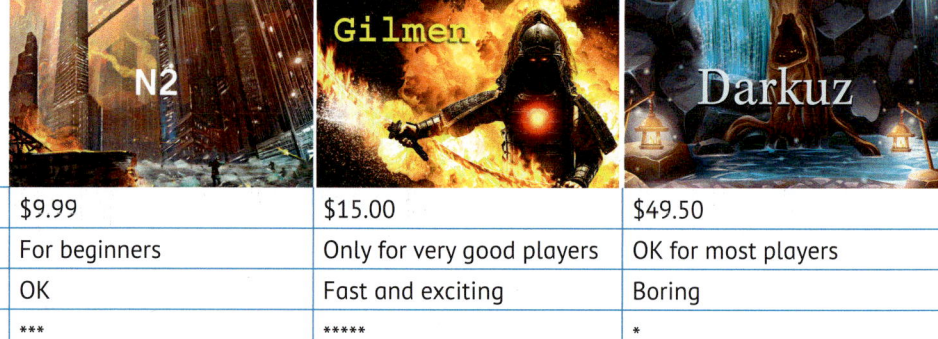

	N2	Gilmen	Darkuz
cheap	$9.99	$15.00	$49.50
easy	For beginners	Only for very good players	OK for most players
exciting?	OK	Fast and exciting	Boring
popular?	***	*****	*

a ⊙ Compare the three games.
1 … is cheaper than …
2 … is easier than …
3 … is the cheapest game.
4 … is the easiest game.

b Copy and complete the FOCUS-box.

> **FOCUS**
>
> **Vergleiche mit kurzen Adjektiven**
>
> | Adjektiv | cheap | Gilmen is cheap. |
> | Komparativ | cheap*er* | N2 is cheap*er* than Gilmen. |
> | Superlativ | cheap*est* | N2 is the cheap*est*. |
>
> Regel: Bei kurzen Adjektiven hängst du … oder … an das Adjektiv. Beim … brauchst du das Wort *than*.

Language file 10 → p. 147

c Look again at the three games. Are these sentences true or false?
Is the information true or false?
1 Darkuz is more exciting than N2.
2 Gilmen is more exciting than Darkuz.
3 Gilmen is the most exciting game.
4 N2 is more popular than Darkuz.
5 N2 is the most popular game.

d Now read this FOCUS-box. Copy and complete the rule.

> **FOCUS**
>
> **Vergleiche mit langen Adjektiven**
>
> | Adjektiv | interesting | Darkuz ist not interesting. |
> | Komparativ | more interesting | N2 is more interesting than Darkuz. |
> | Superlativ | most interesting | Gilmen is the most interesting game. |
>
> Regel: Bei langen Adjektiven setzt du … oder … vor das Adjektiv.
> Beim … brauchst du das Wort *than*.

Language file 10 → p. 147

e 👥 **AND YOU?** Talk to a partner about your favourite games.
… is more difficult than …
… is more interesting than …
… is the most exciting game! It's the best.

86 eighty-six   ➡ Ich kann grammatische Regeln erkennen und anwenden. ✓

2 What do you think?

a Copy the sentences. Put the words in the gaps and make the right sentences for you.
1. I think ... is more popular than ... (tennis / tae kwon do)
2. And I think ... is more exciting than ... (football / ice hockey)
3. I think that ... is more expensive than ... (a skateboard / a bike)
4. And I really think that ... is more dangerous than ... (swimming / cycling)
5. I think ... is more boring than ... (dancing / singing)

b **DOUBLE CIRCLE** **Comparing**
Make two circles and talk to different partners.
Partner A What's more popular, tennis or tae kwon do?
Partner B I think ... is more popular than ...
Partner A What's more exciting, football or ice hockey?
Partner B I think ... is more exciting than ...
Partner A What's more ...

More practice 4 → p. 115

3 Three works of art

a Look at the three photos below.

Street art by Lexi Bella and Miss Zukie in Brooklyn, New York

Balloon Flower (Red) by Jeff Koons in Manhattan, New York

Street art on wall

b Now talk about the works of art with a partner. Use the adjectives in the box.

beautiful • boring • colourful • exciting • interesting • original

I think A is more original than B. Do you agree?

I think C is the most beautiful work of art. Do you agree?

Yes, I think so too. And I think C is more colourful than A. Do you agree?

No, I don't. I think B is more original than A.

Yes, I think so too. And I think B is the most boring work of art. Do you agree?

No, I don't. I think A is the most beautiful work of art.

More practice 5 → p. 115
Workbook 10–12 → p. 47

➡ Ich kann Vergleiche anstellen. ✓

eighty-seven **87**

FOCUS ON LANGUAGE

4 Interesting places in Memphis
Read the information and the four sentences. Are the sentences true or false?

Sun Studio Museum	Zoo	Cotton Museum	Graceland (House only)
$14	Adults $15	Adults $10	Adults $38.75
Ages 5–11 free	Ages 2–11 $10	Ages 6–12 $8	Ages 13–18 $34.90

1 For children Sun Studio is less expensive than the zoo.
2 For children Graceland is less expensive than the Cotton Museum.
3 The Cotton Museum is the least expensive for adults.
4 The Cotton Museum is the least expensive for 10-year-old children.

$ 20	$ 40	$ 60	$ 80	$ 100
the least expensive	less expensive	expensive	more expensive	the most expensive

5 My day in Memphis
Are the missing words *less* or *least*?
My visit to Graceland was the … (1) successful visit in Memphis. This was because we had the cheapest tickets and so we couldn't see Elvis's cars or planes. The zoo was … (2) boring than I expected: I really liked the pandas. The cotton museum was the … (3) interesting for me.
My lunch in the Condor Diner was OK. It's … (4) comfortable than some other cafes and the waiters were the … (5) friendly of all, but the food was good. Memphis is one of the … (6) expensive cities in the USA, and the prices were OK.

6 PRONUNCIATION
British and American English

2.24

a Read the tip, then listen to the sentences.
Is the first speaker British or American?
1 Can I have some bread and bu**t**ter, please?
2 Do you need a bo**tt**le of wa**t**er?
3 I really like my beau**t**iful ci**t**y.
4 I think her par**t**y was be**tt**er than mine.
5 Ge**tt**ing an email is fine – but ge**tt**ing a le**tt**er is be**tt**er.

b 👥 Now read the sentences to a partner.
Choose to say them in British or American English.

The 't' in the middle of a word like *butter, water, better, city* is usually:
[t] in British English
[d] in American English.

Workbook 13–15 → pp. 48–49

SKILLS TRAINING Listening

Weather reports

TIP
The USA uses degrees Fahrenheit for temperature:
32 °F = 0 °C | 59 °F = 15 °C
77 °F = 25 °C | 86 °F = 30 °C

1 Two weather reports
a Look at the three weather maps. Then listen to two weather reports. Which maps do the reports describe?

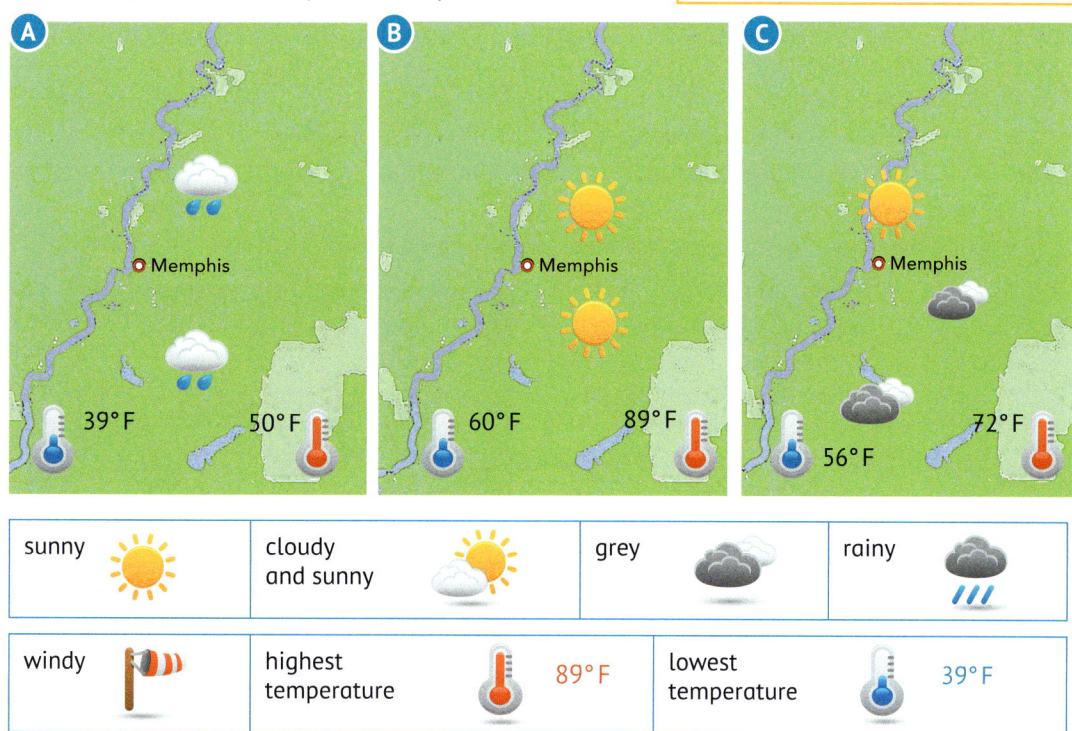

b Listen again. True or false?  → p. 116

Weather report 1
1. The highest temperature was 52 degrees.
2. There was a little rain late in the morning.
3. Tomorrow the weather will be worse.

Weather report 2
1. In the afternoon it was rainy.
2. The night temperatures were just below 40 degrees.

2 The weather tomorrow
a Listen to four weather forecasts (1–4) for tomorrow. Match them with the symbols A–D.

b Listen again. Pick Ⓐ, Ⓑ or Ⓒ.
1. Temperatures tomorrow will be
   Ⓐ the same as today. Ⓑ higher than today. Ⓒ lower than today.
2. Cooler weather will come Ⓐ tomorrow. Ⓑ the day after tomorrow. Ⓒ next week.
3. The highest temperature tomorrow will be Ⓐ 15 °F. Ⓑ 45 °F. Ⓒ 50 °F.
4. Tomorrow it will be Ⓐ hot. Ⓑ cold. Ⓒ sunny.

 → p. 133  → p. 50

 Ich kann Wettervorhersagen verstehen.

SKILLS TRAINING Reading

A DVD cover

1 Different parts of a DVD cover
Look at the DVD cover. Then match sentences 1–8 with parts A–H on the cover.
1 One sentence that tells you what is special about the film.
2 What language(s) the film is in.
3 The name of the actor(s).
4 How long the film is.
5 A category to show you who can see this film (PG = Parental guidance → parents can decide)
6 A short text that makes the reader interested in the film.
7 The title of the film.
8 Good things that newspapers or magazines have said about the film.

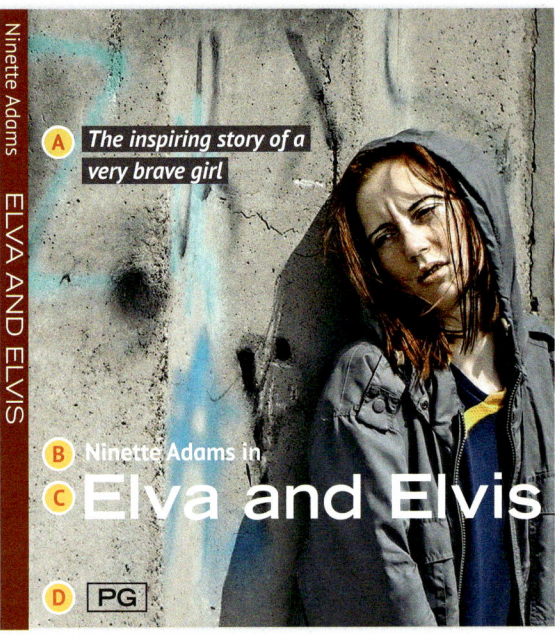

E Elva lives on the streets of Memphis, Tennessee. With the gangs. The drugs. The violence. Then a poster of Elvis gives Elva (Ninette Adams) the inspiration to begin a new life. But it's hard to give up the gangs and the drugs.
You'll laugh and you'll cry – and at the end you'll cheer.

F "Superb" *Memphis Echo*
"The must-see film of the year." *Film Guru*

Bonus features: Interview with Ninette Adams
G 98 minutes
H Languages: English, Spanish

A The inspiring story of a very brave girl
B Ninette Adams in
C Elva and Elvis
D PG

2 Working with a dictionary
Look up these words in a dictionary:
drugs, violence, give up, cheer.
– Check the alphabetical order of the first four letters: *Drugs* comes after *drove*, before *drum*.
– For *give up* look under *give* (not *up*!):
  give → give up
– *cheer* can be a noun or a verb. Look again at the text: is it a noun or a verb in the text?

Skills file 3 → p. 128

3 Where do you read this?
Copy the phrases that tell you that …
1 Elva doesn't have a home.
2 there are big problems on the streets.
3 Elva wants to make a new start.
4 it isn't easy for Elva to start a new life.
5 some scenes are funny and some are sad.
6 the film has a happy ending.

4 AND YOU? Your DVD cover More help → p. 116
Choose a film and make a DVD cover for it. Your cover should include points 1–8 in exercise 1.

Workbook 17 → p. 51

Ich kann den Aufbau eines DVD-Covers erkennen.

SKILLS TRAINING Writing

Formal and informal emails

1 Josh's hotel in Memphis

a Read the two emails.
1 Which email is to a friend, and which is a formal email to a hotel?
2 Why did Josh write to the hotel?

A

Hi Abi
I hope all is OK with you. I'm back from Memphis. We had a terrible hotel there – no towels and a broken shower. And the room wasn't clean. And really unfriendly people. I sure won't go back to that hotel. But Memphis was great.
All the best
Josh

B

Dear Sir / Madam

I am writing to complain about your hotel in Memphis. I stayed there from 15th to 18th August.

My room was not clean and the shower did not work. And there were no towels in the bathroom.

I told the people at reception about these problems, but they were not very friendly.

I will not come back to your hotel!

Yours sincerely
Josh Kane

b Look at the blue phrases from email A. What does Josh write for these phrases in email B?

c WORDS Find the words for pictures A–E.

clean • complain • reception • shower • towels

d You want to complain about a hotel in Memphis. Complete this email.

Dear … (1)
I am writing to … (2) about your hotel in Memphis. I … (3) there from 2nd to 6th July.

My room … (4) not clean and the table lamp … (5) not work.

I told the people at … (6) about these problems, but they were not very friendly.
I … (7) not come back to your hotel!

Yours … (8)
(your name)

Skills file 8 → p. 134-136   Workbook 18 → p. 52

Ich kann formelle und informelle Schreiben unterscheiden.   ninety-one 91

4 SKILLS TRAINING Viewing

Mo's bows

Mo is a boy in Memphis. He has a business: he makes and sells special ties – bow ties. So Mo's business is called "Mo's bows". Here is a film about him.

1 Before you watch

What do *you* think of bow ties? Tell your partner.
Bow ties are boring / smart / cool / stupid / in fashion / …

2 The first half of the film

a Look at the places A–F. Then watch the first half of the film. What's the right order of the places in the film?
   A a shop
   B Mo's school
   C Mo's bedroom
   D a post office
   E Mo's bathroom
   F the kitchen in Mo's house

b Now read sentences A–C below. Which is true: A, B or C?
   A Mo wants to make 100 ties and sell them at a market.
   B Mo wants to sell ties to his dad; his dad will then be proud of him.
   C Mo wants to make 100 ties and sell them at his school.

c Then watch the first half of the film again and check.

3 The second half of the film

a Look at the information in the box and guess:
   1 How many ties will Mo sell?
   2 How much money will Mo make?

> • About 200 people will come to the market
> • Mo will have 100 bow ties.
> • Each tie costs 30 dollars.

Then watch the second half of the film.
Who guessed right?

b Fill the gaps with the people in the box. You won't need all the names.

> aunt • dad • grandma • friend • mom

   1 Mo works with his mom, his sister Taylor, his … (1) and his grandma.
   2 Mo's … (2) says they still have to make 30 ties.
   3 So Mo's … (3) comes to help.
   4 At the end Mo is sad that his … (4) didn't come to the market.

Then watch again and check your answers.

→ Ich kann eine Filmepisode über eine Geschäftsidee verstehen. ✓

TEST AND CHECK!

1 WORDS Unhealthy food

a Write six examples of junk food.
   You can use American or British English. *Hot dogs, ...*

> First test yourself. Then check your answers on page 211.

b Match the words on the left with the phrases on the right.
   1 (to) win   A money
   2 (to) be good   B your bike to a friend
   3 (to) catch   C crazy
   4 (to) go   D at business
   5 (to) sell   E a bus
   6 (to) make   F a competition

2 LANGUAGE Comparing

a Look at this example: *three activities (difficult)*
   Skiing is more difficult than walking. Climbing is the most difficult activity.
   Now compare ...
   1 three supermarkets or shops in your neighbourhood (expensive)
   2 three TV programmes (popular)
   3 three computer games (exciting)

3 LISTENING The Memphis Music Bus Tour

2.27

You are in Memphis with your family.

a Listen to the radio advert for the *Music Bus Tour*.
   Does the advert tell you
   1 what you will see?
   2 the times of the tour?
   3 a phone number?

b Listen again and answer the questions.
   1 What will the guides do? *They will talk and ...*
   2 How long is the tour?
   3 What do tickets cost for adults?
   4 What can you buy for 12 dollars?

4 WRITING A letter

Your hostel in New York was terrible!
Copy and complete the letter to the hostel and complain about your stay.

> Dear ... (1)
> I am writing to complain ... (2) your hostel in New York. I was there ... (3) 3rd–5th August.
> My bed ... (4) not comfortable and the shower in the bathroom ... (5) not work.
> I will not come ... (6) to your hostel!
> Yours ... (7)
> *(signature)*

Workbook → p. 53

Ich kann meinen Lernfortschritt überprüfen. ✓

YOUR TASK

A business plan

You are going to make and present a business plan.

STEP 1 Ideas

a Decide what you can make or sell.

b Decide where you can sell your things.

| in town | in break at school | at a school party | at a market | ... |

STEP 2 Teams

Make teams of three or four students.
Compare your business ideas and decide on one idea for the team.

- I think we could make …
- Good idea.
- Hm, I think we could make …
- We could sell them at school.
- Or maybe in town?

STEP 3 Money

One team wants to sell animal ballons and has made this table.
Make a table like this for your idea.

We need	Cost		We can sell	Price	Profit	
– 50 balloons		4 €	50 balloons	1 € per balloon		50 €
– pens		5 €				– 9 €
	Total:	9 €			Total:	41 €

STEP 4 A poster for your business plan
Make a poster with your business plan.

Our business plan

Make and sell *animal balloons*

What do we need?
Balloons, pens

How much will they cost?
50 balloons cost 4 euros.

STEP 5 Present your business plan
- Then present it to the class.
- Here are some ideas for your presentation:

> Here's our business plan. Our idea is to make *animal balloons* and then sell them.

> First we must buy the balloons. We think that this will cost four euros.

> We think that we can sell 50 balloons and each balloon will cost one euro.
> So we will get 50 euros.
> Our profit will be 46 euros.

> We think that selling balloons is a good idea because:
> – people like …
> – balloons are less expensive than …
> – it's easy to …
> – we can make lots of different …
> – we think that balloons will be more popular than …

STEP 6 Who's best?
Vote for
- the most original idea,
- the best presentation,
- the idea that you think can make the most money.

Skills file 10 → p. 138

Ich kann eine Geschäftsidee vorstellen. ✓

PARTNER B

Unit 1

3 **ROLE-PLAY** Buying tickets   Unit 1 | p.23
Partner B

a You're a sales assistant at the station.
Look at the information.
Act out a role-play.
Your partner starts.

b Now you are travelling.
You want a return ticket to Manchester.
Your partner works at the station.
Act out a role-play.
Note the price and time of your train. Is it on time?

Lösung **London-Quiz:**   Unit 1 | pp. 8–9

1C • 2A • 3B • 4B • 5B • 6C • 7C

DIFF BANK

Unit 1

More practice 1 👥 **The film about London** → Unit 1 | p.9

What other things did you see in the film? Tell your partner. Use words in the box and your own ideas.

> some birds in a park • a bridge • a football stadium • an old boat • lots of big houses • lots of people • some shops • the River Thames • red London buses • a big hospital • a Tube station • some black London taxis • some cows

Partner A I saw …
          What about you?
Partner B I saw … too.

More practice 2 **What do you know about London now?** → Unit 1 | p.11

a Copy and complete the sentences.
  1 Big Ben is in the … of Parliament. (p.8)
  2 Buckingham Palace is the home of … (p.8)
  3 Sherlock Holmes is a London … (p.8)
  4 London … are red. (p.9)
  5 Wembley is famous for its … stadium. (p.9)
  6 Camden has a famous … (p.10)

b Do you remember other interesting information about London? Tell the class.
  London has …   There is / There are …   London is great for …

More practice 3 **Which advert is best?** → Unit 1 | p.13

Read the sentences below. Then choose the best advert (A–F) on page 12.

1 You love music and you're free this evening! But you don't have lots of money.

2 You like clothes and walking around markets and looking at interesting things to buy.

3 You want to travel around London for a day and you want the cheapest ticket.

4 You like going around places that are a bit scary.

5 You love shopping and window-shopping in busy streets.

6 You're a football fan and you'd like to visit a famous English football stadium.

ninety-seven **97**

DIFF BANK

More practice 4 • **About the story** → Unit 1 | p.16

Which sentences give the best information about the story: A or B?

1 About me:
   - A Sherlock is different from his friends.
   - B Sherlock likes books.

2 Saturday plans:
   - A Sherlock's friends laughed.
   - B The kids plan to go shopping.

3 Disaster on the Tube:
   - A Alfie didn't get on the train.
   - B The friends ran to the train.

4 Shopping disaster:
   - A The kids had to leave Harrods.
   - B Things are expensive in Harrods.

5 Disaster in Hyde Park:
   - A Alfie kicked a ball.
   - B The friends had trouble with some teenagers.

6 In the museum:
   - A Everybody liked the museum.
   - B The museum has dinosaurs.

More help **4** **Why and what?** → Unit 1 | p.16

Complete the sentences with the right endings A–F.

1 Sam's friends call him *a geek* because …
2 His friends said "BORING!" when …
3 Alfie didn't get on the Tube train because …
4 They had a problem at Harrods because …
5 The teens in the park ran away when …
6 The friends went to the museum because …

A they heard a noise like a police car.
B they had no money and the museum was free.
C Alfie had a rucksack and they weren't with an adult.
D he likes things like books, history and museums.
E he was too slow.
F Sherlock wanted to go to the Natural History Museum.

1 - D: Sam's friends call him a geek because he likes things like books, history and museums.
2 - …

More practice 5 **A short version of Sherlock's story** → Unit 1 | p.16

What's the right order of the sentences?
- A After Harrods they went to Hyde Park.
- B Sam, Tally and Ruby got the Tube train, but Alfie was too slow.
- C On Saturday Sam met his friends Ruby, Alfie and Tally.
- D Then they went to the Natural History Museum.

E They went to Fulham Tube Station.
F They all really liked the museum, especially the earthquake room.
G When they got out of the Tube they went to Harrods.
H They had trouble with some teenagers because Alfie kicked a ball into their picnic.
I They had trouble with a security man because Alfie had a rucksack.

More practice 6 Sherlock tells about the disaster in the park → Unit 1 | p.16
Write the eight simple past verbs. Then check on page 15.

So next we **TWEN** to Hyde Park. We played football, but we didn't see the teenagers behind a tree. They **AHD** cans of drink with them – and Alfie **CKEDIK** the football into their picnic!
"Hey, you idiot!" a big boy **OTUHSDE**. "We're keeping your football!"
Then I had an idea. I went behind a tree and **OTOK** out my phone. A loud noise came from it – like the noise of a police car. The teenagers **DERAH** it, ran away – and left the football!
"Very clever again, Sherlock," Tally **ASID**. I **ELTF** like a million dollars.

More practice 7 My room → Unit 1 | p.18
What can you see in the room? Use the words in the box and write six sentences with *some* and *any*.
1 There are some books. But there aren't any …

- books
- posters
- clothes
- magazines
- cushions
- toys
- boxes
- photos of my family

More practice 8 A quiz about your lifestyle → Unit 1 | p.19
a Choose the right words and copy sentences 1–8.
1 I don't know somebody/anybody from Turkey.
2 I buy some/any of my clothes online.
3 My neighbourhood has anything/nothing for young people.
4 I know somebody/something who drives a taxi.
5 I never eat anybody/anything between breakfast and lunch.
6 I often watch something/anything on TV in the evening.
7 I never eat some/any meat.
8 Anybody/Nobody in my family is good at maths.

1 DIFF BANK

b Put a tick (✓) if they are true for you, or a cross (✗) if they are false for you.

c WALK AROUND
Try to find somebody who has the same eight answers as you.

> I don't know anybody from Turkey. That's true for me.

> And for me! I buy some of my clothes online. That's true for me too.

> It isn't true for me. Sorry!

More help 3 You only have five minutes! → Unit 1 | p.21

👥 Work with a partner. You have five minutes.
How many words can you find to complete these sentences?
Use words in the box and your own ideas.

1 The best thing about my neighbourhood is the …

> river • sport • football stadium • skate park • bike shop •
> cake shop • cinema • swimming pool • park • video shop • …

2 There's a …

> bus stop • hairdresser's • football stadium • skate park •
> bike shop • cake shop • cinema • swimming pool • museum •
> restaurant • second-hand shop • supermarket • …

and there are …

> lots of cafes • two stadiums • bus stops •
> farms • fields • shops • restaurants • …

near our house.

3 You can …

> go shopping • watch films • go bowling • go swimming • go fishing •
> ride your bike • see farm animals • …

4 But there aren't any …

> parks • music shops • supermarkets • fields •
> restaurants • cinemas • video shops • …

near us.

More practice 9 — In the newspaper
→ Unit 1 | p. 22

What do the red words mean?

> Young swimmers and divers from all parts of Britain were at the London Olympic swimming pool yesterday.
> One winner was John Burns. "I was unwell yesterday," he said in a TV interview. "But today I was lucky and I came first. It's all a bit unreal."

Partner check Compare with a partner.

Unit 2

More practice 1 — PROJECT — The Republic of Ireland
→ Unit 2 | p. 30

a A map of Ireland
Look at the map of Ireland at the beginning of the book. Then copy and complete the table. Put the towns in the right country.

Towns in Ireland	Towns in Northern Ireland

Belfast • Cork • Derry • Dublin • Galway • Limerick

b A quiz about Ireland
Work with a partner. Look on the internet and find the answers.
1 Ireland A is B isn't in the European Union.
2 In Ireland you pay in A euros. B pounds.
3 The population of Ireland is about A 10.2 million. B 4.8 million.
4 Cars in Ireland drive on the A right. B left.
5 Most people in Ireland speak A English. B Irish.
6 The Irish flag is orange, white and A green. B blue.

More practice 2 — WORDS — Everyday talk
→ Unit 2 | p. 32

When good friends talk together they often use special phrases.

a Copy each phrase onto a piece of card.

- All's good.
- Cool!
- That's ace.
- It sucks!
- Oh, come on!
- You're joking!
- Sounds good.
- What a pain!

Pick the right German phrase from the green box and write it on the back of the card.

> Du spinnst wohl! • Cool! • Na, komm schon! • Voll blöd! • Klingt gut. • Es nervt. • Alles gut. • Das ist krass/voll super.

one hundred and one 101

2 DIFF BANK

b Pick good answers from your cards for these sentences.

- I met a really nice boy at the youth club yesterday. …
- How's life? …
- You have to help your dad in the kitchen. …
- What's your new class like? …
- Do you have **50** euros for me? …
- …

Parallel exercise **1c** A new life → Unit 2 | p. 32

What's new for Rob and his parents? Copy and complete the sentences.

> has bought • has found • has met • has seen • hasn't spoken • has started

1 Rob's dad … a new business and he … a new van.
2 Rob's mum … a job in a tennis club and she … nice people there.
3 Rob … a girl on the school bus, but he … to her yet.

More practice 3 The story → Unit 2 | p. 34

a What are the missing words in sentences 1–9?

Who did what?
1 Molly, the … of farmer John Taylor, saved three sheep.
2 John Taylor, Molly's …, was proud of her.
3 Garda Butler spoke to the … for the police.

> father • newspaper • daughter

The story

Where it happened
4 The sheep were in the … so Molly walked into the water.
5 Dogs mustn't run in … where there are animals.
6 People should tell the Garda if they see dogs near the Taylors' …

> farm • river • fields

How things were
7 The water wasn't too … for Molly.
8 But it was … for the sheep.
9 Molly had to work …

> dangerous • deep • hard

b Now look back at page 34 and check your answers.

c ● Now look again at your sentences and tell your partner the story of Molly and the sheep.
Molly, the daughter of farmer John Taylor, saved three sheep. The sheep were …

More practice 4 — You're a reporter! → Unit 2 | p.38

Put sentences A–H in the right order and tell the story for a newspaper.
(B) Molly phoned Rob.
…

A Rob ran to Molly's field with his dog.
B Molly phoned Rob.
C The two police officers couldn't drive home.
D The police said the CCTV was a good idea.
E Rob wrote the number of the car.
F Rob and Molly saw lights of a car at night.
G Rob's dad put up CCTV cameras on the farm.
H Rob's dog Wally found some rubbish.

More practice 5 — Country words → Unit 2 | p.39

Copy the lists. Put the words in the right lists.

COUNTRY WORDS

animals	buildings	water	others
…	…	…	…

birds • cows • farms • fields • fish • grass • hills • lakes • mountains • national park • pigs • ponies • rabbits • rivers • sheep • station • stones • trees

More practice 6 — Regular and irregular verbs → Unit 2 | p.40

a Copy and complete the list for regular verbs:
I work   I've worked
I start   …
I finish   …
He texts   …
She opens   …
He looks   …
She cooks   …

b Look at the list of irregular verbs on pages 214–215 of your student's book. Then complete the list.
I buy   I've bought
I meet   I've …
I speak   …
She has   She's had
He is   He's been
She sees   …
He finds   …

2 DIFF BANK

More practice 7 **Chores** → Unit 2 | p.41

Who has done what in the Blake family?
Look at the list and complete the sentences.
Example: *I have already hoovered the house.*

Mum I ... already ... (hoover) the house.
And I ... ... (go) shopping.
Jody I ... (not fill) the dishwasher yet.
Rob I ... already ... (washed) the car.
And I ... ... (cut) the grass.
Evie I ... (not do) my homework yet.
But I ... ... (tidy) my room.
Dad I ... (not clean) the kitchen yet.
But I ... already ... (cook) dinner.

- hoover house ✔
- go shopping ✔
- fill dishwasher ✘
- wash car ✔
- cut grass ✔
- do homework ✘
- tidy room ✔
- clean kitchen ✘
- cook dinner ✔

Parallel exercise **4b** **AND YOU?** → Unit 2 | p.41

Write six sentences about yourself. Put the verbs in the right form for the present perfect.
I've never ... or *I've ...*

1 (look after) a baby.

2 (speak) to a star.

3 (be) to a beach.

4 (have) a disaster.

5 (find) money in the street.

6 (work) on a farm.

More practice 8   Life in the city – good and bad   → Unit 2 | p.42

A magazine has a page with questions and answers about life in the city.
Complete the answer with *should* or *shouldn't*.

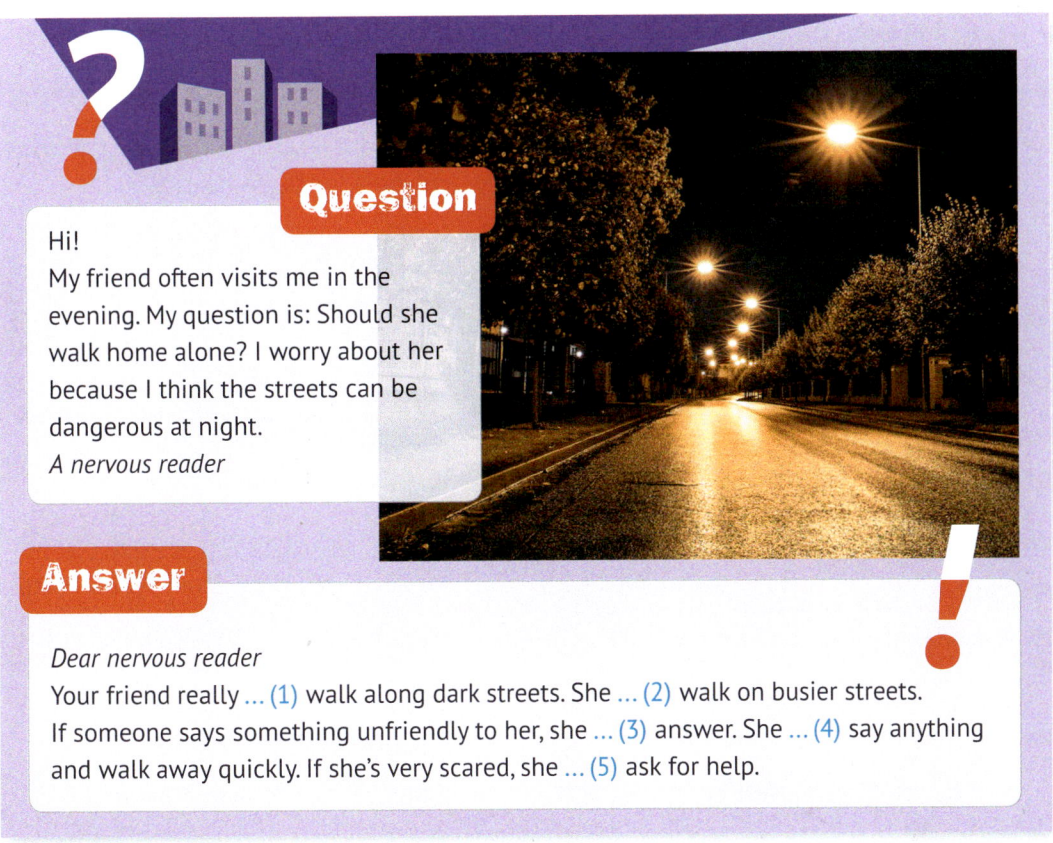

Question

Hi!
My friend often visits me in the evening. My question is: Should she walk home alone? I worry about her because I think the streets can be dangerous at night.
A nervous reader

Answer

Dear nervous reader
Your friend really … (1) walk along dark streets. She … (2) walk on busier streets. If someone says something unfriendly to her, she … (3) answer. She … (4) say anything and walk away quickly. If she's very scared, she … (5) ask for help.

More help   **4**   **AND YOU?**   → Unit 2 | p.43

You're in Dublin. Organize a meeting with a friend.

activity	go – concert in Dublin – Sunday
on	Sunday – 2 pm
meet	bus stop in Clonmel – 9.45 am

Work with a partner. Complete the dialogue.
You   Hi, Yusuf. Would you like to …
Yusuf   Hey, great idea. When is it on?
You   On … When shall we meet?
Yusuf   Can we meet at … at …?
You   OK. See you at … at … Bye, Yusuf.
Yusuf   Bye!

Now read it aloud. Think of the chunks.

DIFF BANK

More help 3 AND YOU? → Unit 2 | p.44

Look at the text below. You can change the words in blue.

I prefer living in the country.

I like it because the people are relaxed and friendly and help you when there's a problem.

Living in the country is quiet and safe.

I love animals and in the country I can go for long walks with my dog Murphy and see lots of animals. Also I like riding my bike. And that's safer and more fun in the country.
So I prefer the country.

More help 2b MEDIATION → Unit 2 | p.45

Alex has found a phone. Is it maybe the phone from advert B?
Tell him the most important information about the lost phone – in German.

Anzeige	Wichtige Information?
LOST My HULALI 3000 smartphone	Ja! Nenne Alex Marke und Modell.
I lost it in or near the Westgate car park.	Ja! Gib diese Information an Alex weiter.
Please help if you can – I desperately need it for work.	Nein! Das brauchst du nicht.
Reward for return of the phone €25	Entscheide selbst, ob das wichtig ist.
Call David 087	Ja! Gib diese Information weiter.

More practice 9 Your advert → Unit 2 | p.45

With a partner, write an advert in English to bring English-speaking tourists to a cafe in your town.
Use and adapt phrases from the *Clonmel Tea Room* advert.
Write 30–50 words.

(name of cafe)
Come and ... at ...
We have ...
We also have ...
In summer months ...
Find out more at ...

Unit 3

More practice 1 Scotland → Unit 3 | p.52

Look again at exercise 1 on page 52.
Then find the correct endings for the sentences.

1 Loch Ness is
2 There is a big castle
3 In summer in Scotland the nights
4 Glasgow is
5 Bagpipes are
6 Scotland's flag is
7 Scotland has
8 Many Scottish road signs

a in Edinburgh.
b the biggest city in Scotland.
c instruments for making music.
d lots of islands.
e are in two languages.
f blue and white
g a big lake in Scotland.
h are very short.

More practice 2 Sports clothes and equipment → Unit 3 | p.54

What things did Macbean's sell?

a Match photos A–H with the right words. Example: A – tents

first-aid kits £4.99

trainers only £12.99

rain jackets from £16.99

sunglasses from £4.99

tents from £29.99

rain trousers from £8.99

boots from £39.99

sleeping bags from £8.99

b 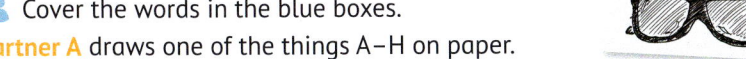 Cover the words in the blue boxes.
Partner A draws one of the things A–H on paper.
Partner B writes the words for each thing next to the picture.
Now look at the words and check that **Partner B** has written them correctly!
Then change roles.

c Now copy and complete the sentences with words from the blue boxes.
1 When you go camping your … is your house and you sleep in a …
2 You need good … if you want to go hiking in mountains.
3 You need a … if you have had an accident.
4 The sun can be bad for your eyes so wear …
5 … are useful because you can wear them in town or for hiking.
6 When you go hiking in bad weather it's a good idea to take a … and …

one hundred and seven 107

3 DIFF BANK

More practice 3 **True or false?** → Unit 3 | p.55

Read the dialogue on page 55.
The decide if the sentences below are true or false.
1. The kids think their dad should go to Glasgow.
2. Mum had a new idea.
3. The Highlands are popular with tourists.
4. Mum says that they could start a B&B.
5. The MacDonalds know a lot about B&Bs.
6. Jamie loves the new idea.

More help **4B** **SPEAKING** → Unit 3 | p.55

a Why should tourists visit Scotland? Make notes – as many as you can.
Use language from pages 52–53.
You should visit Scotland because …

Scotland has lots of	old castles.
	interesting towns.
	…

The Highlands		beautiful.
The mountains	are	interesting.
The lakes		famous.
The towns		great.
…		

You could	see / visit	Edinburgh.
		the Loch Ness Monster!
		the Kelpies.
		lots of castles.
		the Highland Games.
		…
	hear	bagpipes.
	wear / buy	a kilt
		…

b 👥 Tell your partner why he/she should visit Scotland.
Talk for as long as you can!
A You should visit Scotland!
B Why?
A Because the Highlands are beautiful! And you could see the Loch Ness Monster! And …

c 👥 Then swap roles.

More practice 4 Lochside B&B → Unit 3 | p.56

Look at the pictures. Then look again at the Lochside website.
Write the words for the pictures in your exercise book.

A: *a single ...*
B: *...*

More practice 5 More visitors for Lochside B&B → Unit 3 | p.57

a Write the names of the visitors in your exercise book.

b Then listen to them and write the right date next to each name.
2.05
1 Perry
2 Brown
3 Johnson
4 Taylor
5 Jones
6 Schmidt

27th July   31st July   16th August

1st August   15th August   27th August

one hundred and nine   **109**

3 DIFF BANK

More practice 6   Tell the story   → Unit 3 | p.61

a Copy and complete the network with the right adjectives.

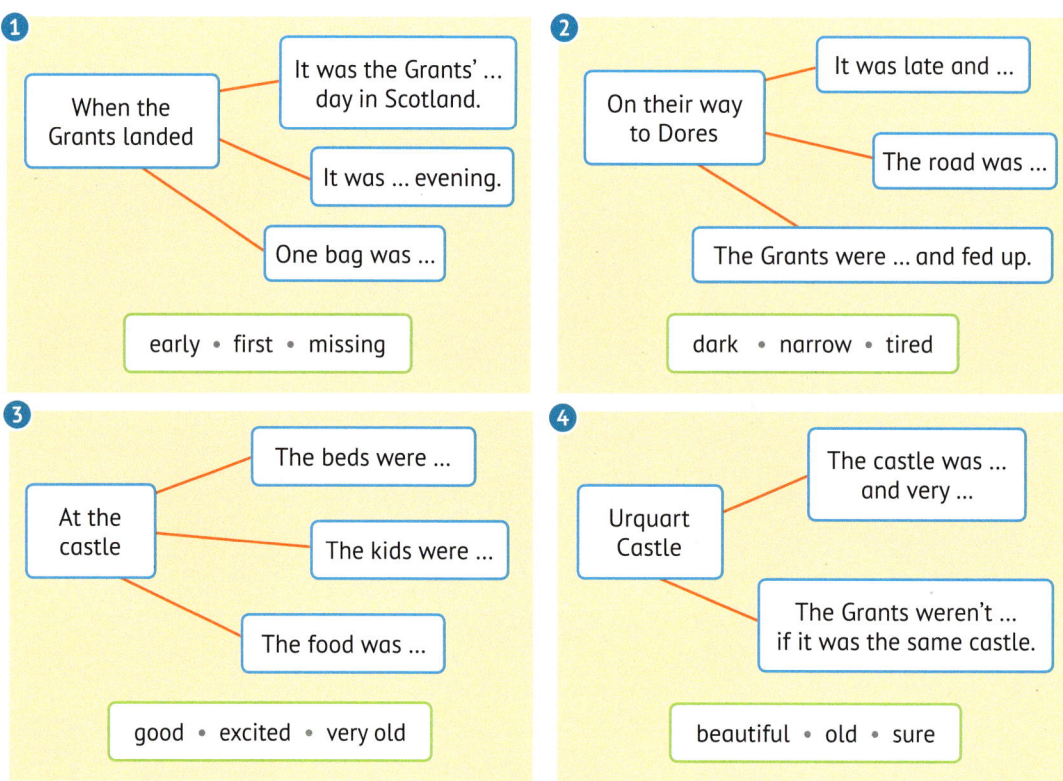

1
- When the Grants landed
  - It was the Grants' … day in Scotland.
  - It was … evening.
  - One bag was …

early • first • missing

2
- On their way to Dores
  - It was late and …
  - The road was …
  - The Grants were … and fed up.

dark • narrow • tired

3
- At the castle
  - The beds were …
  - The kids were …
  - The food was …

good • excited • very old

4
- Urquart Castle
  - The castle was … and very …
  - The Grants weren't … if it was the same castle.

beautiful • old • sure

b Be careful: The verbs are in the wrong sentences!
Write the sentences with the six verbs in the right sentences.

The plane ~~laughed~~.

She ~~looked~~ at her phone.

I ~~hired~~ with grandma.

Grandpa ~~pointed~~.

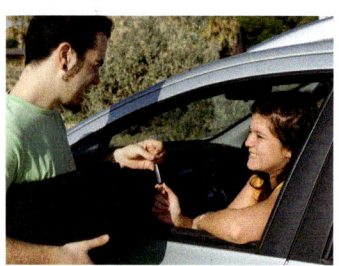

This car isn't mine.
I ~~chatted~~ it.

She ~~landed~~ for the way.

More practice 7 **Excuses for missing homework** → Unit 3 | p.62

a Replace the red words with possessive pronouns (*mine, yours,* etc.)

I'm sorry, Miss. The Queen asked to see our homework, so we gave our homework to her.

And a security man looked in Ella's bag and took her homework.

Sam and Lily made dinner and they cooked their homework by mistake.

Leo's cat ate his homework.

Sorry, Miss. A ghost came into my bedroom and took my homework. I was so scared!

b Write your own excuse.
Use the pronoun *mine* in your answer.
Teacher   Where is your homework?
You   I'm sorry. ...

Ideas:
A snake ...
An accident happened ...
There was an earthquake ...

More practice 8 **The lost phone** → Unit 3 | p.62

Leo has lost his phone. He sees two girls, and talks with one of them.
Replace the red words with possessive pronouns.

Leo   Hi, there. I'm sorry, I've lost my phone. Can I borrow your phone (1)?
Ava   Yes, of course ... Oh, that's funny. I can't find my phone (2)! But I'll ask my sister.
      I'm sure you can use her phone (3). Lily, this boy needs a phone. He has lost his phone (4).
      Can he use your phone (5)?
Lily I'm really sorry, but my phone (6) has no signal.
Leo   Well, thanks for trying.

Leo goes to two new people.

Leo   Hi, could you help me? I've lost my phone, and their phones (7) don't work.
Sam   I think our phones (8) work ...
Ella Yes, no problem. Here, take my phone (9).

3 DIFF BANK

More practice 9 A bad party → Unit 3 | p.63

a Write the seven words in the right lists.

> dancing • drinks • food • friends •
> music • boys • talking • girls

countable	uncountable
...	...

b Now copy and complete the gaps with *lots of*, *much* or *many*.
I went to a party last night, but it wasn't a very good one.
I didn't see ... (1) of my friends there.
There were ... (2) boring boys and there weren't ... (3) interesting girls.
There wasn't ... (4) good food and there weren't ... (5) drinks.
There was ... (6) talking, but there wasn't ... (7) dancing.
And there wasn't ... (8) good music.
I won't go there again!

Unit 4

More practice 1 **WORDS** → Unit 4 | p.78

Find the eight words in the text.
Then take one letter from each word: what word do they make?
1 a group of sport players: t ___ (take the fourth letter)
2 the place where students come to learn: s _____ (take the fifth letter)
3 the meal in the middle of the day: l ___ h (take the second letter)
4 information from your teacher or the principal: a _____ (take the third letter)
5 the morning meal: b _____ (take the last letter)
6 the American word for sweets: c _____ (take the second letter)
7 when somebody thinks rules are very important: s _____ (take the fourth letter)
8 the place where you have meals at school: c _____ (take the seventh letter)

🎧 2.16 *Parallel exercise* **2** **Monday's announcements** → Unit 4 | p.79

a Listen to today's announcements.
  1 Who speaks?
  2 Do they sound bored or excited?

b Listen again. Correct the blue words.
  1 The baseball team won on *Friday*.
  2 The basketball team came *first* in their competition.
  3 This is *A New Start* *month.*
  4 There's news of a new competition in *art* club.
  5 Ben has to go to the principal's *car*.

More practice 2 **Healthy and unhealthy foods** → Unit 4 | p.80

Copy and complete the sentences.
Give as many examples as you can in each sentence.
1 I shouldn't eat so much … and so many …
  I shouldn't eat so much chocolate and so many hot dogs.
2 I shouldn't drink so much … and so many glasses of …
3 I should eat more …
4 I should drink more …

> For food and drink words look at wordbank 4 on page 153.

Parallel exercise **3** **What's the right answer?** → Unit 4 | p.84

Copy the sentences and complete them correctly – A, B, C or D.
1 Ben's dad was unhappy at first because
  A Ben ate the cakes. B Ben had no friends. C the kitchen was messy.
  D the cakes were bad.
2 Ben's dad thinks school is
  A important. B not very important. C a waste of time. D easy.
3 Ben's dad thought the cakes were
  A fantastic. B better than the cakes in his shop. C terrible.
  D OK, but could be better.
4 Ben got his new idea from
  A his friends. B Mrs Fox. C a poster. D a text message.

DIFF BANK

More practice 3 **Tell the story** → Unit 4 | p.84

Put the sentences in the right order and tell the story.

A Ben's dad tried a cupcake and said it was OK – but it had to be something special.
B Ben and his friends made cupcakes in Ben's kitchen.
C Ben got an idea for his business from a poster on the way to school.
D Ben and his friends didn't sell many cupcakes at school, so Ben was fed up.
E Ben told his dad about the competition, but his dad wasn't interested.
F The kitchen was messy and Ben's dad was angry.

More help **6b** **Here and there** **Public holidays** → Unit 4 | p.85

Now choose a day when people in Germany celebrate together.

Make notes:
– the date/name of the day,
– what many people eat, sing, buy, do,
– what you do on that day.

> I want to talk about Christmas/Eid al-Fitr/Fasching/family birthdays/…
> This year Eid/Fasching is on …
> We celebrate Christmas on the evening of …
> Children are happy because … Many families have time together on this day.
> They maybe have dinner/go on a trip/go shopping/go for a walk together.
> People visit their parents/brothers and sisters/grandparents.
> Many people put on funny clothes/sing songs/watch parades.
> They often give presents/have a meal together.
> In the evening there are fireworks/parties in town.
> There are/aren't any important football matches on this day.
> Most people feel … on this day.

More practice 4 **Number One** → Unit 4 | p.87
Copy and complete the sentences.

1 Chatting is one of the ... (popular) activities.
2 Film 1 is the ... (exciting) film in this cinema.
3 The red bike is the ... (expensive) bike in the shop.

4 Maths is the ... (difficult) subject for me.
5 Harry Potter is one of the ... (famous) books in the world.
6 The tiger is the ... (dangerous) animal in this zoo.

More practice 5 **AND YOU?** What do you think? → Unit 4 | p.87

a Copy and complete six of the eight sentences.
1 The most popular place for young people in town is ...
2 The most successful football club in the world is ...
3 The most exciting action film is ...
4 The most dangerous animal in the world is ...
5 The most useful app is ...
6 The most expensive clothes shop in town is ...
7 The most beautiful place I have ever seen is ...
8 The most famous sports person in Germany at the moment is ...

b 👥 Now read your sentences to three different partners. Who do you agree with most often?

DIFF BANK

Parallel exercise **1b** Two weather reports → Unit 4 | p.89

Read the sentences. The information in them is WRONG.
Listen to the weather reports again and correct the sentences.

Weather report 1
1 The highest temperature was 52 degrees.
2 There was a little rain late in the afternoon.
3 Tomorrow the weather will be worse.

Weather report 2
1 In the afternoon it was sunny.
2 The day temperatures were just below 40 degrees.

More help **4** AND YOU? Your DVD cover → Unit 4 | p.90

1 Choose a film and make a DVD cover for it. Write
  – the title of the film
  – the name(s) of actor(s) in the film
  – one sentence that tells you what is special about the film:

The	beautiful exciting famous scary true	story of a	brave amazing modern great successful terrible	boy. girl. man. woman. monster.

2 Say who can see the film. The US categories are:
  G   Everybody can see the film.
  PG/PG-13 Parents can decide if their children should see the film.
  R   People under 17 can see the film only together with an older person.
  NC-17   Only people aged 17 or over can see the film.

3 Write a short text about the film. Make it sound exciting!

(name of character)	lives in/with … meets … tries to … wants to …, but … knows that …

Life is difficult/funny/dangerous/easy because …
Then suddenly …
What will happen to …?

4 Write how long the film is.
5 Can you see the film in English, German, Spanish, …?

Anhänge

Text File

Skills File

Language File

Wordbank

Vocabulary

Dictionary

TEXT FILE

TF 1 London for tourists

Travel …

by tube

The Tube is the popular name for London Underground trains.
It's the oldest underground train system in the world – it opened in 1863! Today there are 270 stations and 11 lines. It's easy to use and about 3 million people go on the Tube every day.

by bus

London's red double-decker buses are famous. The city has more than 700 bus routes and most Londoners live only 400 metres away from one of the 19,500 bus stops. Teens from 11–15 travel free with a Zip Oyster Card. You must apply[1] for this card at least four weeks before you travel.

or by taxi

Taxi drivers must take a very difficult test[2] and must know 25,000 streets in London.
Drivers learn for the test for two to four years. Taxis are expensive if you're alone – but not so expensive for small groups.

Big Ben

Dong, dong, dong, dong! For many people Big Ben is the most famous sound of London.
When Londoners say "Big Ben" they usually mean the clock tower – but Big Ben is really the name of the bell.

You can hear Big Ben very well if you stand next to the Houses of Parliament.

London Eye

Over 3.5 million people ride the London Eye every year. It is 135 metres tall and a tour takes 30 minutes. The Eye moves[3] so slowly that it doesn't stop when people get on. It's open every day (but not on Christmas Day). Travel by Tube to Waterloo station. Or walk over the river from the Houses of Parliament.

---

[1] **(to) apply for** [əˈplaɪ] *beantragen*   [2] **(to) take a test** *eine Prüfung machen*   [3] **(to) move** [muːv] *sich bewegen*

Wembley Stadium

Wembley stadium, the new home of the England national football team, opened in 2007. With space for 90,000 fans and 310 fans in wheelchairs, it's the second largest stadium in Europe. It has 688 places where fans can buy food and drink, and 2618 toilets.

Wembley is a great place for lots of different sports, e.g. American football, rugby and athletics, and for concerts. It's open every day (not Christmas or 1st January, or when there is a game or concert). Travel by Tube or bus. But remember: it's 12 kilometres from the centre of London to Wembley!

Sherlock Holmes

Sherlock Holmes lived at 221B Baker Street … No! That's not true! Sherlock Holmes wasn't a real person. He was a famous detective in books by Arthur Conan Doyle. The first Sherlock Holmes story came out in 1887. But today, 221B Baker Street is a great museum about Sherlock Holmes.

It's open from 9.30 am to 5.30 pm. Travel by Tube to Baker Street, and see the statue of Sherlock Holmes outside the station!

Buckingham Palace

The king or queen lives and works here. When the Queen is at home, you see her flag on top of the palace. The palace has 240 bedrooms, 78 bathrooms and 775 rooms in all. About 800 people work in or for the palace: cooks, cleaners, gardeners, drivers, etc.

Guards[4] with black and red uniforms and big, black hats stand outside the palace. It's free to watch the guards change in front of the palace.

Buckingham Palace is open from July to the end of September. Travel by bus, or take the Tube to St James' Park, or walk! It's only 15 minutes on foot from Big Ben.

Harry Potter

Do you like the Harry Potter films? Some of the places in the films are in London.

The way into the Leaky Cauldron pub is at Leadenhall Market, Harry speaks to a snake in London Zoo, and the train to Hogwarts goes from platform 9¾ at Kings Cross Station.

MEDIATION

Wähle die für dich drei interessantesten Themen oder Sehenswürdigkeiten. Erkläre deinem Partner/deiner Partnerin deine Wahl auf Deutsch.

[4] **guard** [gɑːd] *Wache*

TEXT FILE

TF 2   A German student in Ireland

Read the story. Can you complete Maja's blogs?

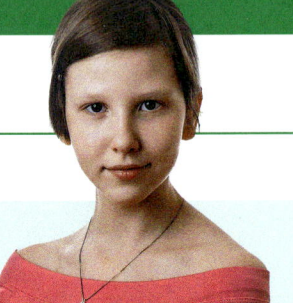

Maja Gschwilm from Munich spent one week with the O'Briens in Dublin. She learned lots of things about living in another country.

PART 1   Maja arrives at the O'Briens
🎧 2.28

Mrs O'Brien, her son Liam and her daughter Emily met Maja at the airport.
Then they drove to their house – a small,
5   cute house, in a line of other houses.

Inside, Maja met two younger boys.
"I'm Maja," she said, and she put out her hand. But the boys didn't take her hand. They only looked at her and said hello. Then a small girl
10   and a dog came out of a room.
"And that's Tess – with Milo the dog,"
Mrs O'Brien said. Maja smiled at Tess, but she didn't put out her hand this time.
"I'll make some tea," said Liam. "Milk and
15   sugar, Maja?"
"No thanks – just black, please,"
Maja answered.
Liam was surprised. And Maja was surprised when she tried the tea.
20   It was very, very strong.
"Oh, I'd like some sugar, please, Mrs O'Brien," she said.
"OK, Maja. But don't call me 'Mrs O'Brien'. My name is Nora, so please call me Nora."
25   "OK, Mrs O'Brien … er I mean Nora."
Maja was surprised. She liked Nora O'Brien already.

Majas Blog (1)

Endlich in Irland angekommen … viel ist anders hier, aber die Familie ist echt nett. Morgen gehe ich mit Liam in die Schule (wir sind beide 14). Ich habe hier schon einiges gelernt, z.B. …   30

PART 2   Maja's first day at school
🎧 2.29

Peep – peep – peep … Emily woke up with a shock.   35
"What's that?" she thought.
"It's only 7 o'clock." It was Maja's alarm!
"Oh Maja, it's too early! School starts at 9 o'clock," Emily said   40
and went back to sleep[1].

But Maja got up because she was so excited.

At 8 o'clock Maja was still in the bathroom. Three O'Brien kids were outside the bathroom. They wanted to go to the toilet – it wasn't   45
funny! When Maja came out at last, she understood the problem.
"Oh I'm sorry," she said. "I forgot that there was only one toilet in the house."

When they got to school, all the students   50
were in school uniform.
"I'm happy that I'm a visitor," thought Maja.
"I don't have to wear a tie!"

The day at school was OK. Lots of kids asked Maja about Germany, her school, her family.   55
She didn't understand everything, but it was fun.

Majas Blog (2)

Heute war ich in der Schule. Alle haben gedacht, dass ich Liams Freundin bin ☺. Auch heute habe ich ein paar Dinge gelernt, z.B. …   60

---

[1] **go back to sleep** *wieder einschlafen*

PART 3 After school

It was a long day at school. Lessons finished at 4 pm, and they got home at 5 pm.
"Hi, Maja," called Nora. "It's tea time."
"Tea?" Maja asked Emily. "I'm hungry!"
Emily smiled. "Don't worry. We say 'tea', but we mean dinner."
Liam cooked sausages, eggs, tomatoes, beans and potatoes.

"Good appetite," Maja said – and one of Liam's brothers laughed.
"Did I say something wrong?" Maja asked.
"Well," Nora answered. "We don't say 'good appetite.' We …, well we just eat."
"Oh, OK," Maja said. And ate.

After tea, Liam said, "Hey Maja, there's a disco at school on Friday. It's for kids under 18. Would you like to come?"
"Yes, OK," Maja said. "But I don't have the right clothes."
"That's no problem," said Emily. "I'll phone some friends."

On Friday after school three girls brought some disco clothes to the house. Maja had lots of fun with the girls. And at the disco Maja met more of Liam's friends. They were very nice and they all had lots of fun that evening.

Majas Blog (3)

Heute war ich mit Liam in der Disco, das war voll genial. Ein paar Mädels haben mir Klamotten ausgeliehen und Makeup – die waren echt entspannt. Ich habe wieder einige Sachen dazu gelernt, z.B. …

PART 4 The last day

On Maja's last day, she and Liam went into Dublin centre on the bus. Maja bought presents for her family and friends.
Then they saw some street musicians and they listened to some good Irish music.
At lunchtime Maja said, "Can we eat something Irish?"
So Liam took Maja to a cafe in the old part of Dublin. "It's the best fish and chip shop in Dublin!" Liam said. Liam asked for two fish and chips.
"Do you want vinegar[2] on the chips?" asked Liam.
"Vinegar?!" Maja said, shocked. "No thanks!"

They took their food to St Patrick's Park. It was nice there.
"Try my chips with vinegar," Liam said to Maja. She tried one … and she liked it!
"What do you put on chips in Germany?" Liam asked.
"Tomato ketchup or mayonnaise," Maja answered.
"Mayonnaise on chips? Yuck!" Liam said, shocked.
"When you come to Germany you can try it. It's great!" Maja answered and smiled.
"You learn a lot when you travel," she thought, "things that you can't learn at school."

Majas Blog (4)

Mein letzter Tag ☹. Ich habe aber immer noch einiges gelernt, z.B. …

---

[2]**vinegar** [ˈvɪnɪɡə] *Essig*

TEXT FILE

TF 3 Scotland

A Geography

Scotland is the country north of England. It's about half as big as England and about as big as Bavaria.

Most people live in the south, in or near the big cities of Edinburgh (the capital) and Glasgow. Aberdeen is the only big city in the north.

Number of people in Scotland's biggest cities:	
Glasgow	– 600,060
Edinburgh	– 489,000
Aberdeen	– 261,960

Oil[1] and gas from the North Sea bring a lot of money and jobs to Aberdeen.

Not many people live in the *Highlands* in the north and west. This is a region of hills and mountains: the highest mountain is Ben Nevis (1344 m).

The longest river is the River Tay (190 kilometres). There are 790 islands (99 with people) and more than 30,000 freshwater lakes *(lochs)*.
The biggest lake in cubic metres is Loch Ness (7,452 million m^3). Loch Ness is the most famous lake because some people think it has a monster – called Nessie!

B History

Scotland is part of the UK. But people from Scotland are proud to be Scottish, so don't call them English!

Older history
For hundreds of years, Scotland and England were two different countries. They often had wars[2]. Sometimes, England won, sometimes Scotland won.

In **1707** Scotland and England became one country – Great Britain. They had one parliament – in London.

Modern history
Scotland has its own flag and national football team.

The Scots have pounds like the English, but Scottish money looks a bit different.

1997: Scotland gets its own parliament again.

2014: The Scottish people vote[3] to stay in the UK.

---

[1] **oil** [ɔɪl] *Öl* [2] **war** [wɔː] *Krieg* [3] **(to) vote** [vəʊt] *für etwas (ab)stimmen*

C Life

Languages
Everybody in Scotland speaks English. But in the *Highlands* some people also speak Gaelic[4]. You'll see roads signs in English and Gaelic.

Sport
Football is the most popular sport in Scotland. Golf is popular too – it started 600 years ago in St Andrews, near Edinburgh. Golf isn't an expensive sport in Scotland, so everybody can play.

In the *Highlands* you can see shinty (a sport a bit like hockey) and traditional sports like tossing the caber[5].

tossing the caber

Festivals
At festivals in Scotland you will see men in kilts and you will hear bagpipes.
There is a long tradition of singing and dancing and Scottish music is very popular.

D The Loch Ness Monster

Is there a monster in Loch Ness?
Most people say 'no', but every year people take photos of something that looks like a monster.

This photo from 1934 is perhaps the most famous picture. For 60 years, people weren't sure if the photo was real or not. But in 1993 the true story came out. It was a trick! It was really a toy submarine[6] with a model of a monster.
In 2012, Marcus Atkinson, a tourist boat captain, was on Loch Ness near Urquhart Castle. Something big followed his boat for more than two minutes. Marcus saw it on his sonar equipment, so he took a photo of the sonar picture. It looks like a big snake. Marcus said: "I was shocked. I showed it to other boat captains and nobody knew what it was."

Experts said it was a photo of plankton (very, very small animals) in the water, but fans of the Loch Ness monster were very excited.
Stories like this explain why thousands of tourists come to Loch Ness every year to look for Nessie. Perhaps you could find Nessie too?

Here and there Scotland and Bavaria
Read the information. What is like Bavaria?
They are part of a bigger country, …
What is different from Bavaria?
Some men wear kilts, …
Write as many examples as you can.

---

[4] **Gaelic** ['geɪlɪk] *Gälisch*   [5] **tossing the caber** [tɒsɪŋ ðəˈkeɪbə] *Baumstammwerfen*
[6] **toy submarine** [tɔɪˈsʌbməriːn] *Spielzeug U-Boot*

TEXT FILE

TF 4 A year of special days in the USA

Read the texts A–I. Then match each text with a photo 1–9.

JANUARY — third Monday

A Martin Luther King Day
Martin Luther King worked against discrimination[1] in the USA and for fairness – especially black people. He won the Nobel Peace Prize[2] in 1964, but was murdered[3] in 1968. Americans celebrate his life's work on the third Monday of January. Some schools close on this day, other schools teach their students about Martin Luther King. And many people do voluntary[4] work on this day, in hospitals or with homeless people in the streets.

FEBRUARY — a Tuesday

B Mardi Gras
Many cities and regions in the USA have their own special days. For example, Mardi Gras is very important in New Orleans. On a Tuesday in February or March, there are big carnival parades – and there's music and colour, everywhere!

MARCH — a Tuesday

MARCH — 17

C St Patrick's Day
St Patrick's Day (March 17th) is a national holiday in Ireland – not in the USA. But 34.5 million people in the USA (11.6% of all Americans) say that they once had some family in Ireland, and many of them wear green and sing Irish songs on St Patrick's day.
Only 4.8 million people live in Ireland – so more people celebrate St Patrick's Day in the USA than in Ireland!

MAY — second Sunday

D Mother's Day and Father's Day
Many countries have days to celebrate mothers and fathers.
In the USA, Mother's Day is the second Sunday in May, and Father's Day is the third Sunday in June.

JUNE — third Sunday

MAY — last Monday

E Memorial Day and Labor Day
Americans don't get long holidays, and these two public holidays are very popular because they are on Mondays.
So people can take long weekends. Memorial Day (when people remember soldiers[5] who died) is on the last Monday in May. That's the beginning of summer, and many swimming pools open on this day.
Labor Day (when people celebrate America's workers) is on the first Monday in September. That's the last public holiday before the winter.

SEPTEMBER — first Monday

JULY — 4

F Independence Day
On the fourth of July there are flags everywhere. Why? Because this public holiday celebrates the day that the USA were born – with independence from the British in 1776. There are lots of special sports events. Many Americans have picnics and watch awesome fireworks in the evening.

NOVEMBER — fourth Thursday

G Thanksgiving Day
Americans celebrate Thanksgiving[6] Day on the fourth Thursday of November. Businesses and schools close on Thursday and Friday, and people often travel hundreds of miles so that they can be with their families. Families have a big meal, often with turkey[7] for dinner. There are parades, and many important sports events. And there are collections[8] of food for poor people too.

---

[1]**discrimination** [dɪskrɪmɪˈneɪʃn] *Diskriminierung, unfaire Behandlung* [2]**Nobel Peace Prize** [nəʊˈbel ˈpiːs praɪz] *Friedensnobelpreis* [3]**(to) murder** [ˈmɜːdə] *ermorden* [4]**voluntary** [ˈvɒləntri] *ehrenamtlich* [5]**soldier** [ˈsəʊldʒə] *Soldat*

OCTOBER 31

H Halloween

Halloween is a fun festival for children They dress up as ghosts, witches⁹ or monsters on the evening of October 31st and go from house to house and get candy from people. People also make eyes, a nose and a mouth in a big pumpkin¹⁰ and put it outside their house. The pumpkins can look very funny.

DECEMBER 25

I Christmas

For most families, Christmas Day (25th December) is the most important festival of the year. People celebrate it as in Europe, with a Christmas tree and a big dinner. Santa Claus brings presents to the children (not Father Christmas, as in Britain). But most Americans have to work on 26th December – it's not a public holiday.

---

⁶ **Thanksgiving** [θæŋksˈɡɪvɪŋ] *Erntedank*   ⁷ **turkey** [ˈtɜːki] *Truthahn*   ⁸ **collection** [kəˈlekʃn] *Sammlung*
⁸ **witch** [wɪtʃ] *Hexe*   ¹⁰ **pumpkin** [ˈpʌmpkɪn] *Kürbis*

one hundred and twenty-five   **125**

SKILLS FILE

SF 1 Vokabeln lernen

→ Unit 4 | p.79

- Führe dein Vokabelheft oder deine Vokabelkartei aus Klasse 6 weiter.
- Lerne nur 5 bis 10 neue Vokabeln auf einmal.
- Versuche, jeden Tag 10 Minuten zu lernen.
- Lerne mit jemandem zusammen. Es macht mehr Spaß, und ihr könnt euch gegenseitig abfragen.
- Schreibe schwierige Vokabeln auf selbsthaftende Zettel. Die klebst du dann zu Hause auf Gegenstände, die du immer wieder ansiehst.

Weitere Tipps zum besseren Merken:

1 Mache Wortfelder
- Ordne die Wörter unter einem Oberbegriff. Du kannst eine Liste machen oder auch ein *wordweb*.
- Oder du arbeitest mit Karteikarten. Schreibe den Oberbegriff in Großbuchstaben auf die Vorderseite einer Karteikarte und die dazu passenden Wörter auf die Rückseite. Später kannst du neue Wörter ergänzen.

2 Finde Gegensatzpaare
Sammle Gegensatzpaare und schreibe sie z.B. auf die letzte Seite deines Vokabelhefts.

3 Lerne *phrases* statt Einzelwörter
Phrases sind Ausdrücke, die aus mehreren Wörtern bestehen, z.B. *a bottle of water* = eine Flasche Wasser. Lerne also nicht *bottle* und *water* als Einzelwörter, sondern den ganzen Ausdruck: *a bottle of water*.

Weitere Beispiele:
- *(to) point* → *(to) point at*
- *allergic* → *allergic to nuts*
- *a form* → *(to) fill in a form*
- *crazy* → *(to) go crazy*

a few

lots of

einen Bus erwischen

(to) catch a bus

SF 2 Unbekannte Wörter verstehen → Unit 1 | p.22 → Unit 3 | p.65

Du kannst englische Texte verstehen – auch wenn du nicht alle Wörter kennst.

1 Schau dir die Bilder an
Bilder zeigen dir oft Dinge aus dem Text. Was bedeuten z. B. *screws, nails* und *screwdriver* im Text rechts?

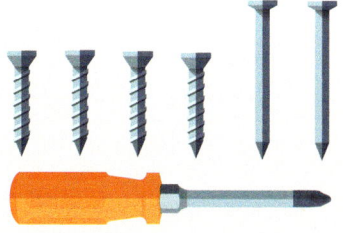

First check if you have all things:
4 **screws**, 2 long **nails** and a **screwdriver**. You also need a **hammer** and some **sandpaper**.

2 Denke an ähnliche Wörter im Deutschen
Viele englische Wörter werden ähnlich wie im Deutschen geschrieben oder klingen ähnlich wie deutsche Wörter:
- *hammer* heißt auf Deutsch „Hammer",
- *sandpaper* bedeutet „Sand- oder Schmirgelpapier".

Was bedeuten die folgenden Wörter auf Deutsch?

> balcony • cable • element •
> flexible • material • optimistic • quality •
> situation • typical

Hmm, *typical* sieht so aus wie das deutsche Wort „typisch", oder?

3 Schau dir den ganzen Satz an
Häufig kannst du die Bedeutung eines unbekannten Wortes aus dem Zusammenhang erschließen. Lies einfach den ganzen Satz und überlege dir, welches Wort hier Sinn machen würde. Was könnten z.B. *alarm* und *go off* bedeuten?

On weekdays the alarm on my mobile goes off at seven o' clock. Then I have to get up.

Also, es geht ums Wecken am Morgen ... ich hab's!

4 Suche Bekanntes in unbekannten Wörtern
Manchmal steckt in einem neuen Wort ein anderes Wort, das du schon kennst. Wie heißen die folgenden Wörter auf Deutsch?

> biker • buyer • dreamer • fruity • icy •
> watery • sunlight • haircut • freshwater

Dream kenne ich schon, das heißt „Traum". Also könnte *dreamer* „Träumer" heißen.

---

1 **screws** Schrauben **nails** Nägel **screwdriver** Schraubendreher 2 **balcony** Balkon **cable** Kabel **element** Element **flexible** flexibel **material** Material **optimistic** optimistisch **quality** Qualität **situation** Situation **typical** typisch 3 **alarm** Wecker **go off** läuten 4 **biker** Fahrradfahrer/in **buyer** Käufer/in **dreamer** Träumer/in **fruity** fruchtig **icy** eisig **watery** wässrig **sunlight** Sonnenlicht **haircut** Haarschnitt **freshwater** Süßwasser

SKILLS FILE

SF 3 Im Wörterbuch nachschlagen

→ Unit 3 | p.65   → Unit 4 | p.90

1 Wörter alphabetisch ordnen

Alles im Wörterbuch ist alphabetisch aufgelistet:
- *U* kommt vor *V*
- *van* kommt vor *vegetables*
- *van* kommt vor *variety*

> °**useful** [ˈjuːsfl] nützlich
> **usually** [ˈjuːʒʊəli] meistens, normalerweise 5
>
> **V**
>
> **van** [væn] Transporter, Lieferwagen 7: 2 (32)
> °**variety (of)** [vəˈraɪəti] Auswahl (an)
> **vegetables** *(pl)* [ˈvedʒtəblz] Gemüse 5

2 Zusammengesetze Ausdrücke finden

Der Haupteintrag (z.B. *easy*) steht farbig oder fett am Anfang. Daneben oder darunter findest du oft zusammengesetzte Wörter oder Redewendungen (z.B. *take it easy*).

> **easy** ► **take it easy** *(umg)* sich nicht aufregen
> ► **easy-going** ungezwungen, gelassen

3 Unterschiedliche Wortbedeutungen beachten

Die Ziffern 1, 2 usw. zeigen, dass ein Wort mehrere Bedeutungen hat.

> Egal, ob du ein englisches oder deutsches Wort suchst: Lies immer den ganzen Eintrag und entscheide dann, welche Bedeutung die richtige ist.

a Englisch-Deutsch

Das Wort *enter* heißt am Computer *eingeben*.
Was aber heißt *enter* in diesen Sätzen?

1. When did you enter the USA? Two weeks ago.
2. Please use the door on the right to enter the building.
3. Please enter your name here at the top of the list.
4. Lots of people were seasick, so they were happy when the ferry entered the harbour.

> **enter** *Verb*
> 1 *(Zimmer)* eintreten
> 2 *(Gebäude)* betreten, hineinkommen
> 3 *(Land)* einreisen
> 4 *(Hafen)* einlaufen
> 5 *(in Liste)* eintragen
> 6 *(Computer)* eingeben

b Deutsch-Englisch

Welches sind die richtigen Wörter für *anmachen* in diesen Sätzen?

1. Kannst du den Salat anmachen?
2. Wieso machst du mich an? Ich habe nichts getan.
3. Bitte mach das Licht an.
4. Sie machte einen Spiegel im Bad an.

> **anmachen** *Verb (umg)*
> 1 *(anbringen)* (to) put up
> 2 *(einschalten)* (to) put on
> 3 *(anzünden)* (to) light
> 4 *(Salat)* (to) dress
> 5 *(kritisieren)* (to) have a go at someone *(umg)*

3a 1 einreisen – 2 hineinkommen – 3 eintragen – 4 einlaufen   3b 1 dress – 2 have a go at me – 3 put on – 4 put up

SF 4 Aus Fehlern lernen

Fehler sind etwas Gutes. Wir ärgern uns zwar über sie, aber sie können zu Helfern werden.

1 Erkenne deine Fehler

Was ist bei deinen Proben oder korrigierten Texten oft angestrichen?
Erkenne, welche Fehler du gemacht hast, und versuche es mit diesen Strategien:

a Leichtsinnsfehler
Vergisst du Buchstaben oder Wörter?
Verwechselst du Buchstaben oder Wörter?
I come form Zwiesel. → from

→ Lass dich nicht ablenken und konzentriere dich auf die Aufgabe. Teile dir die Zeit besser ein. Lies die Arbeit noch einmal durch.

b Vokabelfehler
Kannst du die Wörter nicht richtig schreiben oder aussprechen?
Verwechselst du Vokabeln? Weißt du nicht, was das Wort bedeutet?

→ Beachte die Hinweise auf S. 126 und 127. Lerne und wiederhole regelmäßig. Schreibe die Wörter beim Lernen immer auf.

c Grammatikfehler
Verwendest du die falsche Verbform?
She play football well. → plays
Hast du Probleme mit der Wortstellung?
Machst du Fehler bei den Pronomen?
*My mum was angry.
He said … → She*

→ Suche das betreffende Grammatikkapitel im *Language file* (S. 140–149) und lies es sorgfältig. Hast du alles verstanden? Bitte deine Lehrkraft um Hilfe. Sie kann dir Aufgaben zum Üben geben.

d Verständnisfehler
Weißt du manchmal nicht, was du tun sollst?

→ Lies die Arbeitsanweisung sehr genau durch. Auch zwei- oder dreimal!

2 Erstelle deine persönliche Fehlerliste

Wenn du eine Klassenarbeit oder einen Text korrigiert zurück bekommst, achte auf die Fehler, die du gemacht hast, und erstelle deine persönliche Fehlerliste. Gehe diese immer wieder durch.

SKILLS FILE

SF 5 Proben und Prüfungen

Bei Proben und Prüfungen sind die Arbeitsanweisungen ganz wichtig!
Deshalb:
1. Lies zuerst **alle** Arbeitsanweisungen.
2. Lies die Arbeitsanweisungen **sehr genau** – auch zwei- oder dreimal!
   Sie geben dir wichtige Hinweise und Hilfen.
3. Prüfe am Ende: Hast du alle Anweisungen befolgt? Kannst du alle Punkte abhaken?

1 READING

Hier ist ein Beispiel für eine Leseverstehensaufgabe.

> *First read the text. Then do tasks 1–9:*
> *Decide if the statements are true or false and tick the correct box.*
> *Then finish the sentences.*
> *You can quote from the text.*

1. Lies zuerst die Arbeitsanweisung. Unterstreiche, was du tun sollst:

   > *First <u>read</u> the text.*
   > *Then <u>do</u> tasks 1–9:*
   > *Decide if the statements are true or false and <u>tick</u> the correct box.*
   > *Then <u>finish</u> the sentences.*
   > *You can <u>quote from the text</u>.*

2. Was musst du bei dieser Aufgabe tun:
   - eine Tabelle vervollständigen?
   - Kästchen abhaken?
   - Textstellen suchen?
   - aus dem Text zitieren?
   - falsche Aussagen korrigieren?

I've lived in London since January. At first I didn't like the city because it is very loud and noisy. After some time I really enjoyed it here and I think it's an amazing place for lots of reasons.
Firstly, you can go to many interesting places like the Natural History Museum where you can see dinosaurs. The best thing is: You don't have to pay to get in.
Secondly, you have nice parks, where you can have a break …

1. *He came to London at the beginning of the year. This statement is*
   a) ☐ true   b) ☐ false
   because the text says _____
2. *Now he likes life in the city. This statement is*
   a) ☐ true   b) ☐ false
   because the text says _____
3. …

Du musst Kästchen ankreuzen, Textstellen suchen und aus dem Text zitieren.

2 LISTENING

Lies auch bei Höraufgaben die Arbeitsanweisungen genau und unterstreiche das Wichtigste.

> *First read the tasks 1–6.*
> *Then listen to the discussion.*
> *<u>Tick</u> the correct box or <u>complete</u> the sentences while you are listening.*
> *Tick <u>only one box</u>.*
> *At the end you will <u>hear the discussion again</u>. Now read the tasks 1–6.*
> *You have one minute.*

Was sollst du zuerst tun?

Was wirst du hören?

Musst du bei jeder Aufgabe Kästchen abhaken?

Kannst du mehrere Kästchen abhaken?

Wie oft wirst du den Text hören?

Wie viel Zeit hast du zum Lesen der Aufgaben?

3 WRITING

Hier ist ein Beispiel für eine Schreibaufgabe.

1 Lies zuerst die Arbeitsanweisungen. Welche würdest du unterstreichen?

> *Write an email to your penfriend Steve. Tell him about your last class trip (two things or more). Ask him two questions about his class trip. Write 60 words ore more.*

2 Nun lies Yasins Lösung der Aufgabe.

> Dear Mike
> How are you?
> I feel great. We came back from a class trip last Friday. It was fantastic.
> We spent a week in Habischried. There we went hiking in the mountains.
> One night we made a fire. Our teacher played the guitar and we sang songs.
> That was fun.
> Were did you go on your last class trip?
> Tell me about it.

Hat Yasin die Aufgabe richtig gelöst?

Sind der Anfang und das Ende des Textes wie bei einer Email?

Hat er mindestens zwei Dinge über seine Klassenfahrt geschrieben?

Hat er zwei Fragen gestellt?

Hat er mindestens 60 Wörter geschrieben?

Write an email to your English penfriend Steve. Tell him about your last class trip (two things or more). Ask him two questions about his class trip. Write 60 words or more.
Yasin hat zwei Dinge nicht befolgt: Er hat die Schlussformel der Email vergessen (Best wishes, Yasin) und er hat nur eine Frage zu Steves Klassenfahrt gestellt.

SKILLS FILE

SF 6 Texte besser verstehen → Unit 3 | p.67

1 Skimming

Mit dieser Technik kannst du dir schnell einen Überblick über einen Text verschaffen. Dabei liest du nur ganz kurz und schnell und achtest besonders auf Überschriften, Bilder, Bildunterschriften und fett gedruckte Wörter. Du brauchst nicht jedes Detail zu verstehen.

Du bereitest z.B. einen Vortrag zum Thema *Shinty* vor und suchst allgemeine Informationen zu diesem schottischen Ballspiel. Welcher der beiden Texte eignet sich besser für dein Thema?

Strathglass Shinty Club

Where
The club is based in the village of Cannich near Loch Ness in the Scottish Highlands.

History and teams
The Shinty club has an amazing history. It started in 1879 and today has two junior teams, a First Team and a Second Team.

Success
The First Team presently plays in the National Division. The village is very proud of its sports heroes.

Shinty

Game
Shinty is a team game played with sticks and a ball. It's a bit like hockey.

Rules
There are 12 players on each side.

Players can play the ball in the air and are allowed to use both sides of the stick. They mustn't use their hands – only the goalkeeper can do that.
The winner is the team that scores the most goals.

League system
At present there are these divisions:

2 Scanning

Mit dieser Technik kannst du einen Text nach ganz bestimmten Informationen durchsuchen.
- Du suchst dabei nur nach wichtigen Wörtern (Schlüsselwörtern) und lässt alles andere beiseite.
- Geh dabei mit den Augen und dem Finger schnell über den Text. Das gesuchte Wort wird dir „ins Auge springen". Lies nur dort weiter, um Näheres zu erfahren. Du möchtest z.B. wissen, wie viele Spieler es bei *Shinty* gibt. Suche also nach dem Wort *player*. Wenn du das Wort nicht findest, suche nach ähnlichen Begriffen.

SF 7 Hören und Notizen machen

→ Unit 4 | p. 89

1 Vor dem Hören

Lies immer zuerst die Aufgabe sehr sorgfältig.
Typische Aufgaben sind:
- *multiple-choice* Aufgaben,
- *true / false* Aufgaben,
- Bilder nach einer Reihenfolge ordnen,
- eine Tabelle oder Lücken vervollständigen,
- eigene kurze Sätze oder Satzteile schreiben.

Hier ein Beispiel:

> *Sarah is going to spend the weekend in Memphis.*
> *On Friday morning she listens to the weather report.*
> *What will the weather be like*
> *– on Friday evening?*
> *– on Saturday?*
> *– on Sunday?*
> *You will hear the recording twice.*

Überlege vor dem Hören: Welche Wörter könnten in einer Wettervorhersage vorkommen *(windy, rainy, sunny)*?

Was musst du tun: Kästchen ankreuzen oder eigene Antworten schreiben?

Kannst du dir vor dem Hören schon eine Liste oder Notizen machen?

Es macht nichts, wenn du zuerst nicht alles hast – du hörst den Text zweimal.

2 Beim Hören

- Achte beim Hören auf die Wörter, die in der Aufgabe stehen. Achtung! Die Informationen könnten in einer anderen Reihenfolge auftauchen.

- Mache dir Notizen. Verwende Symbole oder Abkürzungen, z.B. „+" für *and*.

- Gib nicht auf, wenn du etwas nicht verstanden hast. Bleib ruhig und höre weiter zu. Vielleicht verstehst du beim zweiten Hören mehr. Oder vielleicht brauchst du diese Information gar nicht.

3 Nach dem Hören

- Vervollständige deine Notizen sofort.
- Konzentriere dich beim zweiten Hören auf das, was du zuerst nicht gut verstanden hast.

SKILLS FILE

SF 8   Eigene Texte schreiben → Unit 1 | p.21   → Unit 2 | p.44

A   Welche Art von Text willst du verfassen?

1   Persönlicher Brief oder Email

- Beginne mit einer persönlichen Anrede, z.B. *Dear Lily oder Hi Alex!*
- Frage, wie es deinem Freund oder deiner Freundin geht: *How are you?*
- Erzähle, wie es dir geht, und was bei dir Interessantes geschehen ist:
  I'm tired because …
  Yesterday we went … Then we had …
- Frage, was bei deinem Freund oder deiner Freundin so passiert ist:
  What did you do last week /
  in the holidays / …?
- Schreibe am Ende immer einen freundlichen Gruß, z.B. *Best wishes* oder *Lots of love* und deinen Namen.

> Hi Alex!
>
> How are you? I'm tired because I was very busy yesterday. In the morning I went shopping with my dad. In the afternoon I went to the cinema with my friend Charlotte. We saw a funny film and ate lots of popcorn. It was great.
>
> What did you do yesterday? Were you busy too?
>
> Lots of love
> Anna

2   Formeller Brief oder Email

- Beginne mit *Dear Sir / Madam*
- Nenne dann den Grund deines Schreibens:
  I am writing to …
- Verwende keine Kurzformen:
  I'm → *I am*
  wasn't → *was not*
  won't → *will not*
- Schreibe am Ende *Yours sincerely* und deinen Vor- und Nachnamen.

3   Story oder Blog

Wenn du eine Geschichte oder einen Blogeintrag schreiben sollst, denke an diese drei Punkte:
- Mache dir Notizen zu den *wh-questions*:
  Who was in the story?
  When did it happen?
  Where did it happen?
  What happened?
- Verwende *time phrases* und *linking words*.
- Sage, wie sich die Personen gefühlt haben.

> *A great day*
> *Last week I went to the theme park near our town with my friends.*
> *The roller coaster was too expensive so we went on the ghost train.*
> *First we felt scared, but then there was …*

B Folge diesen vier Schritten beim Schreiben:

1 Ideen sammeln

Sammle zuerst wichtige Ideen und Wörter, z. B. in einem Gedankennetz oder einer Liste.

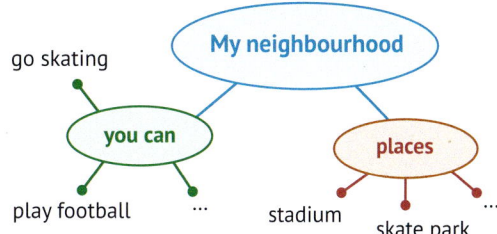

2 Textentwurf machen

- Mache einen Textentwurf auf einem Blatt Papier oder am Computer.
- Schreibst du eine Email oder einen Blog? Beachte die Hinweise auf der linken Seite.
- Überlege dir eine sinnvolle Reihenfolge und mache Absätze bei neuen Punkten.
- Texte aus dem Buch sind oft ein gutes Muster. Schreibe sie aber nicht ab. Ändere sie und ergänze eigene Ideen.

3 Text schreiben

Nun schreibe deinen Text. So wird dein Text besser:
- Verbinde deine Sätze mit *linking words* wie *and, but, so* oder *because* und *time phrases* (*yesterday, at first, then, …*).
- Wenn du eine Geschichte schreibst: Sage, wie sich die Personen fühlten (*happy, disappointed, scared, tired, …*).
- Vergleiche z. B. diese beiden Texte. Welcher klingt besser?

Holidays in Scotland

We flew to Scotland. We went to Loch Ness. We didn't see the monster.

We spent a day in Inverness. Dad bought a kilt. We all watched a game of shinty.

Holidays in Scotland

Last July I flew to Scotland with my parents. We were very excited. On the first day we went to Loch Ness — but we didn't see the monster, so I was disappointed. Then we spent a day in Inverness and dad bought a kilt. He felt so happy with it! The next day we all watched a game of shinty. That was fun!

SKILLS FILE

4 Text überprüfen und korrigieren

Ein Text ist noch nicht fertig, wenn du ihn zu Ende geschrieben hast!
Lies ihn danach noch zweimal durch.

a Groß- und Kleinschreibung
Im Englischen schreibt man fast alles klein. Prüfe also:
- Hast du Wörter wie *football, cinema, train, …* kleingeschrieben?

In manchen Fällen schreibt man aber groß – prüfe also:
- Hast du alle Satzanfänge großgeschrieben?
  Our school starts at 8 o'clock.

- Hast du das Wort *I* (= ich) immer großgeschrieben?
  I like playing football.

b Die richtige Zeitform
- Schreibst du über die Gegenwart?
  Oder über Dinge, die du regelmäßig machst?
  (Signalwörter: *today, often, always*)
  → Dann brauchst du das *simple present*:
    I often meet my friends in the park.

- Oder schreibst du über Sachen, die schon passiert sind? (Signalwörter: *yesterday, last Friday*)
  → Dann brauchst du das *simple past*:
    Last Sunday I went on a bike tour with my family.

- Wenn du vermutest, was in der Zukunft geschehen könnte *(maybe, I think)*, brauchst du das *will-future*:
  Maybe we'll go swimming in the afternoon.

👥 Partner check:
Falls möglich: Suche dir einen Partner/eine Partnerin und tauscht eure Texte aus.
Versteht ihr die Texte des anderen? Findet ihr noch Fehler?

SF 9 Bilder beschreiben

Wenn du ein Bild oder ein Foto beschreiben sollst, dann merke dir die folgenden Schritte:

1 Beginne allgemein

Sage zunächst in ein oder zwei Sätzen, was du allgemein auf dem Bild siehst:

In the picture I can see some people in a park.

2 Teile das Bild in drei Teile

Sage, was sich links, in der Mitte und rechts auf dem Bild befindet.

On the left I can see a man with a dog.

In the middle there's a man who's sleeping on the grass.

On the right there's a boy who's running.

3 Ordne die Personen und Dinge einander zu.

Verwende Präpositionen:

Behind the man with the dog there's a family with two children: a baby and a little boy or girl.
Next to the family a teenage boy and girl are playing football.
Behind the sleeping man in the middle you can see his bag. Next to him there are his shoes.

4 Beschreibe, was die Personen anhaben und was sie gerade tun.

Verwende das *present progressive*:

The man in the middle is sleeping. He's wearing a green suit (= Anzug).
The family is having a picnic. The little boy is eating something.
The man with the dog is wearing brown trousers and a grey shirt.
He's standing and looking at the family.
His dog is looking at the boy who's running.
The boy on the right is wearing trainers, yellow shorts and a blue T-shirt.
The boy behind him is kicking a football. He's wearing orange trousers and a white T-shirt.
He's playing with a girl. She's wearing white trousers and a purple (= purpurfarbenes) T-shirt.

SKILLS FILE

SF 10 Einen Kurzvortrag halten
→ Unit 1 | p.27

1 Erarbeitung

- Entscheide dich für ein Thema.
- Sammle Ideen zu deinem Thema und ordne sie:
  Was passt zum Thema und was nicht?
  Womit fängst du an?
  Welche Reihenfolge ist am besten?
  Womit hörst du auf?
  Schreibe das Wichtigste auf Karteikarten.

- Überlege dir, welche Bilder du zeigen kannst und wie du sie präsentieren möchtest – z. B. als Poster oder am Computer?
  Verwende dabei wenig Text.
  Schreibe groß und lesbar.

- Übe die Präsentation allein vor einem Spiegel oder mit einem Partner/einer Partnerin.
  Das gibt dir Sicherheit.

2 Durchführung

a Am Anfang des Vortrags
- Überprüfe, ob alles vorbereitet ist:
  Ist das Poster aufgehängt? Ist der Computer bereit? Sind die Vortragskarten richtig sortiert?
- Sage, worüber du sprechen möchtest.

b Während des Vortrags
- Verwende typische Redewendungen und sprich langsam und deutlich.
- Schaue deine Zuhörer/innen an.
- Wenn du ein Poster oder Bilder benutzt, zeige während des Vortrags darauf.

c Am Ende des Vortrags
- Sage, wann dein Vortrag zu Ende ist.
- Bedanke dich fürs Zuhören und frage deine Mitschüler/innen, ob sie noch Fragen haben.

SF 11 Mediation

→ Unit 1 | p.17   → Unit 2 | p.45   → Unit 3 | p.56   → Unit 4 | p.95

1 Worum geht es?

Mediation bedeutet, zwischen zwei Sprachen zu vermitteln, z.B.

- englische Informationen auf Deutsch weitergeben:
  Du bist z.B. mit deiner Familie in England. Dein Vater kann nur wenig Englisch und will wissen, was jemand gesagt hat oder was auf einer Broschüre steht.

- deutsche Informationen auf Englisch wiedergeben:
  Vielleicht ist bei dir zu Hause ein Austauschschüler zu Gast, der kein Deutsch spricht.

Was hat er gesagt?

Das Wetter: vereinzelt Regen, …

2 Worauf musst du achten?

- *Mediation* ist keine wörtliche Übersetzung. Deshalb gib nur das Wesentliche wieder und lasse unwichtige Informationen weg.

- Verwende kurze und einfache Sätze.

Is there a campsite nearby?

Ja, es gibt einen. Nicht weit im nächsten Dorf.

Es ist so schön hier. Natur pur. Wir könnten doch länger bleiben. Frag doch mal, ob es in der Nähe einen Campingplatz gibt.

Yes, there's one in the next village. It's nice and cheap – and only two miles from here.

- Beachte die Wortstellung – sie ist im Englischen oft anders als im Deutschen.

When is the shop open?

GEÖFFNET
täglich 9–18 Uhr
außer Dienstags

- Wenn du ein Wort nicht kennst, sage es anders. Beispiele:

  außer Dienstags – but not on Tuesdays   *ermäßigte Eintrittskarten – cheaper tickets*

  der Zug hat 10 Minuten Verspätung – the train is 10 minutes late

  Wie könntest du folgende Ausdrücke umschreiben?
  - *Gibt es hier Übernachtungsmöglichkeiten?* • *Fußballspielen verboten* • *Mindestalter 14 Jahre*

one hundred and thirty-nine **139**

LANGUAGE FILE

LF 1 Revision: *Simple present* → Revision 1 | p.28/29

bejahte Sätze Yes

I / You / We / You / They	start early.
He / She / It	start**s** early.

verneinte Sätze No

I / You / We / They	**don't** start early.
He / She / It	**doesn't** start early.

Fragen mit do/does ?

Do I / Do you / **Does** he/she/it / Do we / Do they	like crabs?

Fragen mit Fragewörtern ?

Where do I go now?
Why do you do this?
What **does** he/she/it do?
When do we arrive?
How do they run?

Mit dem *simple present* (einfache Gegenwart) sagst du, was oft oder jeden Tag passiert und auch was selten oder nie geschieht:
I often go to the sports club.
We never have lunch at school.

Mit *he/she/it* musst du immer ein *-s* ans Verb anhängen. **Achtung:** bei einigen Verben wird *-es* angehängt:
*do – do**es***
*wash – wash**es***
*watch – watch**es***

Wenn du sagen willst, dass etwas nicht passiert oder der Fall ist, setzt du *don't* vor das Verb. Mit *he/she/it* verwendest du *doesn't*.

He doesn't like dogs.

Fragen, auf die man mit *ja* oder *nein* antworten kann, beginnen mit *Do* oder *Does*.

Mit *I/you/we/they* verwendest du *Do*.
Mit *he/she/it* verwendest du *Does*.

Auch Fragen mit Fragewort *(What? When? Where? Who? Why?)* stellst du mit *do* bzw. *does*.

Du verwendest *do* bei *I/you/we/they* und *does* bei *he/she/it*.

Das Fragewort steht wie im Deutschen am Anfang.

LF 2 Revision: *Present progressive*

I'm read**ing** a comic.
Ich lese grade einen Comic.

Dad **is** cook**ing** dinner.
Papa macht gerade das Abendessen.

What **are** you do**ing** at the moment?
Was machst du jetzt gerade?

Mit dem *present progressive* (*ing*-Form) sagst du, was jetzt gerade passiert. Damit beschreibst du auch, was man auf Bildern tut.

Diese Zeitangaben findest du oft in Sätzen im *present progressive*:
now, at the moment, today.

bejahte Sätze	Yes
I'm You're He's She's It's We're You're They're	help**ing**.

Das *present progressive* besteht aus zwei Teilen:

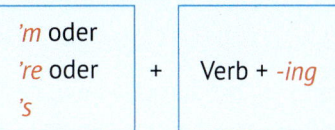

I'm not feel**ing** good today.

verneinte Sätze	No
I'm not You aren't He isn't She isn't It isn't We aren't You aren't They aren't	help**ing**.

Achtung: Bei Verben, die auf *-e* enden, fällt das *e* bei der *ing*-Form weg:

com*e* — coming
mak*e* — making
rid*e* — riding

Bei einigen Verben wird der letzte Buchstabe verdoppelt:

pla**n** — pla**nn**ing
sto**p** — sto**pp**ing
si**t** — si**tt**ing

Fragen	?
Am I Are you Is he Is she Is it Are we Are you Are they	help**ing**?

LANGUAGE FILE

LF 3 Revision: *Simple past*

→ Revision 2 | p.50/51

Yesterday evening I watched TV.
Gestern Abend habe ich ferngesehen/sah ich fern.

Last week I didn't go to football training.
Letzte Woche ging ich nicht zum Fußballtraining.

Did you watch the fireworks last night?
Hast du gestern abend das Feuerwerk gesehen?

bejahte Sätze — Yes

| I / You / He/She/It / We / They | helped. |

verneinte Sätze — No

| I / You / He/She/It / We / They | didn't help. |

Fragen mit did — ?

| Did | I / you / he/she/it / we / they | help? |

Fragen mit Fragewörtern — ?

What	did	she	watch?
When	did	it	finish?
Where	did	they	go?

What did she watch?
She watched the fireworks.

Mit dem *simple past* sprichst du über Dinge, die in der Vergangenheit geschehen sind. Du verwendest es oft mit Zeitangaben wie *yesterday, last week, last year, last summer, in 2015*. Die Vergangenheitsform ist für alle Personen gleich.
Bei regelmäßigen Verben hängst du *-ed* an das Verb: walk – walked   look – looked

Bei Verben, die auf *-e* enden, wird nur *-d* angehängt: arrive – arrived

Unregelmäßige Formen musst du lernen:
buy – bought   find – found
go – went   have – had
make – made   meet – met

Du kannst sie in der zweiten Spalte der *List of irregular verbs* auf den Seiten 214–215 nachschlagen.

Wenn du sagen willst, was nicht geschah, setzt du *didn't* vor das Verb.
Achtung: Das Verb steht dann immer in der Grundform: *He didn't watch.*
❗ nicht: *He didn't watched.*

Fragen im *simple past* bildest du mit *did* und der Grundform des Verbs.
Achtung:
Das Verb bleibt immer in der Grundform: *Did he watch?*
❗ nicht: *Did he watched?*

Manche Fragen beginnen mit Fragewörtern. Auch hier verwendet man *did* bei allen Personen und das Verb in der Grundform: *How did it go?*
❗ nicht: *How did it went?*
Achtung: Bei den Antworten musst du das Verb in die Vergangenheitsform setzen.

Kurzantworten	Yes	No
	Yes, I did. Yes, he/she/it did. Yes, you/we/they did.	No, I didn't. No, he/she/it didn't. No, you/we/they didn't.

Kurzantworten bildest du
nach *Yes* mit *did*:
Yes, I did. / Yes, he did. / …
nach *No* mit *didn't*:
No, I didn't. / No, he didn't. / …

LF 4 Present perfect

→ Unit 2 | p.40

I have already done my homework.
Ich habe meine Hausaufgaben schon gemacht.

My little sister has never been on a plane.
Meine kleine Schwester ist noch nie geflogen.

Have you ever ridden a pony?
Bist du schon einmal geritten?

Mit dem *present perfect* sagst du
– dass du etwas schon gemacht hast.
  Signalwort: *already*.
– dass du etwas schon einmal, öfter oder
  nie gemacht hast.
  Signalwörter:
  ever, never, once, twice, lots of times.

She's only been on a plane once before.

bejahte Sätze	Yes
I You We They	have started early. 've started early.
He She It	has started early.

verneinte Sätze	No
I You We They	haven't started early.
He She It	hasn't started early.

Fragen und Kurzantworten	?
Have you started?	– Yes, I have. – No, I haven't.
Has she started?	– Yes, she has. – No, she hasn't.

Das *present perfect* besteht aus zwei Teilen:
have oder *has* (Kurzformen: *'ve* oder *'s*)
+ *past participle* (eine besondere Verbform)

Wie bildest du das *past participle*?
Bei regelmäßigen Verben hängst du *-ed*
an das Verb:
walk – walked   look – looked

Bei Verben, die auf *-e* enden, wird nur *-d*
angehängt:
arrive – arrived

Unregelmäßige Formen musst du lernen:
 be – been   find – found
 go – gone   have – had
make – made   meet – met

LANGUAGE FILE

LF 5 Revision: *Will*-future

→ Revision 3 | p.72/73

I think you'll have a great birthday party.
Ich glaube, du wirst eine tolle Geburtstagsparty haben.

Maybe we'll have a barbecue in the garden.
Vielleicht grillen wir im Garten.

I'm sure the weather will be nice.
Ich bin sicher, das Wetter wird schön sein.

bejahte Sätze		Yes
It	will / 'll	be sunny tomorrow.

verneinte Sätze		No
It	will not / won't	be sunny tomorrow.

Fragen/Kurzantworten	?
Will it be sunny tomorrow?	Yes, it will. / No, it won't.

Wenn du vermutest, was in der Zukunft geschehen könnte, verwendest du das *will*-future.

Die Sätze beginnen oft mit *I think, maybe, I'm sure*.

Du bildest das *will*-future mit *will* und dem Infinitiv eines Verbs.

Die Kurzform von *will* ist *'ll*.
Die Kurzform von *will not* ist *won't*.

I think I'll have the fish.

LF 6 *Going to*-future*

We're going to have a picnic on Sunday.
Wir haben vor, am Sonntag ein Picknick zu machen.

Oh no, he's going to fall!
Oh nein, er fällt gleich herunter!

Mit *going to* ... sagst du
- was du vorhast oder für die Zukunft geplant hast,
- was wahrscheinlich bald passieren wird.

I'm going to be first!

* Diese Struktur musst du nicht aktiv beherrschen, nur verstehen.

LF 7 Wortstellung

→ Unit 2 | p.42

Hauptsätze

S	V	O
My mum	loves	old cars.

In Aussagesätzen lautet die Reihenfolge wie im Deutschen: Subjekt – Verb – Objekt.

Nebensätze

	S	V	O
He cried when	he	left	his family.
I work because	I	need	the money.

Dies gilt auch in Nebensätzen.
Im Deutschen ist die Wortstellung anders:
He was happy when he got his present.
Er war glücklich, als er sein Geschenk bekam.

Ortsangaben

S	V	O	(Where?)
I	have	lunch	at school.

Ortsangaben (*in town, at home, at school,* etc.) stehen nach dem Verb und Objekt.

Zeitangaben

(When?)	S	V	O	(When?)
At 12.30	he	has	lunch.	
	He	has	lunch	at 12.30.

Zeitangaben (*at 2 o'clock, in the morning, yesterday,* etc.) stehen ganz am Anfang oder ganz am Ende des Satzes.

Orts- und Zeitangaben

S	V	O	(Where?)	(When?)
She	met	him	in Dublin	yesterday.
He	has	lunch	at home	at 12.30.

Bei Orts- und Zeitangaben in einem Satz gilt im Englischen die Regel:

Ort vor Zeit (wie im Alphabet).
Im Deutschen ist es umgekehrt!

LF 8 Mengenangaben *(lots of, much, many)*

→ Unit 3 | p.63

lots of

We've got lots of apples.
I eat lots of fruit.

Mit *lots of, much* oder *many* kannst du über größere Mengen sprechen.

In bejahten Sätzen verwendest du meistens *lots of* – bei zählbaren und nicht zählbaren Dingen.

not many

I don't have many pencils.
My dad doesn't watch many films.

In verneinten Sätzen verwendest du
– *many* bei zählbaren Dingen (nicht viele),
– *much* bei nicht zählbaren Dingen (nicht viel).

not much

I don't eat much chocolate.
There isn't much sugar in my tea.

Zählbare Dinge haben eine Mehrzahlform:
one apple – two apples, one pen – three pens.
Nicht zählbare Dinge kannst du nicht in die Mehrzahl setzen: *fruit, milk, meat, food.*

LANGUAGE FILE

LF 9 · *Some / no / any* und ihre Zusammensetzungen → Unit 1 | p.18/19

some

Some of my friends live in America.
Einige meiner Freunde leben in Amerika.

There's somebody in the kitchen.
Da ist jemand in der Küche.

There's something in your eye.
Da ist etwas in deinem Auge.

Some bedeutet *einige* oder *etwas*.
Es gibt das Wort auch in Zusammensetzungen:

somebody/someone – jemand
something – etwas
somewhere – irgendwo

Du benutzt *some* und seine Zusammensetzungen **in bejahten Sätzen.**

no

I have no money.
Ich habe kein Geld.

Nobody was at home.
Es war niemand zu Hause.

I have nothing to say.
Ich habe nichts zu sagen.

No + Nomen (*no tea, no bread, no juice*) verwendest du **in bejahten Sätzen** für *kein*.

Auch hier gibt es die Zusammensetzungen:
nobody – niemand
nothing – nichts
nowhere – nirgendwo

I'm so hungry and there's nothing to eat.

any

There isn't any tea. Is there any juice?
Es ist kein Tee da. Gibt es Saft?

I don't have anything to wear for the party.
Ich habe für die Party nichts anzuziehen.

Can you see mum anywhere?
Kannst du Mama irgendwo sehen?

In **verneinten Sätzen und Fragen** verwendest du *any* und seine Zusammensetzungen:

not ... anybody – niemand
not ... anything – nichts
not ... anywhere – nirgendwo

anybody – jemand
anything – etwas
anywhere – irgendwo

LF 10 Vergleiche

→ Unit 4 | p.86

Mum is taller than dad. But I'm the tallest.
Mama ist größer als Papa. Aber ich bin der Größte.

This shop is more expensive than the market.
Dieses Geschäft ist teurer als der Markt.

The most expensive bike is not always the best.
Das teuerste Fahrrad ist nicht immer das Beste.

Personen, Sachen und Tiere kann man vergleichen.

I'm stronger than you!

cheap	cheaper	cheapest
near	nearer	nearest
tall	taller	tallest

Bei kurzen Adjektiven hängst du -er bzw. -est an das Adjektiv.

big	bigger	the biggest
hot	hotter	the hottest
noisy	noisier	the noisiest
happy	happier	the happiest

Bei einigen Adjektiven musst du bei der Schreibung aufpassen.

expensive	more expensive	most expensive
exciting	more exciting	most exciting
popular	more popular	most popular

Bei langen Adjektiven setzt du *more* bzw. *most* vor das Adjektiv.

❗ Diese Ausnahmen musst du lernen:

good – better – best
gut – besser – am besten

bad – worse – worst
schlecht – schlechter – am schlechtesten

little – less – least
wenig – weniger – am wenigsten

He's the worst cook in town.

LANGUAGE FILE

LF 11 Revision: Personalpronomen

I like Jan. Jan likes me.
Ich mag Jan. Jan mag mich.

She's good at maths. Let's ask her.
Sie ist gut in Mathe. Fragen wir sie.

They're good songs. Listen to them.
Das sind gute Songs. Hör sie dir an.

Subjektform	Objektform
I	me
you	you
he/she/it	him/her/it
we	us
you	you
they	them

Personalpronomen ersetzen Nomen (z.B. *table* → *it*) oder Eigennamen (z.B. *Ben* → *he*).

Sie kommen in zwei Formen vor, je nachdem ob sie Subjekt oder Objekt des Satzes sind.

Die Objektform steht nach Verben (z.B. *help, meet, see*) oder nach Präpositionen (z.B. *for, with, at*).

Das englische Pronomen *you* kann im Deutschen verschiedene Bedeutungen haben:

You are in my class, Ali. → du
Can you help me, boys? → ihr
Can you tell me the price, please? → Sie

LF 12 Possessivpronomen → Unit 3 | p.62

This is my phone. It's mine.
Das ist mein Handy. Es ist meins.

It think it's her bike. It's hers.
Ich glaube, es ist ihr Fahrrad. Es ist ihres.

I've found this book. Is it yours?
Ich habe dieses Buch gefunden. Ist es deines?

mit Nomen	ohne Nomen
my game	mine
your game	yours
his/her/its game	his/hers/its
our game	ours
your game	yours
their game	theirs

Possessivpronomen zeigen an, wem etwas gehört.

Die Possessivpronomen *my, your, his, her, …* werden vor einem Nomen gebraucht.

Die Possessivpronomen *mine, yours, his, hers, …* stehen allein, ohne Nomen.

These trousers aren't mine!

LF 13 Revision: Der Plural von Nomen

a book	two books
a table	two tables
a bus	two buses
a beach	two beaches
a pony	two ponies
a story	two stories

Die meisten Nomen haben im Plural die Endung s.

Nach -s, -x, -ch oder -sh wird -es angehängt.

Bei Nomen, die auf Konsonant + **y** enden, wird **y** zu -ies. Ausnahmen:

a boy   two boys
a day   two days

Diese unregelmäßigen Pluralformen musst du lernen:

a man   two men   a foot   two feet
a woman   two women   a tooth   two teeth
a child   two children

Einige Nomen haben keinen Singular und werden nur im Plural gebraucht:

jeans   Jeans
trousers   Hose
clothes   Kleidung
news   Nachrichten

three ponies

LF 14 Revision: Der Genitiv mit *of*

the name of the city	der Name der Stadt
the end of the game	das Spielende
a kilo of apples	ein Kilo Äpfel
a bottle of water	eine Flasche Wasser

Den Genitiv mit *of* benutzt man meist bei Dingen.

Der Genitiv mit *of* wird auch in Maß- und Mengenangaben verwendet.

She's having a cup of coffee.

WORDBANK

Wordbank 1: My neighbourhood
Unit 1 | p.21

Transport
airport
bus station
bus stop

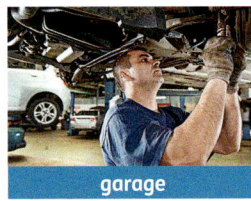
garage

harbour

petrol station

traffic lights
train station
underground station
tram station

Shopping

baker's

butcher's

bookshop
bike shop

chemist's

dry cleaner's

fruit and veg shop
market

newsagent's

phone shop
shopping centre
supermarket

Sport
bowling centre
football field

ice rink

inline skate track

skate park

basketball court

sports club
sports hall
stadium
swimming pool

Other places
bank
cafe

children's playground

cinema
farm

fast food stand

flats
hairdresser's
hospital
houses
museum
nail salon
park
post office
restaurant
river
school
second-hand shop
theatre

> Our nearest … is … minutes away.
> That's good/OK/important/terrible.
> There aren't any … near us.
> That's OK/no problem/a big problem.
> We live near … You can … there.
> There's a big/new/great/good/cool/nice/expensive … near our house.
> There are lots of … in my neighbourhood.
> I think that's great/not so good.

Wordbank 2: City and country

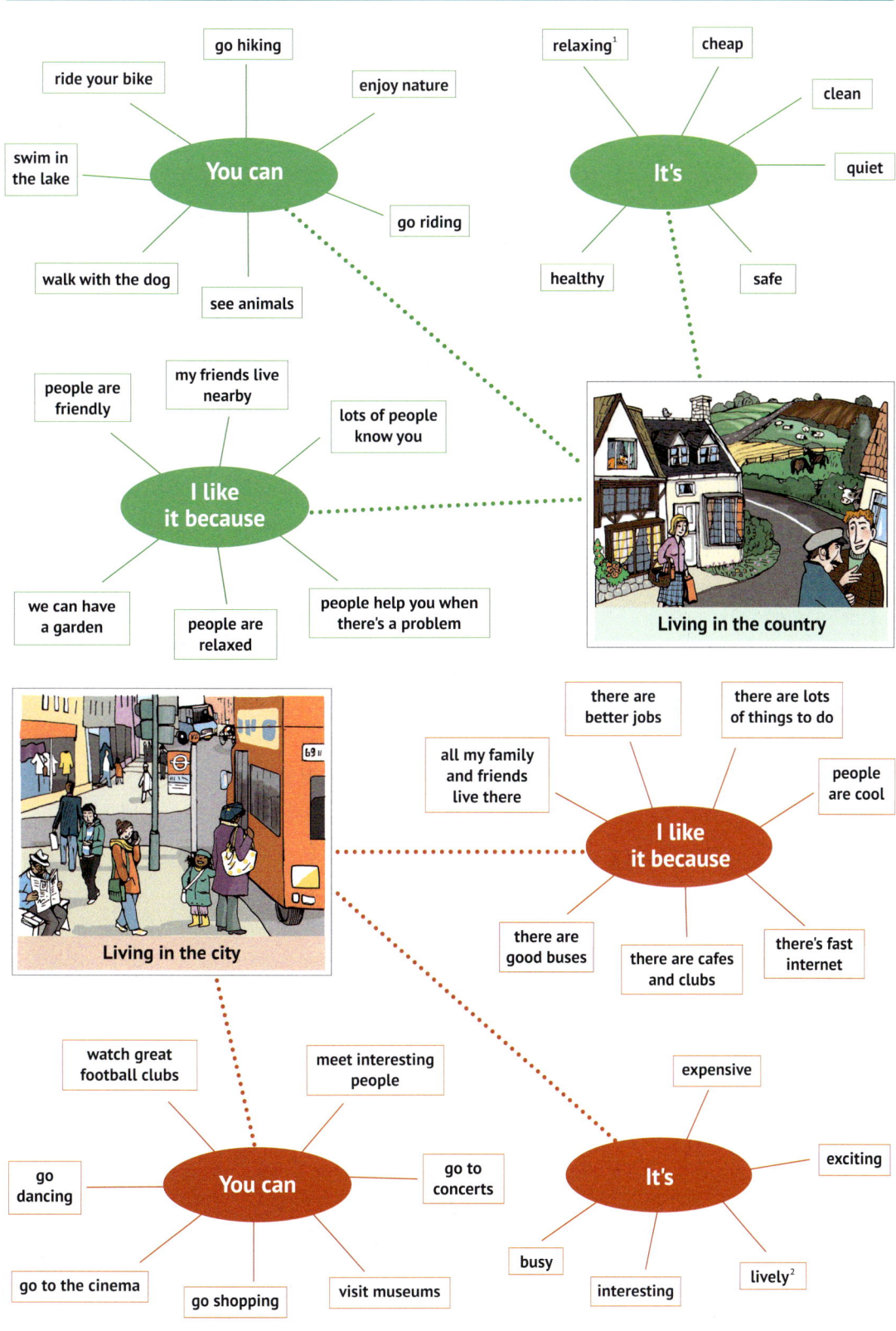

¹**relaxing** [rɪˈlæksɪŋ] *entspannend, erholsam*   ²**lively** [ˈlaɪvli] *lebendig*

WORDBANK

Wordbank 3: Music
Unit 3 | p.66

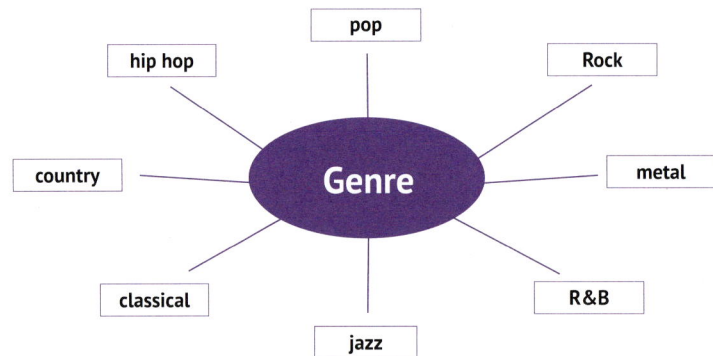

The music/song is ...
fast/slow (schnell/langsam)
lively/sad (beschwingt/traurig)
noisy/calm (laut/ruhig)
exciting/boring (aufregend/langweilig)
relaxing/stimulating
(entspannend/anregend)
aggressive/gentle (aggressiv/sanft)
melodic/rhythmic
(melodisch/rythmisch)
passionate/soulless
(leidenschaftlich/seelenlos)
modern/traditional (modern/traditionell)

I like ...
the melody (die Melodie)
the beat (den Rhythmus)
the instruments (die Instrumente)
the singer's voice (die Stimme des Sängers/der Sängerin)
the mood (die Stimmung)
the performance (die Darbietung)
the lyrics (den Songtext)
the message (die Botschaft)
the video (das Video)
the moves (die Choreografie)

I can hear ...
drums
(ein Schlagzeug)
a guitar (eine Gitarre)
a bass guitar
(einen E-Bass)
a trumpet
(eine Trompete)
a piano (ein Klavier)
a saxophone (ein Saxofon)

The music/song ...
sounds fantastic
(klingt fantastisch)
makes me feel good
(baut mich auf)
calms me down (bringt mich zur Ruhe)
touches my soul (berührt meine Seele)
has a great beat (hat einen guten Rhythmus)
lifts up my energy (gibt mir neue Energie)

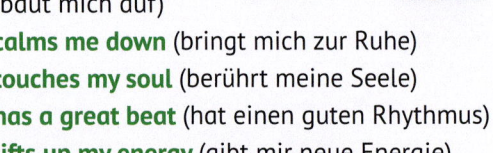

Wordbank 4: Food

Unit 4 | p.79

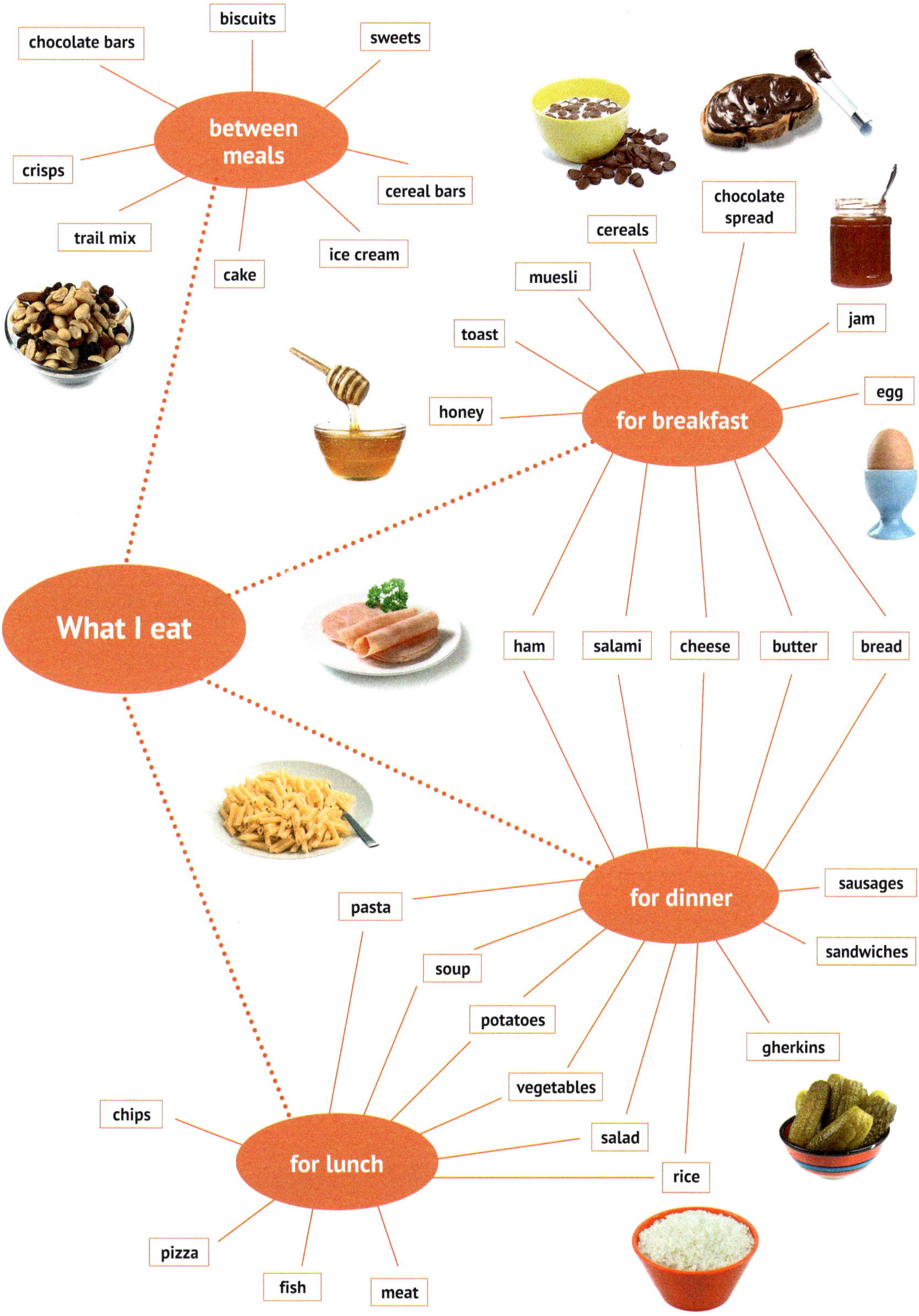

between meals
- chocolate bars
- biscuits
- sweets
- crisps
- cereal bars
- trail mix
- ice cream
- cake

for breakfast
- cereals
- chocolate spread
- muesli
- jam
- toast
- egg
- honey

What I eat

- ham
- salami
- cheese
- butter
- bread

for dinner
- pasta
- sausages
- soup
- sandwiches
- potatoes
- gherkins
- vegetables
- salad
- rice

for lunch
- chips
- pizza
- fish
- meat

Vocabulary

Das **Vocabulary** (Seiten 154–171) enthält alle neuen Wörter und Wendungen des Buches, die du **lernen** musst. Sie stehen in der Reihenfolge, in der sie im Buch zum ersten Mal vorkommen.

Hier siehst du, wie das **Vocabulary** aufgebaut ist:

Die **Lautschrift** zeigt dir, wie ein Wort ausgesprochen wird. Eine Übersicht über die **Lautschriftzeichen** findest du auf Seite 205.

can [kæn]	Dose, Büchse	I don't have time to cook. But here's a **can of** vegetable soup. (= eine Dose Gemüsesuppe)
(to) kick [kɪk]	treten, schießen	
idiot ['ɪdiət]	Idiot/in	❗ Betonung auf der 1. Silbe: **id**iot ['ɪdiət]
keep	halten; behalten	You can **keep** that pen. (behalten) Do you **keep** pets in your house? (halten)
police	Polizei	→ **Police** ist immer Plural: Where **are** the **police**? We have to call **them**. Wo **ist** die **Polizei**? Wir müssen **sie** rufen.
like a million dollars [ə ˌmɪljən ˈdɒləz]	fantastisch	
p.16 earthquake ['ɜːθkweɪk]	Erdbeben	
especially	insbesondere	I love team sports, **especially** basketball.
transport	Verkehrsmittel; Transport(wesen)	❗ Betonung auf der **1.** Silbe: **trans**port ['trænspɔːt]
product	Produkt	❗ Betonung auf der **1.** Silbe: **pro**duct ['prɒdʌkt]
over 18 ['əʊvə]	über 18	over 18 ◀▶ under 18

Focus on language

p.18 department store [dɪˈpɑːtmənt stɔː]	Kaufhaus	
just [dʒʌst]	nur, bloß; einfach	**Just** listen to me for five minutes, please. Don't **just** sit there! Come here and help me.
size [saɪz]	Größe	❗ *English*: What **size** do you **take**? *German*: Welche Größe **hast** du?
(sales) assistant ['seɪlz əsɪstənt]	Verkäufer/in	❕ **assistant** = Helfer/in, Assistent/in Betonung auf der 2. Silbe: as**sis**tant [əˈsɪstənt]
changing room ['tʃeɪndʒɪŋ ruː]	Umkleide(kabine), Anprobe	
p.19 Does **anybody** speak ...? ['enɪbɒdi]	Spricht (irgend)jemand ...?	

Der **blaue Pfeil** heißt: Zu diesem Eintrag gibt es in der rechten Spalte einen blauen Kasten.

Die **blauen Kästen** solltest du dir immer besonders gut ansehen. Dort stehen wichtige Hinweise zu den neuen Wörtern.

Diese Zahl gibt die **Seite** an, auf der die Wörter zum ersten Mal vorkommen: p.16 = Seite 16

Dies ist das „Gegenteil"-Zeichen. **over 18** ◀▶ **under 18** bedeutet: „**over** ist das Gegenteil von **under**".

Das **rote Ausrufezeichen** bedeutet: Vorsicht, hier macht man leicht Fehler!

Tipps zum Wörterlernen findest du im **Skills file** auf Seite 126.

Wir verwenden folgende **Abkürzungen**:

infml = informal (umgangssprachlich) • *p.* = page (Seite) • *sb.* = somebody (jemand) • *sth.* = something (etwas) • *AE* = American English • *BE* = British English • *pl* = plural (Mehrzahl) • *no pl* = no plural (es gibt das Wort nicht in der Mehrzahl)

Wenn du **nachschlagen** möchtest, was ein englisches Wort bedeutet oder wie man es ausspricht, dann solltest du das **Dictionary English – German** auf den Seiten 172–189 verwenden.

Und wenn du vergessen hast, wie etwas auf Englisch heißt, dann kann dir das **Dictionary German – English** auf den Seiten 190–205 eine erste Hilfe sein.

Vocabulary

Unit 1: I love London

p.8	parliament [ˈpɑːləmənt]	Parlament	❗ Beachte die Schreibweise: parl**ia**ment
	bell [bel]	Glocke; Klingel	bells
	tower [ˈtaʊə]	Turm	
	famous (for) [ˈfeɪməs]	berühmt (für, wegen)	Come to our cafe! We're **famous for** our cakes.
	detective [dɪˈtektɪv]	Detektiv/in	❗ Betonung auf der 2. Silbe: de**tec**tive [dɪˈtektɪv]
	palace [ˈpæləs]	Palast	
	king [kɪŋ]	König	king
	queen [kwiːn]	Königin	queen
	president [ˈprezɪdənt]	Präsident/in	❗ Betonung auf der 1. Silbe: **pre**sident [ˈprezɪdənt]
p.9	the Tube [tjuːb]	die U-Bahn *(in London)*	❗ *English:* **on** the Tube *German:* **in** der U-Bahn
	(to) travel [ˈtrævl]	reisen; fahren, sich fortbewegen	Last year we **travelled** to Italy in the holidays. In big cities we always try to **travel** by bus.
	(to) open [ˈəʊpən]	sich öffnen, aufgehen	❗ open = 1. öffnen: **Open** the door, please. 2. sich öffnen, aufgehen: The bridge can **open** for ships.
	high [haɪ]	hoch	What's the **highest** mountain in Germany?

Theme 1

p.10	fashion [ˈfæʃn]	Mode(trend)	
	shopping centre [ˈʃɒpɪŋ sentə]	Einkaufszentrum	
	two years ago [əˈgəʊ]	vor zwei Jahren	We went to London six weeks **ago**. ❗ *English:* **two years/six weeks ago** *German:* **vor** zwei Jahren/sechs Wochen
	culture [ˈkʌltʃə]	Kultur	❗ Betonung auf der 1. Silbe: **cul**ture [ˈkʌltʃə]
	Greek [griːk]	griechisch; Griechisch; Grieche/Griechin	
	half [hɑːf]	halbe(r, s), Halb-	adjective: **half** – noun: **half**, *(pl)* **halves** [hɑːvz] (Hälfte) I'll cut the apple in two **halves**. I don't need more than **half an apple**. (= einen halben Apfel) ❗ Wortstellung: *English:* **half an** apple *German:* **ein halber** Apfel

1 Vocabulary

	Irish [ˈaɪrɪʃ]	irisch, aus Irland	the **Irish** flag
	Scottish [ˈskɒtɪʃ]	schottisch, aus Schottland	the **Scottish** flag
	(to) **be allowed** to do sth. [əˈlaʊd]	etwas tun dürfen	**Are** you **allowed** to use dictionaries in your English tests? Dogs **aren't allowed** in this shop. *(sind ... nicht erlaubt)*
p.11	**title** [ˈtaɪtl]	Titel, Überschrift	
	introduction [ɪntrəˈdʌkʃn]	Einleitung	
	article [ˈɑːtɪkl]	Artikel	❗ Betonung auf der 1. Silbe: **ar**ticle [ˈɑːtɪkl]
	busy [ˈbɪzi]	belebt; verkehrsreich	❗ **busy:** 1. The road **is busy.** = belebt, verkehrsreich 2. I'm **busy.** = Ich bin beschäftigt, ich habe (viel) zu tun.
	museum [mjuˈziːəm]	Museum	

Theme 2

p.13	**advert** [ˈædvɜːt]	Anzeige, Werbung	
	(to) **change** (trains) [tʃeɪndʒ]	umsteigen *(Zug)*	Where do I have to **change (trains)**? *(Wo muss ich umsteigen?)* ❗ **change: 1.** (sich) (ver)ändern; **2.** umsteigen *(Zug)*
	trains/the line **for** ...	Züge / die U-Bahn-Linie nach ...	Change at Earl's Court and take the Piccadilly Line **for** the airport. ❗ **for: 1.** für; **2.** nach
	No worries. *(infml)*	Kein Problem.	

Story

p.14	(to) **call** [kɔːl]	rufen; anrufen; nennen	Please **call** your dog. It's in our garden. *(rufen)* **Call** me tomorrow. Here's my phone number. *(anrufen)* Her name is Jessica, but we **call** her Jess. *(nennen)*
	geek [giːk]	jemand, der sich sehr stark für etwas begeistert (und manchmal von anderen deswegen belächelt wird)	
	dinosaur [ˈdaɪnəsɔː]	Dinosaurier	❗ Betonung auf der **1.** Silbe: **di**nosaur [ˈdaɪnəsɔː]
	disaster [dɪˈzɑːstə]	Katastrophe, Unglück	
p.15	**department store** [dɪˈpɑːtmənt stɔː]	Kaufhaus	
	most famous [məʊst]	der/die/das berühmteste, am berühmtesten	
	the most famous **one**	der/die/das Berühmteste	
	security [sɪˈkjʊərəti]	Sicherheit	This is a **security** check. Would you please open your bags?

	next [nekst]	als Nächstes	First let's eat something. **Next** we can watch a film.
	can [kæn]	Dose, Büchse	I don't have time to cook. But here's a **can of** vegetable soup. (= eine Dose Gemüsesuppe)
	(to) kick [kɪk]	treten, schießen	
	idiot [ˈɪdiət]	Idiot/in	❗ Betonung auf der 1. Silbe: **i**diot [ˈɪdiət]
	(to) keep [kiːp], *simple past:* **kept** [kept]	halten; behalten	You can **keep** that pen. *(behalten)* Do you **keep** pets in your house? *(halten)*
	police *(pl)* [pəˈliːs]	Polizei	→ **Police** ist immer Plural: Where **are** the **police**? We have to call **them**. Wo **ist** die **Polizei**? Wir müssen **sie** rufen.
	like a million dollars [ə ˈmɪljən ˈdɒləz]	fantastisch	a **million** [ˈmɪljən] = eine Million ❗ **millions** of people = **Millionen** (von) Menschen *aber* three **million** people = drei Million**en** Menschen
p.16	**earthquake** [ˈɜːθkweɪk]	Erdbeben	
	especially [ɪˈspeʃəli]	insbesondere	I love team sports, **especially** basketball.
p.17	**transport** [ˈtrænspɔːt]	Verkehrsmittel; Transport(wesen)	❗ Betonung auf der **1.** Silbe: **trans**port [ˈtrænspɔːt]
	product [ˈprɒdʌkt]	Produkt	❗ Betonung auf der **1.** Silbe: **pro**duct [ˈprɒdʌkt]
	over 18 [ˈəʊvə]	über 18	**over** 18 ◄► **under** 18

Focus on language

p.18	**just** [dʒʌst]	nur, bloß; einfach	**Just** listen to me for five minutes, please. Don't **just** sit there! Come here and help me.
	size [saɪz]	Größe	❗ *English:* What **size** do you **take**? *German:* Welche Größe **hast** du?
	(sales) assistant [ˈseɪlz əsɪstənt]	Verkäufer/in	**assistant** = Helfer/in, Assistent/in ❗ Betonung auf der **2.** Silbe: as**sis**tant [əˈsɪstənt]
	changing room [ˈtʃeɪndʒɪŋ ruːm]	Umkleide(kabine), Anprobe	
p.19	Does **anybody** speak …? [ˈenibɒdi]	Spricht (irgend)jemand …?	
	not … anybody [ˈenibɒdi]	niemand	Is **anybody** home? … …Yes, there is **somebody** at home. ◄► No, there is**n't anybody** at home. = No, there's **nobody** at home.
	department [dɪˈpɑːtmənt]	Abteilung	
	somebody who can help	jemand, der helfen kann	Do you know anybody **who** can help me with this German text? – Yes, I have a friend **who** is from Germany.
p.20	**helmet** [ˈhelmɪt]	Helm	helmets
	sock [sɒk]	Socke	

one hundred and fifty-seven **157**

1 Vocabulary

Skills training

p.21	**far** [fɑː]	weit	**far** ◄► **near** You can walk to the station. It's not **far**.
	central [ˈsentrəl]	zentral	❗ **Central** London = London Stadtmitte
	final [ˈfaɪnl]	letzte(r, s), abschließend	Sunday is the **final** day (= the last day) of the festival.
	comment [ˈkɒment]	Kommentar	She didn't want to **make a comment**. (= einen Kommentar abgeben)
p.22	words **that** you know …	Wörter, die du kennst …	Bell? That's a word **that** I don't know. – It's a thing **that** you have on your bike and **that** makes a sound.
	sun [sʌn]	Sonne	In the morning there was **sun**. = It was **sunny**.
	cloud [klaʊd]	Wolke	But in the afternoon there were **clouds**. = It was **cloudy.**
	sleep [sliːp]	Schlaf	verb: (to) **sleep** – noun: **sleep**
p.23	**single (ticket)** [ˈsɪŋgl]	einfache Fahrkarte (nur Hinfahrt)	I'm going to Oxford, but my friend will drive me home tomorrow. So I'll only buy a **single ticket** for the train.
	return (ticket) [rɪˈtɜːn]	Rückfahrkarte	**single (ticket)** ◄► **return (ticket)**
	direct [dəˈrekt]	direkt	You don't have to change. You can take a **direct** train.
p.24	**ringtone** [ˈrɪŋtəʊn]	Klingelton *(Handy)*	

Unit 2: In Ireland

p.30	**Ireland** [ˈaɪələnd]	Irland	noun: **Ireland** – adjective: **Irish**
	its capital [ɪts]	seine Hauptstadt / ihre Hauptstadt	This is my hamster. **Its** name is Joe. **I** – my name **we** – our names **you** – your name **you** – your names **he** – his name **they** – their names **she** – her name **it** – its name
	capital (city) [ˈkæpɪtl]	Hauptstadt	Berlin is the **capital** or **capital city** of Germany.
	northern [ˈnɔːðən]	Nord-, nördlich	northern western eastern southern
	the United Kingdom [juːnaɪtɪd ˈkɪŋdəm] **(the UK** [juː ˈkeɪ])	das Vereinigte Königreich	the **United Kingdom** = Great Britain (England, Scotland, Wales) and Northern Ireland *(Nordirland)*

	one third	ein Drittel	1/2 = a/one **half** *(pl.* **halves***)* 1/5 = a/one **fifth** 1/3 = a/one **third** 1/6 = a/one **sixth** 1/4 = a/one **quarter** ['kwɔːtə]; a/one **fourth** *(AE)* ...
	fast [fɑːst]	schnell	**fast** ◄► **slow**
	most people [məʊst]	die meisten Leute	**many/much – more – most**
p.31	**building** ['bɪldɪŋ]	Gebäude	You don't know this **building**? It's Buckingham Palace!
	(to) **relax** [rɪ'læks]	sich entspannen	❗ *English:* I'm **relaxing**. *German:* Ich entspanne **mich.**

Theme 1

p.32	(to) **move** (to) [muːv]	(um)ziehen (nach/in)	They **moved to** York, **to** a nice flat in town.
	(to) buy: we've **bought** [bɔːt]	kaufen: wir haben gekauft	
	already [ɔːl'redi]	schon	Are you hungry? – No, I've **already** had dinner.
	CCTV [siː siː tiː 'viː]	Überwachungssystem; Überwachungskamera(s)	
	business ['bɪznəs]	Geschäft, Betrieb	My mum's new **business** is on Summer Street: it's a phone shop.
	(to) **start a business**	ein Geschäft aufmachen, einen Betrieb gründen/ eröffnen	My job is terrible. Perhaps I should **start a business**.
	(to) **start**: **he has started**	anfangen: er hat angefangen	I've started – I haven't started he has bought – he hasn't bought
	van [væn]	Transporter, Lieferwagen	a **van**
	(to) **find**: she has **found** [faʊnd]	finden: sie hat gefunden	
	(to) **meet**: she has **met** [met]	treffen: sie hat getroffen	
	pub [pʌb]	Kneipe	
	(to) **see**: I've **seen** [siːn]	sehen: ich habe gesehen	
	(to) **speak**: I've **spoken** ['spəʊkən]	sprechen: ich habe gesprochen	
	not ... yet [jet]	noch nicht	I need more time. I have**n't** finished my homework **yet**.
p.33	(to) **close** [kləʊz]	schließen, zumachen	**open** the door ◄► **close** the door

Vocabulary

gate [geɪt]	Tor	Who left the garden **gate** open?
(to) **become** [bɪˈkʌm], **became** [bɪˈkeɪm], **become**	werden	! (to) **get** = bekommen, kriegen: I **get** lots of emails. (to) **become** = werden: Molly **became** angry when Rob left the gate open.
less [les]	weniger	**less** ◄► **more** **less angry** ◄► **angrier**

Theme 2

p.34	**police officer** [pəˈliːs ɒfɪsə]	Polizeibeamter/-beamtin	English **police officers**
	deep [diːp]	tief	The water is **deep**, but our dog can swim well.
	work **hard** [hɑːd]	hart arbeiten	We must work **hard** at school. ! adjective: **hard** = hart, schwer: It's hard **work**. adverb: **hard** = hart: We work **hard**.
	farmer [ˈfɑːmə]	Bauer, Bäuerin; Landwirt/in	They are **farmers**. = They have a **farm**.
	daughter [ˈdɔːtə]	Tochter	Do they have children? – Yes, they have one **daughter**, Jane.
	(to) **do well**	es gut machen; gut abschneiden, erfolgreich sein	Joe **did well** in his maths test. My sister started a new business, and it's **doing** very **well**.
	(to) **save** [seɪv]	retten	The man **saved** the dog's life.
	(to) **have**: we've **had** [hæd], [həd]	haben: wir haben gehabt	It's been a nice sunny week. We haven't **had** any rain.
	accident [ˈæksɪdənt]	Unfall	a car **accident**
	an accident / accidents **like this** [laɪk]	so ein / ein solcher Unfall; solche Unfälle	! 1. something **like this** / **like that** *(so etwas)* Accidents **like this** / **like that** are terrible. 2. It's always **like this** / **like that**. *(so)* Look, it's easy if you do it **like this** / **like that**. *(so, auf diese Art)*
	before [bɪˈfɔː]	vorher; zuvor	I have**n't** seen this **before**. = Das habe ich noch nie gesehen.
p.35	(to) **take a message**, took, taken	etwas ausrichten	
	Is that Mr Taylor?	Ist da Herr Taylor? *(am Telefon)*	
	Who's speaking?	Wer spricht (da)? *(am Telefon)*	
	This is Rob Blake.	Hier spricht Rob Blake. *(am Telefon)*	John isn't at home. Can I **take** a message? ! (to) **take, took, taken** [ˈteɪkən]

Story

p.36	**bush** [bʊʃ]	Busch, Strauch	**Bushes** are smaller than trees. ❗ Aussprache: bush [bʊʃ]
	suddenly [ˈsʌdənli]	plötzlich	
	(to) **catch** [kætʃ], **caught, caught** [kɔːt]	(ein)fangen	Can he **catch** the ball?
	camera [ˈkæmərə]	Fotoapparat; Kamera	**CCTV camera** = Überwachungskamera
	light [laɪt]	Licht; Lampe	I want to see where I'm going at night, so I have good **lights** on my bike.
	office [ˈɒfɪs]	Büro	I'm a farmer. I like working outside. I couldn't work in an **office** all day!
	fox [fɒks]	Fuchs	a **fox**
p.37	**so (that)** [ˈsəʊ ðət]	sodass	❗ **so** = 1. (*auch* **so that**) = sodass; 2. **so** big/cold/… = so groß/kalt/…; 3. also, daher
	(to) **put**: he has **put**	*(etwas wohin)* tun, legen, stellen, stecken: er hat getan, gelegt, gestellt, gesteckt	
	interested in doing sth. [ˈɪntrəstɪd]	daran interessiert, etwas zu tun	

verb / preposition + *-ing*-form:		
Are you	**interested in**	**learning** to play the piano?
I'm not very	**good at**	**making** new friends.
I'm	**thinking about**	**starting** a business.
Do you	**like**	**playing** football?
No, I	**prefer**	**riding** my pony.
Could you please	**stop**	**playing** this silly game …
… and	**start**	**doing** your homework?

	(to) **put** sth. **up**	etwas anbringen, aufhängen	They're **putting up** a picture.
p.39	**brave** [breɪv]	mutig	Molly was very **brave**. She went into the water to save the sheep.
	dark [dɑːk]	dunkel	It's too **dark** in here. I can't see anything. We need some light!
	quiet [ˈkwaɪət]	ruhig, still, leise	**quiet** ◄► **loud, noisy**
	X-ray [ˈeksreɪ]	Röntgen(strahlen)	an **X-ray fish** = Wasserstieglitz/Sternfleckbuntbarsch
	zebra [ˈzebrə]	Zebra	a zebra

2 Vocabulary

Focus on language

p.40	**questionnaire** [ˌkwestʃəˈneə]	Fragebogen	Please answer all the questions on this **questionnaire**.
	person [ˈpɜːsn]	Person	❗ Nur selten wird der Plural **persons** benutzt. Normalerweise: one **person** – five **people**.
p.41	**island** [ˈaɪlənd]	Insel	Only birds live on this **island**.
p.42	**coat** [kəʊt]	Mantel; Jacke	It's cold. Take a **coat** when you go outside.
	even [ˈiːvn]	sogar, selbst	Everybody tried to help, **even** the children.

Skills training

p.43	(to) **arrange** [əˈreɪndʒ]	vereinbaren, ausmachen (Termin)	Let's **arrange** a date when we can meet.
	meeting [ˈmiːtɪŋ]	Treffen; Zusammenkunft	I'm so tired! I've been in a business **meeting** all afternoon.
	(to) **be on**	stattfinden, gezeigt werden (Kino, Theater)	What's **on** at the theatre this evening?
	… shall we …? [ʃæl], [ʃəl]	… sollen wir …?	Do you have problems? **Shall I** help you?
p.44	**gallery** [ˈɡæləri]	Galerie	The National **Gallery** in London is a museum where you can look at lots of interesting art.
	occasionally [əˈkeɪʒənəli]	gelegentlich	= sometimes, but not very often
	parade [pəˈreɪd]	Parade, Umzug	
p.45	**performance** [pəˈfɔːməns]	Vorstellung, Aufführung	I went to the theatre to see a play. I loved the **performance**!
p.46	**visit** [ˈvɪzɪt]	Besuch	verb: (to) **visit** – noun (person): **visitor** – noun (what you do when you visit people): **visit**
	grandad [ˈɡrændæd]	Opa	grandmother and grandfather = grandma and **grandad**
	(to) **disagree** [ˌdɪsəˈɡriː]	nicht zustimmen, widersprechen	agree ◄► disagree
	rubbish [ˈrʌbɪʃ]	Unsinn, dummes Zeug	❗ **rubbish** = 1. Müll, Abfall; 2. Unsinn, dummes Zeug

irregular verbs							
(to) **become**	became	become	werden	(to) **keep**	kept	kept	(be)halten
(to) **buy**	bought	bought	kaufen	(to) **meet**	met	met	treffen
(to) **catch**	caught	caught	(ein)fangen	(to) **put**	put	put	stellen, legen
(to) **feel**	felt	felt	(sich) fühlen	(to) **see**	saw	seen	sehen
(to) **find**	found	found	finden	(to) **speak**	spoke	spoken	sprechen
(to) **have**	had	had	haben	(to) **take**	took	taken	(mit)nehmen

▶ pp.214–215

Unit 3: Scotland is different

p.52	**Scotland** ['skɒtlənd]	Schottland	noun: **Scotland** – adjective: **Scottish**
	which [wɪtʃ]	der, die, das; die (Relativpronomen)	songs **which** I know / the cat **which** is in our garden **!** Das Relativpronomen **which** benutzt du nur für Dinge und Tiere.
	castle ['kɑːsl]	Burg	a Scottish **castle**
	Europe ['jʊərəp]	Europa	
	bagpipes *(pl)* ['bægpaɪps]	Dudelsack	**!** He's playing **the bagpipes**. Er spielt **Dudelsack**.
	language ['læŋgwɪdʒ]	Sprache	Many people in Scotland speak English and Gaelic, an old Scottish **language**.
p.53	**knife** [naɪf], *pl* **knives** [naɪvz]	Messer	Aussprache – das „k" wird nicht gesprochen: k**nife** [naɪf]
	(to) **cost**: it **cost** [kɒst]	kosten: es kostete, es hat gekostet	

Theme 1

p.54	**unemployed** [ˌʌnɪm'plɔɪd]	arbeitslos	Alec lost his job and is now **unemployed**.
	equipment *(no pl)* [ɪ'kwɪpmənt]	Ausrüstung, Ausstattung	walking **equipment**
	for the last time	zum letzten Mal	
	customer ['kʌstəmə]	Kunde, Kundin	"Do you need any help?" the sales assistant asked the **customer**.
	ours [ɑːz], ['aʊəz]	unsere, unserer, unseres	

Possessivpronomen (Possessive pronouns)

I	**my** dog	**mine**	*meiner, meine, meins*	we	**our** dog	**ours**	*unserer, unsere, unseres*
you	**your** dog	**yours**	*deiner, deine, deins*	you	**your** dog	**yours**	*eurer, eure, eures*
he	**his** dog	**his**	*seiner, seine, seins*	they	**their** dog	**theirs**	*ihrer, ihre, ihr*
she	**her** dog	**hers**	*ihrer, ihre, ihrs*				

	I **have lost** my job. [lɒst]	Ich habe meine Arbeitsstelle verloren.	
p.55	**beautiful** ['bjuːtɪfl]	schön, wunderschön	Your baby sister is a **beautiful** little girl.
	bed and breakfast (B&B)	Frühstückspension; Zimmer mit Frühstück	We stayed at a nice **B&B** in York last year. **Bed and breakfast** is more expensive than camping.

3 Vocabulary

(to) **teach** [tiːtʃ], **taught, taught** [tɔːt]	unterrichten; lehren	Mr Schwarz is a teacher. He **teaches** English.
Help yourselves.	Bedient euch! / Greift zu!	There are very nice biscuits in the kitchen. **Help yourselves!**

myself, yourself, himself … (Reflexivpronomen)

I	listen	to	**myself.**	Ich höre	mir	zu.	/ mich	an.	
You	listen	to	**yourself.**	Du …	dir	…	/ dich	…	
He	listens	to	**himself.**	Er …	sich	…	/ sich	…	
She	listens	to	**herself.**	Sie …	sich	…	/ sich	…	❗ Aussprache und Betonung:
It	listens	to	**itself.**	Es …	sich	…	/ sich	…	-self [-ˈself]
We	listen	to	**ourselves.**	Wir …	uns	…	/ uns	…	-selves [-ˈselvz]
You	listen	to	**yourselves.**	Ihr …	euch	…	/ euch	…	
They	listen	to	**themselves.**	Sie …	sich	…	/ sich	…	

Theme 2

p.56	**guest** [gest]	Gast	= someone who visits someone else
	twin room [twɪn ˈruːm]	Zweibettzimmer	**twin(s)** = Zwilling(e)
	double room [dʌbl ˈruːm]	Doppelzimmer	A **double** room is a room with a **double** bed. **double** = doppelt, Doppel-
	single room [sɪŋgl ˈruːm]	Einzelzimmer	A twin room has two **single** beds. **single** = einzeln, Einzel-
	Wi-Fi [ˈwaɪ faɪ]	WLAN, kabellose Datenübertragung	
	kettle [ˈketl]	Wasserkocher *(elektrisch)*	a **kettle**
	per (person) [pɜː]	pro (Person)	
p.57	(to) **decide** (**to do** sth.) [dɪˈsaɪd]	beschließen, (sich) entscheiden (etwas zu tun)	I didn't feel well, so I **decided** not **to** go to the party.
	(to) **be happy to do** sth.	gerne etwas tun	Look, it's late, it's dark – I'm really **happy to** drive you home.
	(to) **book** [bʊk]	buchen, reservieren	That restaurant is really famous. You should **book** a table. ❗ **book** = 1. Buch; 2. buchen, reservieren
	What sort of …? [sɔːt]	Welche Art/Sorte (von) …?	**What sort of** music do you like?
	(to) **repeat** [rɪˈpiːt]	wiederholen	Could you **repeat** that, please? (= Could you say/do that again, please?)

Story

p.58	**ghost** [gəʊst]	Gespenst	a scary **ghost**
	(to) **exist** [ɪgˈzɪst]	existieren	What do you think: does the Loch Ness Monster **exist**?

	car park [ˈkɑː pɑːk]	Parkplatz	a car park
	musician [mjuˈzɪʃn]	Musiker/in	What's your job? – I'm a musician. I teach the guitar to children in a music school.
p.59	narrow [ˈnærəʊ]	eng, schmal	The road was too narrow for the big bus.
	(to) bring: they brought [brɔːt]	(mit)bringen: sie brachten (mit)	
	(to) point (at/to) [pɔɪnt]	zeigen, deuten (auf)	Look at this map of Ireland. Can you point at Dublin?
	ruin [ˈruːɪn]	Ruine	Urquhart Castle is now a ruin. ❗ Betonung auf der 1. Silbe: ruin [ˈruːɪn]
	wood [wʊd]	Wald; Holz	When you walk through a wood, you see many trees.
	signal [ˈsɪɡnəl]	Signal	❗ Betonung auf der 1. Silbe: signal [ˈsɪɡnəl]
p.60	(to) land [lænd]	landen	verb: (to) land – noun: land (Land)
	(to) hire [ˈhaɪə]	mieten, leihen	I don't have a car. I hire one when I really need one.
	driving licence [ˈdraɪvɪŋ laɪsns]	Führerschein	You need a driving licence if you want to drive a car.
	(to) begin [bɪˈɡɪn], began [bɪˈɡæn], begun [beˈɡʌn]	beginnen, anfangen	= (to) start

Focus on language

p.62	mom (AE) [mɒm]	Mutti, Mama	= BE mum ❗ (AE) zeigt dir, dass dieses Wort besonders in Amerika gebräuchlich ist.
p.63	bacon [ˈbeɪkən]	Speck	Would you like a Scottish breakfast with bacon and tomatoes?
	tomato [təˈmɑːtəʊ], pl tomatoes	Tomate	
	salt [sɔːlt]	Salz	sugar and salt
	sugar [ˈʃʊɡə]	Zucker	
p.64	thousand [ˈθaʊznd]	tausend	one thousand = 1,000
	(to) welcome sb. (to) [ˈwelkəm]	jn. begrüßen (in), jn. willkommen heißen (in)	I'll make tea. Can you welcome the guests?
	the USA [juː es ˈeɪ]	die USA (= die Vereinigten Staaten von Amerika)	
	its own team [əʊn]	seine eigene Mannschaft	❗ English: Do you have your own room? German: Hast du ein eigenes Zimmer?
	world [wɜːld]	Welt	in the world = auf der Welt

3 Vocabulary

	they were born [bɔːn]	sie wurden geboren	! *English:* When **were** you **born**? *German:* Wann **bist** du geboren?

Skills training

p.65	(to) **fill in** [fɪl 'ɪn]	einsetzen; ausfüllen	! **fill in** = 1. ausfüllen – **fill in** a form 2. einsetzen – **fill in** your name / the right word / the missing information
	form [fɔːm]	Formular	If you'd like to work in our shop, please fill in this **form**.
	birth [bɜːθ]	Geburt	**date of birth** = Geburtsdatum **place of birth** = Geburtsort
	nationality [næʃə'næləti]	Staatsangehörigkeit, Nationalität	Betonung auf der **3.** Silbe: nation**a**lity [næʃə'næləti]
	signature ['sɪgnətʃə]	Unterschrift	
	allergic (to) [ə'lɜːdʒɪk]	allergisch (gegen)	I can't eat that. I'm **allergic to** nuts.
p.66	**voice** [vɔɪs]	Stimme	
	electronic [ɪlek'trɒnɪk]	elektronisch	This sounds like a real piano, but it's an **electronic** piano.
	I don't know about ….	Bei … bin ich mir nicht (so) sicher.	! (to) **know**, **knew** [njuː], **known** [nəʊn]
	amazing [ə'meɪzɪŋ]	erstaunlich	24 million people live in Shanghai? **Amazing**!
	(to) **make** sb. **do** sth.	jn. dazu bringen, etwas zu tun	She couldn't **make** him **stay**, so he went away.
	full (of …) [fʊl]	voll; voller …	There's too much traffic here. All the streets are **full of** cars.
	energy ['enədʒi]	Energie	! Betonung auf der **1.** Silbe: **en**ergy ['enədʒi]
p.67	(to) **skim** a text [skɪm]	einen Text überfliegen (um den Inhalt grob zu erfassen)	= (to) read a text quickly to find the most important idea(s)
p.68	**diary** ['daɪəri]	Tagebuch; Kalender	I've arranged to meet Tim on Friday. Let me put this in my **diary**. *(Kalender)* I **keep a diary**. = I write something in my **diary** every day, for example special things that happened. *(Tagebuch, Tagebuch führen)*
	puzzled ['pʌzld]	verwirrt, verwundert	= surprised
	(to) **mean** [miːn], **meant, meant** [ment]	bedeuten; meinen, sagen wollen	! (to) **mean** = 1. bedeuten: What does the word "soccer" **mean**? 2. meinen, sagen wollen: I don't understand. What do you **mean**?
	pizza ['piːtsə]	Pizza	! Aussprache: langes -i-! ['piːtsə]

Irregular verbs							
(to) **begin**	**began**	**begun**	*beginnen*	(to) **lose**	**lost**	**lost**	*verlieren*
(to) **bring**	**brought**	**brought**	*(mit)bringen*	(to) **make**	**made**	**made**	*machen*
(to) **cost**	**cost**	**cost**	*kosten*	(to) **mean**	**meant**	**meant**	*meinen; bedeuten*
(to) **know**	**knew**	**known**	*kennen; wissen*	(to) **teach**	**taught**	**taught**	*unterrichten*

▶ pp.214–215

USA – here we come

p.74 **state** [steɪt] — (Bundes-)Staat

Unit 4: In the heart of the USA

p.76 **heart** [hɑːt] — Herz — a **heart**

European [jʊərə'piːən] — europäisch; Europäer/in — adjective: **European** – noun: **Europe**

pyramid ['pɪrəmɪd] — Pyramide — ❗ Betonung auf der **1.** Silbe: **py**ramid ['pɪrəmɪd]

son [sʌn] — Sohn — A prince is a king's or queen's **son**.
brother ◄► sister
son ◄► daughter

plane [pleɪn] — Flugzeug — a **plane**

mural ['mjʊərəl] — Wandgemälde — = a picture on a wall or a building

artist ['ɑːtɪst] — Künstler/in — ❗ Betonung auf der **1.** Silbe: **ar**tist ['ɑːtɪst]

civil rights *(pl)* [sɪvl 'raɪts] — Bürgerrechte — ❗ **right** = **1.** richtig; **2.** rechts; **3. rights** *(pl)* = Rechte

protest ['prəʊtest] — Protest(demonstration) — ❗ noun: **protest** ['prəʊtest] – verb: (to) **protest** [prə'test]

entertainment park [entə'teɪnmənt pɑːk] — Erholungspark, Vergnügungspark

march [mɑːtʃ] — Marsch — noun: **march** – verb: (to) **march** (marschieren)

Theme 1

p.78 **announcement** [ə'naʊnsmənt] — Durchsage, Ansage — Did you hear that **announcement**? Our plane is an hour late!

(to) **sell** [sel], **sold, sold** [səʊld] — verkaufen — **buy** ◄► **sell**

(potato) chips *(pl, AE)* [pə'teɪtəʊ tʃɪps] — (Kartoffel-)Chips — = *BE* **crisps**

French fries *(pl, AE)* [frentʃ 'fraɪz] — Pommes frites — = *BE* **chips**

p.79 **competition** [kɒmpə'tɪʃn] — Wettbewerb — The World Cup is a **competition** for teams from many different countries in the world.

4 Vocabulary

opposite [ˈɒpəzɪt]	Gegenteil	The **opposite** of 'big' is 'small'.
against [əˈgenst]	gegen	We're not allowed to eat junk food at school. It's **against** the school rules.
Yours sincerely [sɪnˈsɪəli]	Mit freundlichen Grüßen (Briefschluss)	
ham [hæm]	(gekochter) Schinken	**ham**
meal [miːl]	Mahlzeit, Essen	Do you eat a hot **meal** at lunchtime? *(warme Mahlzeit)*

Theme 2

p.80	(to) **make money**	Geld verdienen	I want a new phone. But first I must find a job and **make** some **money**.
	chocolate bar [ˈtʃɒklət bɑː]	Schokoriegel	I sometimes eat a **chocolate bar**, but usually I eat healthy food.
p.81	**a few** [fjuː]	ein paar, einige	You're hungry? There are a **few** apples in the kitchen. **in the last few weeks** = in den letzten paar Wochen
	business (studies) [ˈbɪznəs]	Wirtschaft(slehre)	I like **business studies** at school. In those lessons we learn how the **business** world works.
	profit [ˈprɒfɪt]	Gewinn, Profit	I made a **profit** of £15 when I sold my bike. ❗Betonung auf der 1. Silbe: **pro**fit [ˈprɒfɪt]
	successful [səkˈsesfl]	erfolgreich	Her business did very well. Her business idea was very **successful**.
	least [liːst]	(der/die/das) wenigste, am wenigsten	**least successful** = am wenigsten erfolgreich less ◄► more least ◄► most
	independence (from) [ɪndɪˈpendəns]	Unabhängigkeit (von)	**Independence Day** = Unabhängigkeitstag
	(to) **take part (in)** [teɪk ˈpɑːt]	teilnehmen (an), mitmachen (bei)	More than 200 singers **took part** in the concert.

Story

p.82	**past** [pɑːst]	Vergangenheit	the **past** ◄► the **future** ❗**past** = 1. Vergangenheit: Things were easier in the **past**. 2. vorbei an: We walked **past** a bike shop.
	crazy [ˈkreɪzi]	verrückt	What a stupid thing to do! Are you **crazy**?
	(to) **go crazy**	verrückt werden	❗**Go** *(werden)* wird nur in bestimmten Zusammenhängen verwendet, z.B. für Farben oder bei Verschlechterungen. The vegetables **have gone** [gɒn] bad. Apples can **go** brown.

(to) **forget (about)** sth. [fə'get], **forgot** [fə'gɒt], **forgotten** [fə'gɒtn]	etwas vergessen	It's dad's birthday tomorrow. Don't **forget** it. **forget** sth. ◄► **remember** sth.
China ['tʃaɪnə]	China	❗ Aussprache: ['tʃaɪnə]
(to) **leave school**	von der Schule abgehen	She **left school** and started her own business.
little ['lɪtl]	wenig	**little – less – least** ◄► **much – more – most** ❗ **little = 1.** wenig; **2. a little =** ein wenig, ein bisschen
p.83 (to) **catch (a bus/train/…)** [kætʃ]	(einen Bus/Zug/…) nehmen, erwischen	❗ (to) **catch = 1.** (ein)fangen; **2.** *(Bus, Zug etc.)* nehmen, erwischen
p.84 (to) **send (to)** [send], **sent, sent** [sent]	schicken, senden (an)	We bought a nice birthday card and **sent** it to Grandma.
lots and lots of cupcakes	unheimlich viele Cupcakes	Their business is very successful. They sell **lots and lots** of their special T-shirts.
waste [weɪst]	Verschwendung	What a **waste** of time!
skill [skɪl]	Fähigkeit, Fertigkeit	Jane's computer **skills** are amazing.
p.85 **score** [skɔː]	Spiel-/Punktestand; Punkt *(Spiel/Sport)*	noun: **score** – verb: (to) **score** (einen Punkt / ein Tor erzielen)
public holiday [pʌblɪk 'hɒlədeɪ]	(gesetzlicher) Feiertag	Next Monday we're not going to school: it's a **public holiday**.
Christmas ['krɪsməs]	Weihnachten	**Christmas Day** = der 1. Weihnachtstag (25.12.)

Focus on language

p.86 **beginner** [bɪ'gɪnə]	Anfänger/in	I'm not very good at judo yet. I'm still a **beginner**.
original [ə'rɪdʒənl]	originell	adjective: **original** – noun: **original** (Original)
p.87 **colourful** ['kʌləfl]	farbenfroh, bunt	a **colourful** duck
I think so. **I don't think so.**	Ich glaube/denke ja. Das glaube/denke ich nicht.	I hope **so**. *(Das hoffe ich.)* He said **so**. *(Das hat er gesagt.)*
p.88 **age** [eɪdʒ]	Alter	**ages** 5–11 free = Kinder im Alter von 5–11 frei children **aged** 7 = Kinder im Alter von 7 Jahren
cotton ['kɒtn]	Baumwolle	
(to) **expect** [ɪk'spekt]	erwarten	Writing this text was harder than I **expected**. It was a lot of work!
waiter ['weɪtə], **waitress** ['weɪtrəs]	Kellner, Kellnerin	a **waiter** and two customers

4 Vocabulary

British English / American English

sounds:
In **American English**, the **t** between two vowels sounds more like a **d**:

better	['bedə]
butter	['bʌdə]
city	['sɪdi]
party	['pɑːdi]
photo	['fəʊdəʊ]
Saturday	['sædədeɪ]
water	['wɔːdə]

spelling: BE -tre **spelling:** AE -ter

centre	center
metre	meter
theatre	theater

words BE **words** AE

sweets	candy
crisps	(potato) chips
biscuit	cookie
chips	French fries
school year	grade
mum	mom
cinema	movie theater

Skills training

p.89 | **report** [rɪ'pɔːt] | Bericht | **weather report** = Wetterbericht
noun: **report** – verb: (to) **report** (berichten)

degree [dɪ'griː] | Grad | It'll be 14 **degrees** (14°) and very cloudy.

grey [greɪ] | grau | They're **grey**.

low [ləʊ] | niedrig, tief | **high** temperatures ◄► **low** temperatures
it's warm/hot ◄► it's cold

below [bɪ'ləʊ] | unter(halb von); unten | Write your name **below** all the other names on the list, please. *(unter)*
Look at the pictures **below**. *(unten)*

p.90 | **actor** ['æktə] | Schauspieler/in | Which **actor** played the detective in this famous crime series?

category ['kætəɡəri] | Kategorie | ❗ Betonung auf der 1. Silbe: **cat**egory ['**kæt**əɡəri]

drug [drʌɡ] | Droge, Rauschgift; Arzneimittel

violence ['vaɪələns] | Gewalt; Gewalttätigkeit | noun: **violence** – adjective: **violent** ['vaɪələnt] (gewalttätig)

(to) **give** sth. **up**, **gave**, **given** | etwas aufgeben, aufhören mit etwas | I'll never learn to dance. I **give up**!
(to) **give**, **gave**, **given** ['ɡɪvn]

(to) **cheer** [tʃɪə] | jubeln, (Sportler/innen) anfeuern | verb: (to) **cheer** – noun: **cheer** (Beifallsruf, Hurra(geschrei))

Spanish ['spænɪʃ] | spanisch; Spanisch | I'd like to learn another language. – What about **Spanish**? You can use it in many different countries.

p.91 | **formal** ['fɔːml] | formell | When you write to the hotel manager, your letter should be **formal**.

informal [ɪn'fɔːml] | informell, locker | But your emails to your friends can be **informal**.

(to) **break** [breɪk], **broke** [brəʊk], **broken** ['brəʊkən] | (zer)brechen; kaputtgehen; kaputtmachen | ❗ something is **broken** = etwas ist gebrochen, zerbrochen, kaputt

shower ['ʃaʊə] | Dusche; Schauer

clean [kliːn]	sauber	adjective: **clean** – verb: (to) **clean** (sauber machen, putzen)
All the best	Mit besten Grüßen, Alles Gute *(Briefschluss)*	
Dear Sir/Madam [sɜː], [ˈmædəm]	Sehr geehrte Damen und Herren	
(to) **complain (about/of)** [kəmˈpleɪn]	sich beschweren (über); jammern	They **complained about** the food. *(sich beschweren)* "That's unfair!" he **complained**. *(jammern)*
reception [rɪˈsepʃn]	Empfang *(auch beim Telefon)*; Rezeption	**in reception** = an der Rezeption
p.92 **bow tie** [bəʊ ˈtaɪ]	Fliege *(Krawatte)*	**bow** = Schleife
(to) **be called** [kɔːld]	genannt werden, heißen	Do you know this song? Do you know what the band **is called**? (= the name of the band)
each [iːtʃ]	jede(r, s) (einzelne)	**Each** cupcake *(jeder einzelne Cupcake)* costs 50p. = The cupcakes cost 50p **each**. *(jeweils 50p)*

Irregular verbs

(to) **break**	broke	**broken**	(zer)brechen	(to) **leave**	left	**left**	verlassen
(to) **forget**	forgot	**forgotten**	vergessen	(to) **say**	said	**said**	sagen
(to) **give**	gave	**given**	geben	(to) **sell**	sold	**sold**	verkaufen
(to) **go**	went	**gone**	gehen; fahren	(to) **send**	sent	**sent**	schicken, senden

▶ *pp. 214–215*

DICTIONARY

English – German

Im **Dictionary** werden folgende **Abkürzungen und Symbole** verwendet:

sb. = somebody   sth. = something   jn. = jemanden   jm. = jemandem
pl = *plural* (Mehrzahl)   BE = *British English*   AE = *American English*   infml = *informal* (umgangssprachlich)

° Mit diesem Kringel sind Wörter markiert, die nicht zum Lernwortschatz gehören. Die Fundstellenangaben zeigen, in welchem Band ein Wort zum ersten Mal vorkommt: 5 = Highlight 5; 6 = Highlight 6.
Beim vorliegenden Band mit genauer Unit- und Seitenangabe: 7: 4 (78) = Highlight 7, Unit 4, Seite 78.

A

a [ə] ein/e 5 **once a week** einmal pro Woche 6
about [əˈbaʊt]:
1. ungefähr 5
2. über 5
What about you? Und du? / Was ist mit dir? 5 **What's special about him?** Was ist das Besondere an ihm? 6 **write about** schreiben über 5
accident [ˈæksɪdənt] Unfall 7: 2 (34)
°**accommodation** [əkɒməˈdeɪʃn] Unterkunft; Wohnung, Zimmer
°**accompany** [əˈkʌmpəni]: **they must be accompanied by …** sie müssen von … begleitet werden
°**ace** [eɪs]: **That's ace.** *(infml)* Das ist krass/genial/super.
°**acrobat** [ˈækrəbæt] Akrobat/in
°**across cultures** [əˈkrɒs] (quer) über/durch die Kulturen
act [ækt]:
1. Theater spielen; schauspielern 6
2. aufführen, spielen 6
°**act out** vorspielen, aufführen
activity [ækˈtɪvəti] Aktivität, Beschäftigung 6
actor [ˈæktə] Schauspieler/in 7: 4 (90)
°**adapt (to)** [əˈdæpt] (sich) anpassen (an)
address [əˈdres] Adresse 5
adult [ˈædʌlt] Erwachsene/r 6
adventure [ədˈventʃə] Abenteuer 6
advert [ˈædvɜːt] Anzeige, Werbung 7: 1 (13)
°**advice** [ədˈvaɪs] Rat; Ratschläge
aerobics [eəˈrəʊbɪks] Aerobic 6
after school [ɑːftə ˈskuːl] nach der Schule 5
afternoon [ɑːftəˈnuːn] Nachmittag 5 **in the afternoon(s)** nachmittags, am Nachmittag 5
again [əˈɡen] wieder, noch einmal 5
against [əˈɡenst] gegen 7: 4 (79)
age [eɪdʒ] Alter 7: 4 (88)
°**age limit** [ˈeɪdʒ lɪmɪt] Altersgrenze, Mindestalter

aged [eɪdʒd]: **children aged 7** Kinder im Alter von 7 Jahren 7: 4 (88)
ago [əˈɡəʊ]: **two years ago** vor zwei Jahren 7: 1 (10)
agree [əˈɡriː]: **agree (with sb.)** (jm.) zustimmen 6 °**agree (on)** sich einigen (auf), vereinbaren
airport [ˈeəpɔːt] Flughafen 6
all [ɔːl] alle(s) 5 **all day** den ganzen Tag (lang) 6 **not … at all** überhaupt nicht … 5 °**all of them** sie alle °**all over Ireland** überall in Irland, in ganz Irland
allergic (to) [əˈlɜːdʒɪk] allergisch (gegen) 7: 3 (65)
allowed [əˈlaʊd]: **be allowed** erlaubt sein 7: 1 (10) **be allowed to do sth.** etwas tun dürfen 7: 1 (10)
alone [əˈləʊn] allein(e) 6
along the street [əˈlɒŋ] die Straße entlang 6
°**aloud** [əˈlaʊd]: **read sth. aloud** etwas laut (vor)lesen
°**alphabet** [ˈælfəbət] Alphabet
°**alphabetical** [ælfəˈbetɪkl] alphabetisch
already [ɔːlˈredi] schon 7: 2 (32)
also [ˈɔːlsəʊ] auch 6
always [ˈɔːlweɪz] immer 5
am [æm]: **I'm (= I am)** ich bin 5
am [eɪ ˈem]: **11 am** 11 Uhr morgens/vormittags 5
amazing [əˈmeɪzɪŋ] erstaunlich 7: 3 (66)
American [əˈmerəkən]:
1. Amerikaner/in 6
2. amerikanisch 6
an [ən] ein/e (vor Vokalen) 5
and [ænd], [ənd] und 5
angry [ˈæŋɡri] wütend, ärgerlich 5
animal [ˈænɪml] Tier 5
announcement [əˈnaʊnsmənt] Durchsage, Ansage 7: 4 (78)
another [əˈnʌðə] ein/e andere(r, s); noch ein/e 5
answer [ˈɑːnsə]:
1. Antwort 5
2. antworten (auf), beantworten 5
any [ˈeni]: **Do you have any questions?** Hast du/Habt ihr

(irgendwelche) Fragen? 6 **We don't have any pets.** Wir haben keine (Haus-)Tiere. 5
anybody [ˈenibɒdi]: **Does anybody speak …?** Spricht (irgend)jemand …? 7: 1 (19) **not … anybody** niemand 7: 1 (19)
anything [ˈeniθɪŋ]: **Anything else?** Sonst noch etwas? 5 **not (…) anything** nichts 6
apple [ˈæpl] Apfel 5
April [ˈeɪprəl] April 5
are [ɑː] bist, sind, seid 5 **They're £ 90.** Sie kosten 90 Pfund. 5
arm [ɑːm] Arm 6
around [əˈraʊnd] umher- 5 **run around** umherrennen; herumlaufen 6
arrange [əˈreɪndʒ] vereinbaren, ausmachen *(Termin)* 7: 2 (43)
°**arrival** [əˈraɪvl]: **date of arrival** Ankunftsdatum
arrive (at) [əˈraɪv] ankommen (in/an/bei) 5
art [ɑːt] Kunst 5 **work of art** Kunstwerk 7: 4 (77)
article [ˈɑːtɪkl] Artikel 7: 1 (11)
artist [ˈɑːtɪst] Künstler/in 7: 4 (76)
°**arts and crafts** *(pl)* [ɑːts ən ˈkrɑːfts] Kunsthandwerk
as [æz], [əz] wie 5 **as in …** wie in … 5 °**as many as you can** so viele (wie) du kannst
ask [ɑːsk] fragen 5 **ask sb. about sth.** sich bei jm. nach etwas erkundigen, jn. nach etwas fragen 6 °**ask for sth.** um etwas bitten, nach etwas fragen
assistant [əˈsɪstənt]:
1. Helfer/in, Assistent/in 7: 1 (18)
2. Verkäufer/in 7: 1 (18)
at [æt], [ət] an, bei 5 **at a restaurant** in einem Restaurant 5 **at Eggbuckland** auf der Eggbuckland-Schule 5 **at Ellie's house** bei Ellie daheim, bei Ellie zu Hause 5 **at home** zu Hause 5 **at least** mindestens, wenigstens 6 **at MARTINS** bei MARTINS 5 **at night** nachts, in der Nacht 5 **at school** in der Schule 5 **at the**

172   one hundred and seventy-two

cinema im Kino 5 **at the top (of)** oben, am oberen Ende (von); an der Spitze (von) 6 **at this school** auf/an dieser Schule 5 **not ... at all** überhaupt nicht ... 5 °**at reasonable prices** zu vernünftigen Preisen
ate [eɪt], [et] *siehe* **eat**
August [ˈɔːɡəst] August 5
aunt [ɑːnt] Tante 6
°**available** [əˈveɪləbl] verfügbar; erhältlich; möglich
away [əˈweɪ] weg, fort 5
°**awesome** [ˈɔːsəm] *(AE, infml)* klasse, stark, großartig

B

baby [ˈbeɪbi] Baby 5
babysitter [ˈbeɪbɪsɪtə] Babysitter 5
back [bæk] zurück 5 °**at the back of the shop** hinten im Geschäft/Laden
bacon [ˈbeɪkən] Speck 7: 3 (63)
bad [bæd] schlecht; schlimm 5
°**badge** [bædʒ] Anstecknadel, Button
badminton [ˈbædmɪntən] Badminton, Federball 6
bag [bæɡ] Tasche 5
bagpipes *(pl)* [ˈbæɡpaɪps] Dudelsack 7: 3 (52)
ball [bɔːl] Ball 5
°**balloon** [bəˈluːn] Ballon
banana [bəˈnɑːnə] Banane 5
band [bænd] Band, Musikgruppe 5
bank [bæŋk] Bank *(Geldinstitut)* 6
°**barbecue** [ˈbɑːbɪkjuː] Grillfest, Grillparty
baseball [ˈbeɪsbɔːl] Baseball 6
basketball [ˈbɑːskɪtbɔːl] Basketball 5
bathroom [ˈbɑːθruːm] Bad(ezimmer) 5
Bavaria [bəˈveərɪə] Bayern 6
Bavarian [bəˈveərɪən]:
1. Bayer/in 6
2. bayerisch 6
be [biː], **was/were, been** sein 5
beach [biːtʃ] Strand 5 **on the beach** am Strand 5
bear [beə] Bär 5
beat [biːt] *(Musik)* Beat, Rhythmus 7: 3 (66)
beautiful [ˈbjuːtɪfl] schön, wunderschön 7: 3 (55)
became [bɪˈkeɪm] *siehe* **become**
because [bɪˈkɒz] weil 5
become [bɪˈkʌm], **became, become** werden 7: 2 (33)

bed [bed] Bett 5 **go to bed** ins Bett gehen, schlafen gehen 5
bed and breakfast (B&B) [bed ən ˈbrekfəst] Frühstückspension; Zimmer mit Frühstück 7: 3 (55)
bedroom [ˈbedruːm] Schlafzimmer 5
been [biːn], [bɪn] *siehe* **be**
before [bɪˈfɔː]:
1. vor *(zeitlich)* 5
2. vorher; zuvor 7: 2 (34)
3. **before (you read)** bevor (du liest) 5
began [bɪˈɡæn] *siehe* **begin**
begin [bɪˈɡɪn], **began, begun** anfangen, beginnen 7: 3 (60)
beginner [bɪˈɡɪnə] Anfänger/in 7: 4 (86)
°**beginning** [bɪˈɡɪnɪŋ] Anfang
begun [bɪˈɡʌn] *siehe* **begin**
behind [bɪˈhaɪnd] hinter 5
bell [bel] Glocke; Klingel 7: 1 (8)
below [bɪˈləʊ] unter(halb von); unten 7: 4 (89)
best [best] beste(r, s); am besten 5 **All the best** Mit besten Grüßen, Alles Gute *(Briefschluss)* 7: 4 (91) **like sth. best** etwas am liebsten mögen 5
better [ˈbetə] besser 6 **do better** besser abschneiden 6 **like sth. better** etwas lieber mögen 6
between [bɪˈtwiːn] zwischen 6
°**beware of** [bɪˈweər əv] sich in Acht nehmen vor
big [bɪɡ] groß 5
bike [baɪk] Fahrrad 5 **ride a bike** Rad fahren 5
bikini [bɪˈkiːni] Bikini 7: 1 (19)
bird [bɜːd] Vogel 5
birth [bɜːθ] Geburt 7: 3 (65)
birthday [ˈbɜːθdeɪ] Geburtstag 5 **Happy birthday!** Herzlichen Glückwunsch zum Geburtstag! 5 **It's her birthday.** Sie hat Geburtstag. 5 **When is your birthday?** Wann hast du Geburtstag? 5
biscuit [ˈbɪskɪt] Keks, Plätzchen 6
bit [bɪt] Teil, Stück(chen) 7: 1 (12) **a bit** ein bisschen 5
black [blæk] schwarz 5
blog [blɒɡ] Blog *(Internet-Tagebuch)* 6
blue [bluː] blau 5
blues [bluːz] Blues *(Musikrichtung)* 7: 4 (76)
°**board** [bɔːd] Tafel *(im Klassenraum)*
boat [bəʊt] Boot; Schiff 5

bonfire [ˈbɒnfaɪə] *(Freuden-)*Feuer 6
bonus [ˈbəʊnəs] Bonus- 7: 4 (90)
book [bʊk]:
1. Buch 5
2. buchen, reservieren 7: 3 (57)
bookshop [ˈbʊkʃɒp] Buchladen 6
boot [buːt] Stiefel 6
°**bored** [bɔːd] **be bored** Langeweile haben, gelangweilt sein
boring [ˈbɔːrɪŋ] langweilig 5
born [bɔːn] **they were born** sie wurden geboren 7: 3 (64)
borrow [ˈbɒrəʊ] (aus)leihen, sich borgen 5
bossy [ˈbɒsi] herrisch 5
°**botanic garden** [bəˈtænɪk ˈɡɑːdn] botanischer Garten
°**both** [bəʊθ] beide
bottle [ˈbɒtl] Flasche 5
bought [bɔːt] *siehe* **buy**
bow [bəʊ] Schleife 7: 4 (92)
bow tie [bəʊ ˈtaɪ] Fliege *(Krawatte)* 7: 4 (92)
bowling [ˈbəʊlɪŋ]: **go bowling** Bowling spielen gehen 5
box [bɒks] Box, Kasten 5
boy [bɔɪ] Junge, Bub 5
boyfriend [ˈbɔɪfrend] (fester) Freund 6
brave [breɪv] mutig 7: 2 (39)
bread [bred] Brot 6
break [breɪk] Pause 5
break [breɪk], **broke, broken** (zer)brechen 7: 4 (91)
breakfast [ˈbrekfəst] Frühstück 5 **have breakfast** frühstücken 5
bridge [brɪdʒ] Brücke 6
brilliant [ˈbrɪljənt] genial 5
bring [brɪŋ], **brought, brought** bringen, mitbringen 5
Britain [ˈbrɪtn] Großbritannien 6
British [ˈbrɪtɪʃ] britisch 5
brochure [ˈbrəʊʃə] Broschüre, Prospekt 5
broke [brəʊk] *siehe* **break**
broken [ˈbrəʊkən] *siehe* **break be broken** gebrochen; zerbrochen, kaputt sein 7: 4 (91)
brother [ˈbrʌðə] Bruder 5
brought [brɔːt] *siehe* **bring**
brown [braʊn] braun 5
building [ˈbɪldɪŋ] Gebäude 7: 2 (31)
burger [ˈbɜːɡə] Hamburger *(Frikadelle)* 6
bus [bʌs] Bus 5
°**bus service** [ˈsɜːvɪs] Busverbindung
bus stop [ˈbʌs stɒp] Bushaltestelle 6

DICTIONARY

English – German

bush [bʊʃ] Busch, Strauch 7: 2 (36)
business [ˈbɪznəs]:
1. Geschäft, Betrieb 7: 2 (32) **start a business** ein Geschäft aufmachen, einen Betrieb gründen/eröffnen 7: 2 (32)
2. (= business studies) Wirtschaftslehre 7: 4 (81)
business studies (pl) [ˈbɪznəs stʌdiz] Wirtschaftslehre 7: 4 (81)
busy [ˈbɪzi]:
1. belebt; verkehrsreich 7: 1 (11)
2. **be busy** beschäftigt sein, (viel) zu tun haben 6
but [bʌt] aber 5
butter [ˈbʌtə] Butter 6
buy [baɪ], **bought, bought** kaufen 5
by [baɪ]: **by Berry** (geschrieben) von Berry 5 **by bus** mit dem Bus 5
Bye. [baɪ] Tschüs./Servus. 5

C

cafe [ˈkæfeɪ] Café 5
cage [keɪdʒ] Käfig 5
cake [keɪk] Kuchen 5
calculator [ˈkælkjuleɪtə] Taschenrechner 5
calendar [ˈkælɪndə] Kalender 5
call [kɔːl]:
1. rufen; anrufen; nennen 7: 1 (14)
2. (kurz für: **phone call**) (Telefon-)Anruf 6
called [kɔːld]: **be called** genannt werden, heißen 7: 4 (92)
came [keɪm] siehe **come**
camera [ˈkæmərə] Fotoapparat; Kamera 7: 2 (36)
°**camogie** [kəˈməʊgi] Camogie (dem Hurling ähnlicher Sport für Frauen und Mädchen)
camping [ˈkæmpɪŋ] Camping 5
campsite [ˈkæmpsaɪt] Campingplatz, Zeltplatz 5
can [kæn], [kən] können 5
can [kæn] Dose, Büchse 7: 1 (15)
°**candy** [ˈkændi] (AE) Süßigkeiten
canoe [kəˈnuː] Kanu, Paddelboot 5
can't (= cannot) [kɑːnt], [ˈkænt] nicht können 5
canteen [kænˈtiːn] (Schul-)Mensa, Kantine 5
°**canyon** [ˈkænjən] Cañon
capital (city) [ˈkæpɪtl] Hauptstadt 7: 2 (30)
°**caption** [ˈkæpʃn] Bildunterschrift
car [kɑː] Auto 5

car number [ˈkɑː nʌmbə] Autokennzeichen 7: 2 (37)
car park [ˈkɑː pɑːk] Parkplatz 7: 3 (58)
card [kɑːd] Karte 5
careful [ˈkeəfl] vorsichtig; sorgfältig 6
carefully [ˈkeəfəli]: **listen carefully** ganz genau zuhören 6
carrot [ˈkærət] Möhre, Karotte 6
cartoon [kɑːˈtuːn] Zeichentrickfilm; Comic 6
castle [ˈkɑːsl] Burg 7: 3 (52)
cat [kæt] Katze 5
catch [kætʃ], **caught, caught** (ein)fangen 7: 2 (36) **catch (a bus/train/…)** (einen Bus/Zug/…) nehmen, erwischen 7: 4 (83)
category [ˈkætəgəri] Kategorie 7: 4 (90)
caught [kɔːt] siehe **catch**
CCTV [siː siː tiː ˈviː] Überwachungssystem; Überwachungskamera(s) 7: 2 (32)
CCTV camera [siː siː tiː ˈviː kæmərə] Überwachungskamera 7: 2 (36)
CD [siːˈdiː] CD 5
CD player [siːˈdiː pleɪə] CD-Spieler 6
celebrate [ˈselɪbreɪt] feiern 6
°**Celtic** [ˈkeltɪk] keltisch
°**center** [ˈsentə] (AE) Zentrum, (Stadt-)Mitte
central [ˈsentrəl] zentral 7: 1 (21) **Central London** London Stadtmitte 7: 1 (21)
centre [ˈsentə] Zentrum, (Stadt-)Mitte 6
chair [tʃeə] Stuhl 5
change [tʃeɪndʒ] (ver)ändern, sich (ver)ändern 6 **change (trains)** umsteigen (Zug) 7: 1 (13)
changing room [ˈtʃeɪndʒɪŋ ruːm] Umkleide(kabine), Anprobe 7: 1 (18)
°**character** [ˈkærəktə] Figur, Person (in Roman, Film usw.)
charity [ˈtʃærəti] wohltätige Organisation 6
charity shop [ˈtʃærəti ʃɒp] Geschäft, das gespendete Waren für wohltätige Zwecke verkauft 6
chat [tʃæt]:
1. **chat (with)** plaudern (mit); „chatten" (mit) 5
2. Gespräch, Unterhaltung; Chat 6
have a chat sich unterhalten, reden 6
°**chat show** [ˈtʃæt ʃəʊ] Talkshow

cheap [tʃiːp] billig, preiswert 6 **It's cheaper than that.** So viel kostet das nicht. 6
check [tʃek]:
1. (über)prüfen, kontrollieren 6
2. (Über-)Prüfung, Kontrolle 6
cheer [tʃɪə]:
1. Beifallsruf, Hurra(geschrei) 7: 4 (90)
2. jubeln, (Sportler/innen) anfeuern 7: 4 (90)
cheese [tʃiːz] Käse 5
°**cheesecake** [ˈtʃiːzkeɪk] Käsekuchen
chicken [ˈtʃɪkɪn] Huhn; (Brat-)Hähnchen 5
child, pl **children** [tʃaɪld], [ˈtʃɪldrən] Kind 5
chill [tʃɪl] (infml) relaxen, sich ausruhen 6
China [ˈtʃaɪnə] China 7: 4 (82)
chips (pl) [tʃɪps] Pommes frites 5 **(potato) chips** (AE) (Kartoffel-)Chips 7: 4 (78)
chocolate [ˈtʃɒklət] Schokolade; Praline 5 **hot chocolate** Kakao, heiße (Trink-)Schokolade 6
chocolate bar [ˈtʃɒklət bɑː] Schokoriegel 7: 4 (80)
°**choice** [tʃɔɪs] (Aus-)Wahl
°**choose** [tʃuːz] (aus)wählen
chores [tʃɔːz]: **do chores** (Haus-)Arbeiten erledigen 6
Christmas [ˈkrɪsməs] Weihnachten 7: 4 (85) **Christmas Day** 1. Weihnachtstag (25.12.) 7: 4 (85)
cinema [ˈsɪnəmə] Kino 5
°**circle** [ˈsɜːkl] Kreis
circus [ˈsɜːkəs]:
1. Zirkus 6
°2. runder Platz (in einer Stadt)
city [ˈsɪti] (Groß-)Stadt 5
civil rights (pl) [sɪvl ˈraɪts] Bürgerrechte 7: 4 (76)
class [klɑːs] (Schul-)Klasse 5 **in class** im Unterricht 5
class teacher [ˈklɑːs tiːtʃə] Klassenlehrer/in 5
°**classification** [klæsɪfɪˈkeɪʃn] (Alters-)Einstufung, Klassifizierung
classroom [ˈklɑːsruːm] Klassenzimmer 5
clean [kliːn]:
1. sauber machen, putzen 5
2. sauber 7: 4 (91)
clear [klɪə] deutlich, klar 6
clearly [ˈklɪəli]: **speak clearly** deutlich sprechen 6

clever [ˈklevə] schlau, klug 7:1 (14)
climb [klaɪm] klettern (auf) 6
climbing [ˈklaɪmɪŋ] (das) Klettern (Sport) 6
clock [klɒk] Uhr 5
close [kləʊz] schließen, zumachen 7:2 (33)
closed [kləʊzd]: **be closed** geschlossen sein, zu sein 6
clothes (pl) [kləʊðz] Kleidung 5
cloud [klaʊd] Wolke 7:1 (22)
cloudy [ˈklaʊdi] wolkig, bewölkt 6
club [klʌb] Klub, Verein 5
coat [kəʊt] Mantel; Jacke 7:2 (42)
coffee [ˈkɒfi] Kaffee 5
cold [kəʊld] kalt 5
collect [kəˈlekt] sammeln 6
colour [ˈkʌlə] Farbe 5
colourful [ˈkʌləfl] farbenfroh, bunt 7:4 (87)
°**column** [ˈkɒləm] (Text-)Spalte
come [kʌm], **came, come** (mit)kommen 5 **come (in) first** Erste/r werden (z.B. Rennen) 7:4 (79) **come in** hereinkommen 6 **Come on!** Na los! / Komm(t) (schon)! 5
comedy [ˈkɒmədi] Comedyshow; Komödie 6
comfortable [ˈkʌmftəbl] bequem, gemütlich 6
comic [ˈkɒmɪk] Comic(heft) 6
comment [ˈkɒment] Kommentar 7:1 (21) **make a comment** einen Kommentar abgeben 7:1 (21)
°**company** [ˈkʌmpəni] Gesellschaft, Firma
°**compare** [kəmˈpeə] vergleichen
°**competition** [kɒmpəˈtɪʃn] Wettbewerb 7:4 (79)
complain (about/of) [kəmˈpleɪn] sich beschweren (über); jammern 7:4 (91)
°**complete** [kəmˈpliːt] vervollständigen
computer [kəmˈpjuːtə] Computer 5
concert [ˈkɒnsət] Konzert 5
°**contact** [ˈkɒntækt] Kontakt
cook [kʊk] kochen 5
°**cookie** [ˈkʊki] (AE) Keks, Plätzchen
cool [kuːl]:
 1. cool 5
 2. kühl 5
°**copy** [ˈkɒpi] kopieren, abschreiben
correct [kəˈrekt]:
 1. korrekt 6
 2. korrigieren, berichtigen 6

cost [kɒst], **cost, cost** kosten 5
cottage [ˈkɒtɪdʒ] Häuschen, Hütte 6
cotton [ˈkɒtn] Baumwolle 7:4 (88)
could [kʊd]:
 1. **she could** sie konnte 6
 2. **we could** wir könnten 5
country [ˈkʌntri] Land 5 **in the country** auf dem Land 5
°**county** [ˈkaʊnti] Grafschaft, Bezirk
°**cousin** [ˈkʌzn] Cousin, Cousine
cover [ˈkʌvə]:
 1. Hülle (DVD, CD); Einband, Umschlag (Buch) 7:4 (90)
 °2. abdecken, zudecken
cow [kaʊ] Kuh 5
crab [kræb] Krebs (Tier) 5
crazy [ˈkreɪzi] verrückt 7:4 (82)
cream [kriːm] Sahne 5
cricket [ˈkrɪkɪt] Kricket (Mannschaftssportart) 6
crime series, pl **crime series** [ˈkraɪm sɪəriːz] Krimiserie 6
crisps (pl) [krɪsps] (Kartoffel-)Chips 5
cross [krɒs]:
 1. überqueren 6
 2. Kreuz 6
cry [kraɪ] weinen 6
culture [ˈkʌltʃə] Kultur 7:1 (10)
cupcake [ˈkʌpkeɪk] Cupcake (kleiner runder Kuchen) 7:4 (82)
cushion [ˈkʊʃn] Kissen 5
customer [ˈkʌstəmə] Kunde, Kundin 7:3 (54)
cut [kʌt], **cut, cut** schneiden; (Rasen) mähen 6
cute [kjuːt] niedlich, süß 5
cycle [ˈsaɪkl] Rad fahren 6
cycle track [ˈsaɪkl træk] Radweg 7:2 (42)
cycling [ˈsaɪklɪŋ] (das) Radfahren 5

D

dad [dæd] Papa, Vati 5
dance [dɑːns] tanzen 5
dancer [ˈdɑːnsə] Tänzer/in 7:1 (22)
dancing [ˈdɑːnsɪŋ] (das) Tanzen 5
dangerous [ˈdeɪndʒərəs] gefährlich 5
dark [dɑːk] dunkel 7:2 (39)
date [deɪt] Datum 5
date of birth [deɪt əv ˈbɜːθ] Geburtsdatum 7:3 (65)
daughter [ˈdɔːtə] Tochter 7:2 (34)
day [deɪ] Tag 5
day out, pl **days out** [deɪ ˈaʊt] (Tages-)Ausflug 6

daylight [ˈdeɪlaɪt] Tageslicht 7:3 (52)
deal [diːl] Geschäft; Vereinbarung 6 **It's a deal!** Abgemacht! 6 **make a deal** ein Geschäft abschließen/vereinbaren 6
dear [dɪə]: **Dear …** Liebe/r … 5 **Dear Sir/Madam** Sehr geehrte Damen und Herren 7:4 (91) **Oh dear.** Oje! 6
December [dɪˈsembə] Dezember 5
decide (to do sth.) [dɪˈsaɪd] beschließen, (sich) entscheiden (etwas zu tun) 7:3 (57)
deep [diːp] tief 7:2 (34)
degree [dɪˈɡriː] Grad 7:4 (89)
Denmark [ˈdenmɑːk] Dänemark 6
department [dɪˈpɑːtmənt] Abteilung 7:1 (19)
department store [dɪˈpɑːtmənt stɔː] Kaufhaus 7:1 (15)
°**departure** [deɪt əv dɪˈpɑːtʃə]: **date of departure** Abreisedatum
describe [dɪˈskraɪb] beschreiben 6
desk [desk] Schreibtisch 5
°**desperately** [ˈdespərətli] verzweifelt; unbedingt
°**detail** [ˈdiːteɪl] Detail, Einzelheit
detective [dɪˈtektɪv] Detektiv/in 7:1 (8)
°**diagram** [ˈdaɪəɡræm] Diagramm
°**dialogue** [ˈdaɪəlɒɡ] Dialog
diary [ˈdaɪəri] Tagebuch; Kalender 7:3 (68) **keep a diary** Tagebuch führen 7:3 (68)
dictionary [ˈdɪkʃənri] Wörterbuch, (alphabetisches) Wörterverzeichnis 5
did [dɪd] siehe **do He didn't do his homework.** Er hat seine Hausaufgaben nicht gemacht. 5
die [daɪ] sterben 6
difference [ˈdɪfrəns] Unterschied 5 **make a difference** etwas bewirken, etwas ausmachen 5
different [ˈdɪfrənt] unterschiedlich, verschieden, anders 5
difficult [ˈdɪfɪkəlt] schwierig, schwer 6
diner [ˈdaɪnə] (AE) Imbissstube, Lokal 6
dinner [ˈdɪnə] Abendessen 5 **have dinner** (zu) Abend essen 5
dinosaur [ˈdaɪnəsɔː] Dinosaurier 7:1 (14)
direct [dəˈrekt] direkt 7:1 (23)
°**director** [dəˈrektə] Regisseur/in
disagree [dɪsəˈɡriː] nicht zustimmen, widersprechen 7:2 (46)

DICTIONARY

English – German

disappointed (with sb./sth.) [dɪsə'pɔɪntɪd] enttäuscht 6
disaster [dɪ'zɑːstə] Katastrophe, Unglück 7: 1 (14)
dishwasher ['dɪʃwɒʃə] Geschirrspülmaschine 6
dive [daɪv] einen Kopfsprung machen 5
diver ['daɪvə] Kunst-/Turmspringer/in 7: 1 (22)
diving ['daɪvɪŋ] (das) Tauchen (Sport) 6
DJ ['diː dʒeɪ] DJ (Discjockey) 7: 3 (66)
do [duː], **did, done** machen, tun 5 **do a trip** einen Ausflug machen 6 **do sport** Sport treiben 5 **50p will do** 50 Pence reichen (auch) 6 **I do my homework** ich mache (meine) Hausaufgaben 5
doctor ['dɒktə] Arzt/Ärztin, Doktor/in 6
dog [dɒg] Hund 5
dogs' home [dɒgz 'həʊm] Hundeheim 6
dollar ($) ['dɒlə] Dollar 7: 1 (15) **like a million dollars** fantastisch 7: 1 (15)
°**done** [dʌn] siehe **do**
donkey ['dɒŋki] Esel 5
door [dɔː] Tür 6
double ['dʌbl] doppelt, Doppel- 7: 3 (56)
double room [dʌbl 'ruːm] Doppelzimmer 7: 3 (56)
down the hill [daʊn] den Hügel hinunter / runter 5
drama ['drɑːmə] Schauspiel, darstellende Kunst 5
drank [dræŋk] siehe **drink**
°**draw** [drɔː], **drew, drawn** zeichnen
°**drawn** [drɔːn] siehe **draw**
dream [driːm] Traum 6
dress [dres] Kleid 6
°**dressing room** ['dresɪŋ ruːm] Umkleide(kabine)
°**drew** [druː] siehe **draw**
drink [drɪŋk]:
1. Getränk 5
2. **drink, drank, drunk** trinken 5
drive [draɪv], **drove, driven** (mit dem Auto) fahren 6
°**driven** ['drɪvn] siehe **drive**
driver ['draɪvə] Fahrer/in 7: 1 (22)
driving licence ['draɪvɪŋ laɪsns] Führerschein 7: 3 (60)
drove [drəʊv] siehe **drive**
drug [drʌg] Droge, Rauschgift; Arzneimittel 7: 4 (90)

drums (pl) [drʌmz] Schlagzeug; Trommeln 5
°**drunk** [drʌŋk] siehe **drink**
duck [dʌk] Ente 5
°**dungeon** ['dʌndʒən] Kerker, Folterkammer
DVD [diːviː'diː] DVD 5

E

each [iːtʃ] jede(r, s) (einzelne) 7: 4 (92) **50 p each** jeweils 50 pence 7: 4 (92)
ear [ɪə] Ohr 6
early ['ɜːli] früh 5
earthquake ['ɜːθkweɪk] Erdbeben 7: 1 (16)
east [iːst] Osten; östlich; Ost- 6
eastern ['iːstən] östlich, Ost- 7: 2 (30)
easy ['iːzi] einfach, leicht 6
eat [iːt], **ate, eaten** essen; fressen 5
°**eaten** ['iːtn] siehe **eat**
°**e.g.** [iː 'dʒiː] z.B. (= zum Beispiel)
°**egg** [eg] Ei
eight [eɪt] acht 5
electronic [ɪlek'trɒnɪk] elektronisch 7: 3 (66)
elephant ['elɪfənt] Elefant 5
eleven [ɪ'levn] elf 5
else [els]: **Anything else?** Sonst noch etwas? 5
email ['iːmeɪl] E-Mail 5
empty ['empti]:
1. leer 6
2. leeren 6
end [end] Ende, Schluss 5 **at the end (of ...)** am Ende (von ...) 5 **in the end** schließlich, zum Schluss 5
ending ['endɪŋ] Ende (Text, Geschichte); Endung 6 **happy ending** Happy End 6
energy ['enədʒi] Energie 7: 3 (66)
England ['ɪŋglənd] England 5
English ['ɪŋglɪʃ] Englisch; englisch 5
°**English-speaking** ['ɪŋglɪʃ spiːkɪŋ] englischsprachig
enjoy [ɪn'dʒɔɪ] genießen 6
enough [ɪ'nʌf] genug 6
entertainment park [entə'teɪnmənt pɑːk] Erholungspark, Vergnügungspark 7: 4 (76)
°**episode** ['epɪsəʊd] Episode; Folge (z.B. einer TV-Serie)
equipment [ɪ'kwɪpmənt] Ausrüstung, Ausstattung 7: 3 (54)

e-reader ['iː riːdə] E-Book-Reader 6
especially [ɪ'speʃəli] insbesondere 7: 1 (16)
etc. [et'setərə] (aus dem Lateinischen) usw. (und so weiter) 6
°**EU (= European Union)** [iː 'juː] EU (Europäische Union)
°**euro**, pl **euros** ['jʊərəʊ] Euro
Europe ['jʊərəp] Europa 7: 3 (52)
European [jʊərə'piːən]:
1. europäisch 7: 4 (76)
2. Europäer/in 7: 4 (76)
°**European Union** [jʊərəpiːən 'juːniən] Europäische Union
even ['iːvn] sogar, selbst 7: 2 (42)
evening ['iːvnɪŋ] Abend 5 **in the evening(s)** abends, am Abend 5
°**event** [ɪ'vent] Ereignis
ever ['evə] je(mals) 6 **Have you ever been ...?** Warst du schon mal ...? / Bist du schon mal ... gewesen? 6 °**the most exciting programme ever** das aufregendste Programm aller Zeiten
every ['evri] jede(r, s) 5
everybody ['evribɒdi] jeder; alle 5
everyone ['evriwʌn] jeder; alle 6
°**everywhere** ['evriweə] überall(hin)
example [ɪg'zɑːmpl] Beispiel 5 **for example** zum Beispiel 5
°**exchange sth.** [ɪks'tʃeɪndʒ] etwas austauschen
excited [ɪk'saɪtɪd] aufgeregt, gespannt 5
exciting [ɪk'saɪtɪŋ] aufregend 5
°**excuse** [ɪk'skjuːs] Ausrede
Excuse me, ... [ɪks'kjuːz mi] Entschuldigung, ... 6
exercise ['eksəsaɪz] Übung, Aufgabe 5
exercise book ['eksəsaɪz bʊk] Schulheft, Übungsheft 5
exist [ɪg'zɪst] existieren 7: 3 (58)
expect [ɪk'spekt] erwarten 7: 4 (88)
expensive [ɪk'spensɪv] teuer 5
°**explain** [ɪk'spleɪn] erklären
eye [aɪ] Auge 6

F

factory ['fæktri] Fabrik 6
fall [fɔːl], **fell, fallen** fallen; hinfallen 5 **fall off sth.** herunterfallen von etwas (Fahrrad, Pferd) 5
°**fallen** ['fɔːlən] siehe **fall**
°**falls** (pl) [fɔːlz] Wasserfall
false [fɔːls] falsch, unrichtig 6

family, *pl* **families** ['fæməli] Familie 5

family tree [fæməli 'triː] (Familien-)Stammbaum 5

family-friendly [fæməli 'frendli] familienfreundlich 7: 3 (56)

famous (for) ['feɪməs] berühmt (für, wegen) 7: 1 (8)

fan [fæn] Fan 5

fantastic [fæn'tæstɪk] fantastisch 6

far [fɑː] weit 7: 1 (21) °**so far** bis jetzt, bis hierher

farm [fɑːm] Bauernhof 5

farmer ['fɑːmə] Bauer, Bäuerin; Landwirt/in 7: 2 (34)

fashion ['fæʃn] Mode(trend) 7: 1 (10)

fast [fɑːst] schnell 7: 2 (30)

father ['fɑːðə] Vater 5

favourite ['feɪvərɪt] Lieblings- 5 **favourite thing** Lieblingssache 5

°**feature** ['fiːtʃə] Merkmal, Eigenschaft; Bestandteil

February ['februəri] Februar 5

°**fed** [fed] *siehe* **feed**

fed up [fed 'ʌp]: **feel fed up** genervt sein, sauer sein; die Nase voll haben 5

feed [fiːd], **fed, fed** füttern 5

feel [fiːl], **felt, felt** sich fühlen; fühlen 5

°**feeling** ['fiːlɪŋ] Gefühl

fell [fel] *siehe* **fall**

felt [felt] *siehe* **feel**

ferry ['feri] Fähre 5

festival ['festɪvl] Fest 6

few [fjuː]: **a few** ein paar, einige 7: 4 (81) **in the last few weeks** in den letzten paar Wochen 7: 4 (81)

field [fiːld] Feld; Weide 5 **in the field** auf dem Feld/der Weide 5

°**file** [faɪl] Datei; Ordner

fill [fɪl] füllen 6 **fill in** einsetzen; ausfüllen 7: 3 (65)

film [fɪlm]:
1. Film 5
2. filmen 7: 2 (39)

film star ['fɪlm stɑː] Filmstar 7: 1 (8)

final ['faɪnl] letzte(r, s), abschließend 7: 1 (21)

°**finalist** ['faɪnəlɪst] Finalist/in

find [faɪnd], **found, found** finden 5 **find out** herausfinden 6 °**find out about sth.** sich über etwas informieren

fine [faɪn] gut, schön 5 **I'm fine.** Es geht mir gut. 5

finish ['fɪnɪʃ] beenden; enden 6

fire ['faɪə] Feuer 6

firefighter ['faɪəfaɪtə] Feuerwehrmann, Feuerwehrfrau 5

firework ['faɪəwɜːk] Feuerwerkskörper 6 **fireworks** (*pl*) Feuerwerk 6

first [fɜːst]:
1. zuerst 5
2. (= 1st) erste, erster, erstes 5
at first zuerst, am Anfang 6

first aid [fɜːst 'eɪd] Erste Hilfe 6

first-aid kit [fɜːst 'eɪd kɪt] Erste-Hilfe-Set, Verbandkasten 6

fish, *pl* **fish** [fɪʃ] Fisch 5

°**fishing** ['fɪʃɪŋ]: **go fishing** angeln gehen

fit [fɪt] fit 6

°**fit** [fɪt] passen

fitness ['fɪtnəs] Fitness 6

five [faɪv] fünf 5 **Give me five!** Gib mir fünf! (*Aufforderung zum Abklatschen, Geste der Freude/Begrüßung*) 6

flag [flæg] Fahne, Flagge 6

flat [flæt] Wohnung 5

°**flour** ['flaʊə] Mehl

°**fluent** ['fluːənt] flüssig, fließend (Sprache)

°**focus** ['fəʊkəs] Schwerpunkt **focus on language** (etwa) Schwerpunkt: Sprache

foggy ['fɒgi] nebelig 6

°**follow** ['fɒləʊ] folgen **follow in sb.'s footsteps** in js. Fußstapfen treten **the following words** die folgenden Wörter

food [fuːd] Essen, Lebensmittel; Futter 5

°**foot** [fʊt]: **by foot** zu Fuß

football ['fʊtbɔːl] Fußball 5 **playing football** Fußballspielen 5

footballer ['fʊtbɔːlə] Fußballspieler/in 7: 1 (22)

°**footstep** ['fʊtstep]: **follow in sb.'s footsteps** in js. Fußstapfen treten

for [fɔː], [fə] für 5 **for 100 metres** 100 Meter weit 6 **for the last time** zum letzten Mal 7: 3 (54) **trains/the line for ...** Züge/die U-Bahn-Linie nach ... 7: 1 (13)

forecast ['fɔːkɑːst] Vorhersage 6

forget (about) [fə'get], **forgot, forgotten** vergessen 7: 4 (82)

forgot [fə'gɒt] *siehe* **forget**

forgotten [fə'gɒtn] *siehe* **forget**

form [fɔːm] Formular 7: 3 (65)

°**form** [fɔːm] bilden

formal ['fɔːml] formell 7: 4 (91)

found [faʊnd] *siehe* **find**

four [fɔː] vier 5

fox [fɒks] Fuchs 7: 2 (36)

free [friː]:
1. frei 5
Are you free at one o'clock? Hast du um ein Uhr Zeit? 5
2. **(for) free** kostenlos 5

French [frentʃ] Französisch; französisch 5

French fries (*pl*) [frentʃ 'fraɪz] (AE) Pommes frites 7: 4 (78)

Friday ['fraɪdeɪ], ['fraɪdi] Freitag 5

friend [frend] Freund/in 5 **make friends** Freunde finden 6

friendly ['frendli] freundlich, nett 6

fries (*pl*) [fraɪz]: **French fries** (AE) Pommes frites 7: 4 (78)

from [frɒm]:
1. aus 5
from Plymouth aus Plymouth 5
2. von 5
from Monday to Friday von Montag bis Freitag 5 **a text from mum** eine SMS von Mama 5

front [frʌnt]: **in front of** vor 5

fruit [fruːt] Früchte, Obst; Frucht 5

full [fʊl] voll 7: 3 (66) **full of ...** voller ... 7: 3 (66) °**full sentences** ganze Sätze

fun [fʌn] Spaß 5 **... is fun.** ... macht Spaß. 5 **they're fun** es macht Spaß, mit ihnen zusammenzusein 5

funny ['fʌni] lustig; seltsam 5

future ['fjuːtʃə] Zukunft 6

G

°**Gaelic** ['gælɪk] gälisch; Gälisch

°**Gaelic football** [gælɪk 'fʊtbɔːl] gälischer Fußball (*Mannschaftssportart, die dem Rugby ähnlich ist*)

gallery ['gæləri] Galerie 7: 2 (44)

game [geɪm] Spiel 6

gang [gæŋ] Gang (*Bande*) 7: 4 (90)

°**gap** [gæp] Lücke

garage ['gærɑːʒ] Garage 5

garage sale ['gærɑːʒ seɪl] Garagenflohmarkt (*privater Flohmarkt*) 5

garden ['gɑːdn] Garten 5

gate [geɪt] Tor 7: 2 (33)

gave [geɪv] *siehe* **give**

geek [giːk] jemand, der sich sehr stark für etwas begeistert (und manchmal von anderen deswegen belächelt wird) 7: 1 (14)

DICTIONARY

English – German

geography [dʒɪˈɒgrəfi] Geografie, Erdkunde 5
German [ˈdʒɜːmən] Deutsch; deutsch; Deutsche/r 5
Germany [ˈdʒɜːməni] Deutschland 5
get [get]**, got, got** bekommen, kriegen 5 **get (to)** kommen, gelangen (nach) 5 **get off a bus** aussteigen aus einem Bus 5 **get on a bus** einsteigen in einen Bus 5 **get out** herauskommen 5 **get sth.** (sich) etwas holen, besorgen 6 **get up** aufstehen 5
ghost [gəʊst] Gespenst 7: 3 (58)
ginger [ˈdʒɪndʒə]:
 1. Ingwer 6
 2. rotblond *(Haare)* 6
girl [gɜːl] Mädchen 5
girlfriend [ˈgɜːlfrend] (feste) Freundin 6
give [gɪv]**, gave, given** geben 5 **give sth. up** etwas aufgeben, aufhören mit etwas 7: 4 (90) **give a talk** einen Vortrag halten 6 **Give me five!** Gib mir fünf! *(Aufforderung zum Abklatschen, Geste der Freude/Begrüßung)* 6
given [ˈgɪvn] *siehe* **give**
glad [glæd]**: I'm glad.** Ich bin froh. 6
glass [glɑːs] Glas 6
glasses *(pl)* [ˈglɑːsɪz] Brille 6
glove [glʌv] Handschuh 6
°**gluten** [ˈgluːtn] Gluten
go [gəʊ]**, went, gone**:
 1. gehen; fahren 5
 go away weggehen 5 **go out** ausgehen; hinausgehen 6 **I'm going to help** ich werde helfen 6
 2. **go crazy** verrückt werden 7: 4 (82)
gone [gɒn] *siehe* **go**
good [gʊd] gut 5 **Good morning.** Guten Morgen. 5 **Good night.** Gute Nacht. 5 **be good at sth.** etwas gut können, gut sein in etwas 6 **Have a good day.** Ich wünsche dir einen schönen Tag. / Schönen Tag noch. 5
Goodbye. [gʊdˈbaɪ] Auf Wiedersehen. 5
got [gɒt] *siehe* **get**
GPS [dʒiː piː ˈes] GPS 7: 3 (57)
°**grade** [greɪd] *(AE)* Klasse, Jahrgang; (Schul-)Note
grandad [ˈgrændæd] Opa 7: 2 (46)
grandfather [ˈgrænfɑːðə] Großvater 5

grandma [ˈgrænmɑː] Oma 5
grandmother [ˈgrænmʌðə] Großmutter 5
grandpa [ˈgrænpɑː] Opa 5
grandparents *(pl)* [ˈgrænpeərənts] Großeltern 5
grass [grɑːs] Gras 6
great [greɪt] großartig, toll 5 **have a great time** viel Spaß haben 5
Great Britain [greɪt ˈbrɪtn] Großbritannien 6
Greek [griːk] griechisch; Griechisch; Grieche/Griechin 7: 1 (10)
green [griːn] grün 5
°**grew** [gruː] *siehe* **grow**
grey [greɪ] grau 7: 4 (89)
ground [graʊnd] Erde *(Erdboden)* 6
group [gruːp] Gruppe 6
°**grow** [grəʊ]**, grew, grown** anbauen, anpflanzen
°**grown** [grəʊn] *siehe* **grow**
°**guess** [ges] (er)raten
guest [gest] Gast 7: 3 (56)
°**guide** [gaɪd] Reiseleiter/in, Fremdenführer/in
guitar [gɪˈtɑː] Gitarre 5
guys *(pl)* [gaɪz] Leute *(Anrede)* 6
gymnastics [dʒɪmˈnæstɪks] Turnen, Gymnastik 6

H

had [hæd], [həd] *siehe* **have**
hair [heə] Haar, Haare 6
hairdresser [ˈheədresə] Frisör/in 6
hairdryer [ˈheədraɪə] Föhn, Haartrockner 6
hairy [ˈheəri] behaart, haarig 6
half [hɑːf]:
 1. halbe(r, s), Halb- 7: 1 (10)
 half price zum halben Preis 7: 1 (18)
 2. *pl* **halves** Hälfte 7: 1 (10)
°**hall** [hɔːl] Halle; Saal
ham [hæm] *(gekochter)* Schinken 7: 4 (79)
hamster [ˈhæmstə] Hamster 5
hand [hænd] Hand 6
hang-gliding [ˈhæŋ glaɪdɪŋ] Drachenfliegen 6
happen [ˈhæpən] geschehen, passieren 6
happy [ˈhæpi] glücklich, froh 5 **Happy birthday!** Herzlichen Glückwunsch zum Geburtstag! 5 **happy ending** Happy End 6 **be happy to do sth.** gerne etwas tun 7: 3 (57)
harbour [ˈhɑːbə] Hafen 5

hard [hɑːd] schwer; schwierig; hart 5 **work hard** hart arbeiten 7: 2 (34)
has [hæz], [həz]**: he/she/it has** er/sie/es hat 5
hat [hæt] Hut, Mütze 5
have [hæv]**, had, had** haben 5 **Have a good day.** Ich wünsche dir einen schönen Tag. / Schönen Tag noch. 5 **have to do sth.** etwas tun müssen 6
he [hiː] er 5 **he's (= he is)** er ist 5
headache [ˈhedeɪk]**: have a headache** Kopfschmerzen haben 6
health [helθ] Gesundheit 6
healthy [ˈhelθi] gesund 6
hear [hɪə]**, heard, heard** hören 5
heard [hɜːd] *siehe* **hear**
heart [hɑːt] Herz 7: 4 (76)
°**by heart** auswendig
Hello. [həˈləʊ] Hallo./Servus. 5
helmet [ˈhelmɪt] Helm 7: 1 (20)
help [help]:
 1. helfen 5
 Help yourselves. Bedient euch! / Greift zu! 7: 3 (55)
 2. Hilfe 5
helper [ˈhelpə] Helfer/in 6
her [hɜː]:
 1. **her dad** ihr Vater 5
 2. *(zu „she")* sie; ihr 5
 for her für sie 5 **with her** mit ihr 5
here [hɪə] hier; hierher 5 **Here you are.** Bitte schön. / Hier, bitte. 5
hers [hɜːz] ihre/r, ihrs *(zu „she")* 7: 3 (54)
herself [hɜːˈself] sie/sich selbst *(zu „she")* 7: 3 (55)
Hi! [haɪ] Hallo. 5
high [haɪ] hoch 7: 1 (9)
°**high street** [ˈhaɪ striːt] Hauptstraße; Einkaufsstraße
°**Highland Games** *(pl)* [ˈhaɪlənd ˈgeɪmz] traditionelle schottische Veranstaltung mit sportlichen Wettkämpfen
hiking [ˈhaɪkɪŋ] *(das)* Wandern 6
hill [hɪl] Hügel 5
hilly [ˈhɪli] hügelig 7: 1 (22)
him [hɪm] ihn; ihm 5
himself [hɪmˈself] er/sich selbst 7: 3 (55)
hire [ˈhaɪə] mieten, leihen 7: 3 (60)
his [hɪz]**: his bike** sein Fahrrad *(zu „he")* 5 **the bike is his** das Fahrrad ist seins *(zu „he")* 7: 3 (54)
history [ˈhɪstri] Geschichte 5
hobby [ˈhɒbi] Hobby 5

hockey [ˈhɒki] (Feld-)Hockey 7: 2 (30)
°**hold** [həʊld] halten
holiday [ˈhɒlədeɪ] Urlaub 5 **holidays** (pl) Ferien 5 **a week's / six weeks' holiday** eine Woche / sechs Wochen Urlaub 6
home [həʊm]:
1. nach Hause 5
I'm home ich bin zu Hause 5
2. Heim, Zuhause 5
at home zu Hause 5 **dogs' home** Hundeheim 6
3. Startseite (Internet) 7: 2 (44)
°**home-made** [həʊmˈmeɪd] hausgemacht, selbstgemacht
homework [ˈhəʊmwɜːk] Hausaufgabe/n 5 **I do my homework** ich mache (meine) Hausaufgaben 5
hoodie [ˈhʊdi] Kapuzenpullover 5
°**Hooray!** [huˈreɪ] Hurra!
hoover [ˈhuːvə] staubsaugen 6
hope [həʊp] hoffen 5
hospital [ˈhɒspɪtl] Krankenhaus 5
hot [hɒt] heiß, warm 6
hot chocolate [hɒt ˈtʃɒklət] Kakao, heiße (Trink-)Schokolade 6
hot dog [ˈhɒt dɒg] Hot Dog 7: 4 (80)
hotel [həʊˈtel] Hotel 7: 4 (91)
hour [aʊə] Stunde 6 **for hours and hours** stundenlang 6
house [haʊs] Haus 5
houseboat [ˈhaʊsbəʊt] Hausboot 6
how [haʊ] wie 5 **How are you?** Wie geht's? / Wie geht es dir/euch? 5 °**That's how you'll get a good job.** So bekommst du einen guten Job.
hundred [ˈhʌndrəd]: **a/one hundred** (ein)hundert 5
hungry [ˈhʌŋgri]: **Are you hungry?** Hast du / habt ihr Hunger? 5
°**hurling** [ˈhɜːlɪŋ] Hurling (dem Hockey ähnlicher Sport in Irland)

I

I [aɪ] ich 5 **I'm (= I am)** ich bin 5
ice cream [aɪs ˈkriːm] (Speise-)Eis 5
ice hockey [ˈaɪs hɒki] Eishockey 7: 4 (87)
ice skating [ˈaɪs skeɪtɪŋ] Schlittschuhlaufen 6
ICT (information and communication technology) [aɪ siː ˈtiː], [ɪnfəˈmeɪʃn ənd kəmjuːnɪˈkeɪʃn tekˈnɒlədʒi] Informations- und Kommunikationstechnologie 5

°**ID (= identification)** [aɪ ˈdiː], [aɪdentɪfɪˈkeɪʃn] Ausweis, Identifizierung, Legitimation
idea [aɪˈdɪə] Idee 5
idiot [ˈɪdiət] Idiot/in 7: 1 (15)
if [ɪf] wenn, falls 6
ill [ɪl] krank 6
important [ɪmˈpɔːtənt] wichtig 5
in [ɪn]:
1. herein, hinein 6
2. in 5
in English auf Englisch 5 **in the afternoon(s)** nachmittags, am Nachmittag 5 **in the country** auf dem Land 5 **in the evening(s)** abends, am Abend 5 **in the field** auf dem Feld/der Weide 5 **in the morning(s)** morgens, am Morgen 5 **in the photo** auf dem Foto 5 **in the street** auf der Straße 6
°**include** [ɪnˈkluːd] einschließen
°**including** [ɪnˈkluːdɪŋ] einschließlich, inklusive
independence (from) [ɪndɪˈpendəns] Unabhängigkeit (von) 7: 4 (81)
Independence Day [ɪndɪˈpendəns deɪ] Unabhängigkeitstag 7: 4 (81)
informal [ɪnˈfɔːml] informell, locker 7: 4 (91)
information (about) [ɪnfəˈmeɪʃn] Information(en) (über) 6
inside [ɪnˈsaɪd] (nach) drinnen 6
°**inspiration** [ɪnspəˈreɪʃn] Anregung, Inspiration
°**inspiring** [ɪnˈspaɪərɪŋ] begeisternd, inspirierend
instrument [ˈɪnstrəmənt] Instrument 5
interest [ˈɪntrəst] Interesse 6
interested [ˈɪntrəstɪd]: **interested in doing sth.** daran interessiert, etwas zu tun 7: 2 (37) **be interested in** sich interessieren für, interessiert sein an 6
interesting [ˈɪntrəstɪŋ] interessant 6
°**international** [ɪntəˈnæʃnəl] international
internet [ˈɪntənet] Internet 6
interview [ˈɪntəvjuː]:
1. Interview 5
°2. befragen, interviewen
°**interviewer** [ˈɪntəvjuːə] Interviewer/in
into [ˈɪntu], [ˈɪntə] in (... hinein) 6
introduction [ɪntrəˈdʌkʃn] Einleitung 7: 1 (11)

invitation (to) [ɪnvɪˈteɪʃn] Einladung (zu, nach) 5
invite [ɪnˈvaɪt] einladen 5
Ireland [ˈaɪələnd] Irland 7: 2 (30)
Irish [ˈaɪrɪʃ] irisch, aus Irland 7: 1 (10)
is [ɪz] (er/sie/es) ist 5 **It's £ 31.** Es kostet 31 Pfund. 5
island [ˈaɪlənd] Insel 7: 2 (41)
it [ɪt] es, (bei Dingen und Tieren:) er, sie 5 **it's (= it is)** es ist (Dinge/Tiere auch: er ist, sie ist) 5
°**Italian** [ɪˈtæliən] Italiener/in; italienisch
Italy [ˈɪtəli] Italien 6
its [ɪts] sein/e; ihr/e (Dinge/Tiere) 7: 2 (30)
itself [ɪtˈself] es/sich selbst 7: 3 (55)

J

jacket [ˈdʒækɪt] Jacke, Jackett 5
jam [dʒæm] Marmelade 5
January [ˈdʒænjuəri] Januar 5
jealous (of) [ˈdʒeləs] eifersüchtig (auf); neidisch (auf) 6
jeans (pl) [dʒiːnz] Jeans 5
°**jigsaw** [ˈdʒɪgsɔː] Puzzle
job [dʒɒb] Job, Stelle 6
jogging [ˈdʒɒgɪŋ] Jogging 6
join [dʒɔɪn] mitmachen (bei); (einem Klub) beitreten 6
joke [dʒəʊk] Witz, Scherz 6
°**You're joking!** Du machst wohl Witze!
°**journey** [ˈdʒɜːni] Reise
judo [ˈdʒuːdəʊ] Judo 6
juice [dʒuːs] Saft 5
July [dʒuˈlaɪ] Juli 5
June [dʒuːn] Juni 5
junk food [ˈdʒʌŋk fuːd] Junkfood (ungesundes Essen) 6
just [dʒʌst]:
1. nur, bloß; einfach 7: 1 (18)
2. **just like Berry** genau wie Berry 6

K

keep [kiːp], **kept, kept** halten; behalten 7: 1 (15)
°**kelpie** [ˈkelpi] Wassergeist (Schottland)
kept [kept] siehe **keep**
kettle [ˈketl] Wasserkocher (elektrisch) 7: 3 (56)
°**keyword** [ˈkiːwɜːd] Stichwort, Schlagwort
kick [kɪk] treten, schießen 7: 1 (15)
kid [kɪd] Kind, Jugendliche/r 5

DICTIONARY — English – German

kilometre (km) ['kɪləmiːtə] Kilometer 6
kilt [kɪlt] Kilt *(Schottenrock)* 7: 3 (52)
kind [kaɪnd] freundlich, nett 6
kind (of) [kaɪnd] Art/Sorte (von) 6
king [kɪŋ] König 7: 1 (8)
Kingdom ['kɪŋdəm]: **the United Kingdom (the UK)** das Vereinigte Königreich 7: 2 (30)
kitchen ['kɪtʃɪn] Küche 5
kitten ['kɪtn] Kätzchen, junge Katze 6
knew [njuː] *siehe* **know**
knife, *pl* **knives** [naɪf], [naɪvz] Messer 7: 3 (53)
know [nəʊ], **knew, known** wissen; kennen 5 **I don't know about ...** Bei ... bin ich mir nicht (so) sicher. 7: 3 (66)
known [nəʊn] *siehe* **know**

L

lake [leɪk] (Binnen-)See 6
lamp [læmp] Lampe 5
land [lænd]:
  1. Land 7: 3 (60)
  2. landen 7: 3 (60)
language ['læŋgwɪdʒ] Sprache 7: 3 (52)
°**language file** ['læŋgwɪdʒ faɪl] Anhang zum Thema Sprache
lantern ['læntən] Laterne 6
laptop ['læptɒp] Laptop 5
lasagne [ləˈzænjə] Lasagne 6
last [lɑːst] letzte(r, s) 5 **last week** vorige/letzte Woche 6 °**at last** schließlich, endlich
late [leɪt] (zu) spät 5 **my bus is late** mein Bus hat Verspätung 5
later ['leɪtə] später 5
laugh [lɑːf] lachen 5
leader ['liːdə] Leiter/in, (An-)Führer/in 6
°**leading** ['liːdɪŋ] führend
learn [lɜːn] lernen 6
least [liːst] (der/die/das) wenigste, am wenigsten 7: 4 (81) **at least** mindestens, wenigstens 6
leave [liːv], **left, left**:
  1. verlassen 6
  leave school von der Schule abgehen 7: 4 (82)
  2. zurücklassen; abfahren 6
left [left] links; nach links 5 **on the left** links, auf der linken Seite 5
left [left] *siehe* **leave**
leg [leg] Bein 5

lemonade [leməˈneɪd] Limonade 6
less [les] weniger 7: 2 (33)
lesson ['lesn] (Unterrichts-)Stunde 5
let's (= let us) [lets], ['let əs] lass(t) uns 5 **Let's see.** Lass(t) uns (mal) sehen. 6
letter ['letə]:
  1. Brief 5
  °2. Buchstabe
licence ['laɪsns]: **driving licence** Führerschein 7: 3 (60)
life, *pl* **lives** [laɪf], [laɪvz] Leben 5
lifestyle ['laɪfstaɪl] Lebensstil 6
light [laɪt] Licht; Lampe 7: 2 (36)
like [laɪk] mögen 5 **I'd (= I would) like** ich hätte gern, ich möchte (...) haben 5 **I'd (= I would) like to join** ich würde/möchte gern mitmachen 6
like [laɪk] wie 5 **like this** so, auf diese Art 7: 2 (34) **a hat like that** so(lch) eine Mütze 7: 2 (34) **an accident / accidents like this** so ein/ein solcher Unfall; solche Unfälle 7: 2 (34) **I don't feel like it.** Mir ist nicht danach. 6 **just like Berry** genau wie Berry 6 **What's it like?** Wie ist es? / Wie sieht es aus? 5
line [laɪn]:
  1. Linie, Reihe 6
  2. U-Bahn-Linie 7: 1 (13)
list [lɪst] Liste 5
listen ['lɪsn]: **listen (to)** zuhören; *(sich etwas)* anhören 5 **listen for sth.** auf etwas horchen, *(beim Zuhören)* auf etwas achten 6
little ['lɪtl] wenig 7: 4 (82) **a little** ein wenig, ein bisschen 7: 4 (82)
live [lɪv] leben, wohnen 5
live [laɪv] live 7: 4 (76)
lives [laɪvz] *Plural von* **life** 5
living room ['lɪvɪŋ ruːm] Wohnzimmer 5
°**local** ['ləʊkəl] örtlich, lokal, Orts-, Lokal-
Londoner ['lʌndənə] Londoner/in 7: 1 (10)
lonely ['ləʊnli] einsam 6
long [lɒŋ] lang; lange 6 °**as long as you can** so lang(e) (wie) du kannst
look [lʊk]:
  1. aussehen 6
  2. sehen, schauen 5
  Look, Adam. Sieh mal, Adam. / Schau mal, Adam. 5

look after sich kümmern um; aufpassen auf 5 **look at** anschauen 5 **look for** suchen 5
  3. Blick 7: 2 (30)
lose [luːz], **lost, lost** verlieren 6 **I have lost ...** Ich habe ... verloren. 7: 3 (54)
lost [lɒst] *siehe* **lose**
lot [lɒt]: **a lot (of); lots (of)** viel(e) 5 **lots and lots of ...** unheimlich viel/e ... 7: 4 (84)
loud [laʊd] laut 6
love [lʌv]:
  1. lieben, sehr mögen 5
  I'd love to come. (= I would love to come.) Ich komme sehr gern. / Ich würde sehr gern kommen. 5
  2. Liebling, Schatz 5
low [ləʊ] niedrig, tief 7: 4 (89)
lucky ['lʌki]: **Lucky you!** Du Glückliche/r! 6 **you're lucky** du hast Glück 5
lunch [lʌntʃ] Mittagessen 5 **have lunch** (zu) Mittag essen 5
lunchtime ['lʌntʃtaɪm]: **at lunchtime** mittags, zur Mittagszeit 6

M

madam ['mædəm]: **Dear Sir/Madam** Sehr geehrte Damen und Herren 7: 4 (91)
made [meɪd] *siehe* **make**
magazine [mægəˈziːn] Zeitschrift, Magazin 6
make [meɪk], **made, made** machen, herstellen 5 **make a deal** ein Geschäft abschließen/vereinbaren 6 **make friends** Freunde finden 6 **make money** Geld verdienen 7: 4 (80) **make sb. do sth.** jn. dazu bringen, etwas zu tun 7: 3 (66) **What makes a perfect weekend?** Was macht ein perfektes Wochenende aus? 6
make-up ['meɪkʌp] Make-up 6
man, *pl* **men** [mæn], [men] Mann 5
manager ['mænɪdʒə] Geschäftsführer/in, Manager/in 7: 3 (54)
many ['mæni] viele 5 **how many?** wie viele? 5
map [mæp] Landkarte, Stadtplan 5
March [mɑːtʃ] März 5
march [mɑːtʃ]:
  1. Marsch 7: 4 (76)
  2. marschieren 7: 4 (76)
°**Mardi Gras** [mɑːdi ˈgrɑː] Karnevalsdienstag
market ['mɑːkɪt] Markt 5
°**married** ['mærɪd] verheiratet

180 one hundred and eighty

mask [mɑːsk] Maske 6
°match [mætʃ] Spiel (z.B. Fußball)
°match with [ˈmætʃ wɪð] zuordnen
maths [mæθs] Mathematik 5
May [meɪ] Mai 5
maybe [ˈmeɪbi] vielleicht 6
me [mi] mir; mich 5 **Me too.** Ich auch 5 **It's me.** Ich bin's. 5
meal [miːl] Mahlzeit, Essen 7: 4 (79) **hot meal** warme Mahlzeit 7: 4 (79)
mean [miːn]:
1. gemein, fies 5
2. geizig 6
mean [miːn], meant, meant meinen, sagen wollen 7: 3 (68)
meant [ment] siehe **mean**
meat [miːt] Fleisch 6
°mediation [miːdiˈeɪʃn] Vermittlung, Sprachmittlung
meet [miːt], met, met kennenlernen; (sich) treffen 5 **meet sb.** jn. abholen 6 **Nice to meet you.** Schön, dich/euch/Sie kennenzulernen. 6
meeting [ˈmiːtɪŋ] Treffen; Zusammenkunft 7: 2 (43)
men [men] Plural von **man** 5
message [ˈmesɪdʒ]:
1. Nachricht, Mitteilung 5 **message in a bottle** Flaschenpost 5 **take a message** etwas ausrichten 7: 2 (35)
2. Nachrichten schicken/austauschen 6
messy [ˈmesi] unordentlich 5
met [met] siehe **meet**
metre [ˈmiːtə] Meter 6
mice [maɪs] Plural von **mouse** 6
middle [ˈmɪdl] Mitte 5
°middle school [ˈmɪdl skuːl] (AE) Mittelschule (für 11- bis 14-Jährige)
mile [maɪl] Meile (ca. 1,6 km) 6
milk [mɪlk] Milch 5
milkshake [ˈmɪlkʃeɪk] Milchshake 6
million [ˈmɪljən] Million 7: 1 (15) **like a million dollars** fantastisch 7: 1 (15)
mine [maɪn] meine/r; meins 7: 3 (54)
mineral water [ˈmɪnərəl wɔːtə] Mineralwasser 6
minute [ˈmɪnɪt] Minute 5
miss [mɪs] vermissen 5
missing [ˈmɪsɪŋ] vermisst 6 **be missing** fehlen 7: 3 (59) **the missing bags** die fehlenden Taschen 7: 3 (59)

°mistake [mɪˈsteɪk] Fehler **by mistake** aus Versehen
mobile (phone) [məʊbaɪl ˈfəʊn] Handy 5
°modern [ˈmɒdn] modern
mom [mɒm] (AE) Mutti, Mama 7: 3 (62)
°moment [ˈməʊmənt] Moment **at the moment** im Moment
Monday [ˈmʌndeɪ], [ˈmʌndi] Montag 5
money [ˈmʌni] Geld 5 **make money** Geld verdienen 7: 4 (80)
monitor [ˈmɒnɪtə] Monitor 7: 2 (36)
monkey [ˈmʌŋki] Affe 5
monster [ˈmɒnstə] Monster 7: 3 (53)
month [mʌnθ] Monat 5
more [mɔː] mehr, weitere 6 **more popular** beliebter, populärer 6 **one more thing** noch eine Sache 6
morning [ˈmɔːnɪŋ] Morgen 5 **Good morning.** Guten Morgen. 5 **in the morning(s)** morgens, am Morgen 5 **on Friday morning(s)** freitagmorgens, am Freitagmorgen 5
most [məʊst]: **most famous** der/die/das berühmteste, am berühmtesten 7: 1 (15) **most people** die meisten Leute 7: 2 (30)
mother [ˈmʌðə] Mutter 5
mountain [ˈmaʊntən] Berg 6
mouse, pl mice [maʊs], [maɪs] Maus 6
°mouth [maʊθ] Mund; (Tier) Schnauze
move (to) [muːv] (um)ziehen (nach/in) 7: 2 (32) °**move on to ...** weiter gehen/ziehen zu ...
°movie theater [ˈmuːvi θɪətə] (AE) Kino
Mr Lee [ˈmɪstə] Herr Lee 5
Mrs Lee [ˈmɪsɪz] Frau Lee 5
Ms Lee [mɪz] Frau Lee 5
much [mʌtʃ] viel 5 **How much is / How much are ...?** Was (Wie viel) kostet ... / Was (Wie viel) kosten ...? 5 **miss/like/love sb. so much** jn. so sehr vermissen/mögen/lieben 6 **Thanks very much.** Vielen Dank. 6
mud [mʌd] Matsch, Schlamm 6
mum [mʌm] Mama, Mutti 5
Munich [ˈmjuːnɪk] München 6
mural [ˈmjʊərəl] Wandgemälde 7: 4 (76)
museum [mjuˈziːəm] Museum 7: 1 (11)
music [ˈmjuːzɪk] Musik 5

musician [mjuˈzɪʃn] Musiker/in 7: 3 (58)
must [mʌst] müssen 5
mustn't do [ˈmʌsnt] nicht tun dürfen 6
my [maɪ] mein/e 5
myself [maɪˈself] ich/mich/mir selbst 7: 3 (55)

N

name [neɪm] Name 5 **What's your name?** Wie heißt du? 5
narrow [ˈnærəʊ] eng, schmal 7: 3 (59)
national [ˈnæʃnəl] national 6
national day [ˈnæʃnəl ˈdeɪ] Nationalfeiertag 7: 2 (30)
national park [ˈnæʃnəl ˈpɑːk] Nationalpark (staatliches Naturschutzgebiet) 6
nationality [ˌnæʃəˈnæləti] Staatsangehörigkeit, Nationalität 7: 3 (65)
°natural [ˈnætʃrəl] natürlich, Natur-
near [nɪə] in der Nähe von, nahe (bei) 6
nearly [ˈnɪəli] fast, beinahe 7: 3 (64)
need [niːd] brauchen 5 °**need to do sth.** etwas tun müssen
neighbour [ˈneɪbə] Nachbar/in 6
neighbourhood [ˈneɪbəhʊd] Nachbarschaft, Viertel, Gegend 6
nervous [ˈnɜːvəs] nervös, aufgeregt 6
°network [ˈnetwɜːk] Netz(werk); Wortnetz
never [ˈnevə] nie, niemals 5
new [njuː] neu 5
news [njuːz] Nachrichten; Neuigkeiten 5
newsletter [ˈnjuːzletə] Mitteilungsblatt, Informationsblatt 6
newspaper [ˈnjuːzpeɪpə] (Tages-)Zeitung 6
next [nekst]:
1. nächste(r, s) 5 **the next day** am nächsten Tag 6
2. als Nächstes 7: 1 (15)
next to [ˈnekst tə] neben 5
nice [naɪs] nett, schön 5 **Nice to be together again.** Schön, wieder zusammen zu sein. 6 **Nice to meet you.** Schön, dich/euch/Sie kennenzulernen. 6
night [naɪt] Nacht 5 **at night** nachts, in der Nacht 5 **Good night.** Gute Nacht. 5
nine [naɪn] neun 5

DICTIONARY — English – German

nineties [ˈnaɪntiz]: **the 90s** die Neunzigerjahre 6
no [nəʊ]:
1. nein 5
2. kein/e 5
nobody [ˈnəʊbədi] niemand 6
noise [nɔɪz] Geräusch; Lärm 5
noisy [ˈnɔɪzi] laut, voller Lärm 5
normal [ˈnɔːml] normal 5
north [nɔːθ] Norden; nördlich; Nord- 6
north-east [nɔːθˈiːst] Nordosten, nordöstlich 6
northern [ˈnɔːðən] Nord-, nördlich 7: 2 (30)
north-west [nɔːθˈwest] Nordwesten, nordwestlich 6
°**nose** [nəʊz] Nase
not [nɒt] nicht; kein/e 5 **not ... at all** überhaupt nicht ... 5
°**note** [nəʊt]:
1. Notiz
make notes (sich) Notizen machen (zur Vorbereitung) **take notes** (sich) Notizen machen (beim Lesen oder Zuhören)
2. notieren; beachten
nothing [ˈnʌθɪŋ] nichts 5
November [nəʊˈvembə] November 5
now [naʊ] nun, jetzt 5
number [ˈnʌmbə] Zahl, Ziffer, Nummer; Anzahl 5 **car number** Autokennzeichen 7: 2 (37)
nut [nʌt] Nuss 6

O

occasionally [əˈkeɪʒənəli] gelegentlich 7: 2 (44)
o'clock [əˈklɒk]: **at one o'clock** um 1 Uhr / um 13 Uhr 5
October [ɒkˈtəʊbə] Oktober 5
°**odd one out** [ɒd wʌn ˈaʊt] Ding, das nicht zu den anderen passt
of [ɒv], [əv] von 5 **the last day of the holidays** der letzte Tag der Ferien 5
of course [əv ˈkɔːs] natürlich, selbstverständlich 6
off [ɒf] von ... herunter/hinunter 5 **fall off sth.** herunterfallen von etwas (Fahrrad, Pferd) 5 **get off a bus** aussteigen aus einem Bus 5
°**offer** [ˈɒfə] anbieten
office [ˈɒfɪs] Büro 7: 2 (36)
often [ˈɒfn], [ˈɒftən] oft 5
oh [əʊ] Null (im gesprochenen Englisch) 5

OK [əʊˈkeɪ]: **I'm OK.** Es geht mir gut. 5
old [əʊld] alt 5 **How old are you?** Wie alt bist du? 5
°**Olympic** [əˈlɪmpɪk] olympisch
on [ɒn]:
1. auf 5
on Friday morning(s) freitagmorgens, am Freitagmorgen 5 **on his birthday** an seinem Geburtstag 5 **on Monday** am Montag 5 **on Mondays** (immer) am Montag, montags 5 **on page 18** auf Seite 18 5 **on the bus** im Bus 5 **get on a bus** einsteigen in einen Bus 5
2. **be on** stattfinden, gezeigt werden (Kino, Theater) 7: 2 (43)
once [wʌns] einmal; einst 6
one [wʌn] eins 5 **the most famous one** der/die/das Berühmteste 7: 1 (15)
online [ɒnˈlaɪn] online, Online- 6
only [ˈəʊnli]:
1. nur, bloß; erst 5
2. **the only student** der einzige Schüler / die einzige Schülerin 5
°**onto** [ˈɒntu] auf (... hinauf)
open [ˈəʊpən]:
1. offen, geöffnet 5
2. öffnen, aufmachen 6
3. sich öffnen, aufgehen 7: 1 (9)
opposite [ˈɒpəzɪt] Gegenteil 7: 4 (79)
or [ɔː] oder 5
orange [ˈɒrɪndʒ]:
1. orange(farben) 5
2. Orange 5
°**order** [ˈɔːdə] Reihenfolge
°**order sth.** [ˈɔːdə] etwas bestellen
°**organic (eggs)** [ɔːˈɡænɪk] Bio-(Eier)
°**organize** [ˈɔːɡənaɪz] organisieren
original [əˈrɪdʒənl]:
1. Original 7: 4 (87)
2. originell 7: 4 (87)
other [ˈʌðə] andere(r, s) 5
our [ˈaʊə], [ɑː] unser/e 5
ours [ɑːz], [ˈaʊəz] unsere/r, unseres 7: 3 (54)
ourselves [aʊəˈselvz] wir/uns selbst 7: 3 (55)
out [aʊt] hinaus, heraus, raus 6 **be out** unterwegs sein 5 **go out** ausgehen; hinausgehen 6
out of ... [ˈaʊt əv] aus ... (heraus/hinaus) 6
outside [aʊtˈsaɪd]:
1. draußen; nach draußen 5
2. außerhalb (von), vor 5

over [ˈəʊvə]:
1. vorbei 5
2. **over 18** über 18 7: 1 (17)
°**14 or over** 14 (Jahre alt) oder darüber/älter, mindestens 14 °**all over Ireland** überall in Irland, in ganz Irland
over here [əʊvə ˈhɪə] hier drüben; hier herüber 6
over there [əʊvə ˈðeə] da drüben; da hinüber 5
own [əʊn]: **its own team** seine eigene Mannschaft 7: 3 (64) °**your own ideas** deine eigenen Ideen

P

p [piː]: **50p** 50 Pence 5
pack [pæk] packen, einpacken 6
page (= p.) [peɪdʒ] (Buch-, Heft-)Seite 5
paid [peɪd] siehe **pay**
°**pain** [peɪn]: **What a pain!** So ein Mist! / Es nervt!
pair [peə] Paar 6
palace [ˈpæləs] Palast 7: 1 (8)
panda [ˈpændə] Panda 7: 4 (88)
panic [ˈpænɪk] Panik bekommen 6 **Don't panic.** Keine Panik. / Immer mit der Ruhe. 6
paper [ˈpeɪpə] Zeitung 6 **do a paper round** Zeitungen austragen 6
parade [pəˈreɪd] Parade, Umzug 7: 2 (44)
°**parallel** [ˈpærəlel] parallel, Parallel-
°**parental guidance (PG)** [pərentl ˈɡaɪdns] elterliche Aufsicht empfohlen (Kino)
parents (pl) [ˈpeərənts] Eltern 5
park [pɑːk] Park 5
park (a car) [pɑːk] parken 6
parliament [ˈpɑːləmənt] Parlament 7: 1 (8)
part [pɑːt] Teil 6 **take part (in)** teilnehmen (an), mitmachen (bei) 7: 4 (81)
partner [ˈpɑːtnə] Partner/in 5
partner work [ˈpɑːtnə wɜːk] Partnerarbeit 5
party [ˈpɑːti] Party 5 **have a party** eine Party feiern 5
past [pɑːst] Vergangenheit 7: 4 (82)
past the shop [pɑːst] am Geschäft vorbei 6
pasty [ˈpæsti] Pastete (mit Fleisch- oder Gemüsefüllung) 6
°**pause** [pɔːz] Pause
pay [peɪ], **paid, paid** (be)zahlen 6

PE (physical education) [piː ˈiː], [fɪzɪkl edʒuˈkeɪʃn] (Schul-)Sport 5
pen [pen] Kugelschreiber, Stift; Füller 5
pencil [ˈpensl] Bleistift 5
pencil case [ˈpensl keɪs] Federmäppchen 5
pencil sharpener [ˈpensl ʃɑːpnə] Bleistiftanspitzer 5
penfriend [ˈpenfrend] Brieffreund/in 6
penny, *pl* **pence** [ˈpeni], [pens] Penny *(kleinste britische Münze)* 6
people [ˈpiːpl] Leute, Menschen 5
pepper [ˈpepə] Pfeffer 6
per (person) [pɜː] pro (Person) 7: 3 (56)
perfect [ˈpɜːfɪkt] perfekt 6
performance [pəˈfɔːməns] Vorstellung, Aufführung 7: 2 (45)
perhaps [pəˈhæps] vielleicht 6
person [ˈpɜːsn] Person 7: 2 (40)
°**personality** [pɜːsəˈnæləti] Persönlichkeit
pet [pet] Haustier 5
pet shop [ˈpet ʃɒp] Zoogeschäft, Tierhandlung 5
°**PG (= parental guidance)** [pərentl ˈɡaɪdns] elterliche Aufsicht empfohlen *(Kino)*
phone [fəʊn]:
 1. anrufen 5
 2. Telefon 5
phone call [ˈfəʊn kɔːl] (Telefon-)Anruf 6
phone number [ˈfəʊn nʌmbə] Telefonnummer 5
photo [ˈfəʊtəʊ] Foto 5 **in the photo** auf dem Foto 5 **take a photo** ein Foto machen 6
phrase [freɪz] Ausdruck, (Rede-)Wendung 5
piano [piˈænəʊ] Klavier 5
pick [pɪk] (aus)wählen 5
picnic [ˈpɪknɪk] Picknick 5 **have a picnic** ein Picknick machen 5
picture [ˈpɪktʃə] Bild 5
°**piece** [piːs] Stück
pig [pɪɡ] Schwein 5
pink [pɪŋk] rosa 5
pity [ˈpɪti]: **That's a pity.** Das ist schade. 5
pizza [ˈpiːtsə] Pizza 7: 3 (68)
place [pleɪs] Ort, Platz, Stelle 5
place of birth [pleɪs əv ˈbɜːθ] Geburtsort 7: 3 (65)
plan [plæn]:
 1. Plan 5
 2. planen 5

plane [pleɪn] Flugzeug 7: 4 (76)
°**plant** [plɑːnt] Pflanze
plastic [ˈplæstɪk] Plastik, Kunststoff 6
plastic bag [plæstɪk ˈbæɡ] Plastiktüte 6
platform [ˈplætfɔːm] Bahnsteig 6
play [pleɪ]:
 1. spielen 5
 playing football Fußballspielen 5
 2. Theaterstück 6
player [ˈpleɪə] Spieler/in 6
please [pliːz] bitte 5
°**Pledge of Allegiance** [pledʒ əv əˈliːdʒəns] Treuegelöbnis
pm [piː ˈem]: **6 pm** 6 Uhr abends, 18 Uhr 5
pocket [ˈpɒkɪt] Tasche *(an Kleidungsstücken)* 6
pocket money [ˈpɒkɪt mʌni] Taschengeld 6
poem [ˈpəʊɪm] Gedicht 6
point (at/to) [pɔɪnt] zeigen, deuten (auf) 7: 3 (59)
police *(pl)* [pəˈliːs] Polizei 7: 1 (15)
police officer [pəˈliːs ɒfɪsə] Polizeibeamter/-beamtin 7: 2 (34)
°**polite** [pəˈlaɪt] höflich
pony [ˈpəʊni] Pony 5
poor [pʊə] arm 6 **poor Mrs Trent** (die) arme Mrs Trent 6 **Poor you!** Du Arme/r! 6
popular [ˈpɒpjələ] beliebt, populär 6
°**population** [pɒpjuˈleɪʃn] Bevölkerung, Einwohner(zahl)
°**possible** [ˈpɒsəbl] möglich **as often as possible** so oft wie möglich
post [pəʊst] Post *(Teil eines Blogs)* 5
post office [ˈpəʊst ɒfɪs] Post(amt) 6
postcard [ˈpəʊstkɑːd] Postkarte 6
posted by [ˈpəʊstɪd baɪ] gepostet von *(im Internet veröffentlicht)* 5
poster [ˈpəʊstə] Poster 5
potato, *pl* **potatoes** [pəˈteɪtəʊ] Kartoffel 6
potato chips *(pl)* [pəˈteɪtəʊ tʃɪps] *(AE)* Kartoffelchips 7: 4 (78)
pound (£) [paʊnd] Pfund *(britische Währung)* 5
°**practice** [ˈpræktɪs] Übung(en); Training
°**practise** [ˈpræktɪs] üben
prefer sth. to sth. [prɪˈfɜː] etwas lieber mögen als etwas, etwas einer Sache vorziehen 6

°**prepare (for)** [prɪˈpeə] vorbereiten; sich vorbereiten (auf)
present [ˈpreznt] Geschenk 5
°**present sth.** [prɪˈzent] etwas präsentieren, vorstellen
°**presentation** [preznˈteɪʃn] Referat, Präsentation **give a presentation** ein Referat halten
president [ˈprezɪdənt] Präsident/in 7: 1 (8)
price [praɪs] (Kauf-)Preis 5 **half price** zum halben Preis 7: 1 (18)
prince [prɪns] Prinz 5
principal [ˈprɪnsəpl] Schulleiter/in 5
prize [praɪz] Preis *(Gewinn)* 5
problem [ˈprɒbləm] Problem 5
product [ˈprɒdʌkt] Produkt 7: 1 (17)
profit [ˈprɒfɪt] Gewinn, Profit 7: 4 (81)
programme [ˈprəʊɡræm] (Fernseh-)Sendung 5
°**project** [ˈprɒdʒekt] Projekt
°**pronunciation** [prənʌnsiˈeɪʃn] Aussprache
protest [prəˈtest] protestieren 7: 4 (76)
protest [ˈprəʊtest] Protest(demonstration) 7: 4 (76)
proud (of) [praʊd] stolz (auf) 5
°**prove** [pruːv] nachweisen, beweisen
pub [pʌb] Kneipe 7: 2 (32)
public holiday [pʌblɪk ˈhɒlədeɪ] (gesetzlicher) Feiertag 7: 4 (85)
pullover [ˈpʊləʊvə] Pullover 5
put [pʊt], **put, put** *(etwas wohin)* tun, legen, stellen 6 **put in** einsetzen 6 **put sth. on** etwas anziehen *(Kleidung)*; etwas aufsetzen *(Hut, Brille)* 6 **put sth. up** etwas anbringen, aufhängen 7: 2 (37) **He puts it with the other things.** Er legt sie zu den anderen Dingen. 6
puzzled [ˈpʌzld] verwirrt, verwundert 7: 3 (68)
pyramid [ˈpɪrəmɪd] Pyramide 7: 4 (76)

Q

quarter [ˈkwɔːtə] Viertel 7: 2 (30)
queen [kwiːn] Königin 7: 1 (8)
question (to sb.) [ˈkwestʃən] Frage (an jn.) 5 **ask a question** eine Frage stellen 5
questionnaire [kwestʃəˈneə] Fragebogen 7: 2 (40)
quick [kwɪk] schnell 5

DICTIONARY

English – German

quiet ['kwaɪət] ruhig, still, leise 7: 2 (39)
quiz [kwɪz] Quiz 5

R

rabbit ['ræbɪt] Kaninchen 5
°**radio** ['reɪdiəʊ] Radio
rain [reɪn]:
1. Regen 6
2. regnen 6
rain jacket ['reɪn dʒækɪt] Regenjacke 6
rain trousers (pl) ['reɪn traʊzəz] Regenhose 6
rainy ['reɪni] regnerisch 6
ran [ræn] siehe **run**
rang [ræŋ] siehe **ring**
ranger ['reɪndʒə] Aufseher/in in einem Nationalpark 6
rap [ræp]:
1. Rap 5
2. rappen 5
rapper ['ræpə] Rapper/in 5
rat [ræt] Ratte 5
read [red] siehe **read**
read [riːd], **read, read** lesen 5
°**Read the texts to …** Lies/Lest … die Texte vor.
reader ['riːdə] Leser/in 7: 1 (22)
reading ['riːdɪŋ] (das) Lesen 5
real [rɪəl] echt, wirklich 5
reality [riˈæləti] Realität, Wirklichkeit 6
really nice ['rɪəli] wirklich nett 5
°**reasonable** ['riːznəbl] vernünftig, angemessen
reception [rɪˈsepʃn] Empfang (auch beim Telefon); Rezeption 7: 4 (91) **in reception** an der Rezeption 7: 4 (91)
°**record** [rɪˈkɔːd] aufnehmen, aufzeichnen
red [red] rot 5
°**regular** ['regjələ] regelmäßig
relax [rɪˈlæks] sich entspannen 7: 2 (31)
remember [rɪˈmembə]:
1. sich erinnern an 5
2. daran denken, nicht vergessen 5
repeat [rɪˈpiːt] wiederholen 7: 3 (57)
°**replace (with)** [rɪˈpleɪs] ersetzen (durch)
report [rɪˈpɔːt]:
1. Bericht 7: 4 (89) **weather report** Wetterbericht 7: 4 (89)
2. **report (from)** berichten (von/aus) 7: 4 (89)
reporter [rɪˈpɔːtə] Reporter/in 7: 1 (10)
°**republic** [rɪˈpʌblɪk] Republik
°**reserve** [rɪˈzɜːv] reservieren
restaurant ['restrɒnt] Restaurant 5
°**return** [rɪˈtɜːn] Rückgabe
return (ticket) [rɪˈtɜːn] Rückfahrkarte 7: 1 (23)
°**revision** [rɪˈvɪʒn] Wiederholung (von Lernstoff)
reward [rɪˈwɔːd] Belohnung 6
°**rhyme** [raɪm] Reim
°**ridden** ['rɪdn] siehe **ride**
ride [raɪd], **rode, ridden**:
1. reiten 5
ride a pony auf einem Pony/ein Pony reiten 5
2. fahren 5
ride a bike Rad fahren 5
right [raɪt] rechts; nach rechts 5
on the right rechts, auf der rechten Seite 5
right [raɪt] richtig 5 **that's right** das stimmt, das ist richtig 5
rights (pl) [raɪts] Rechte 7: 4 (76)
civil rights Bürgerrechte 7: 4 (76)
ring [rɪŋ], **rang, rung** läuten, klingeln 6
ringtone ['rɪŋtəʊn] Klingelton (Handy) 7: 1 (24)
river ['rɪvə] Fluss 6
road [rəʊd] Straße (Landstraße zwischen Orten / Straße in Orten) 5
rock (music) ['rɒk mjuːzɪk] Rock(musik) 6
rock and roll [rɒk ənd 'rəʊl] Rock and Roll (Musikrichtung) 7: 4 (76)
°**rode** [rəʊd] siehe **ride**
°**role** [rəʊl] Rolle (Theater, Rollenspiel)
°**role-play** ['rəʊl pleɪ] Rollenspiel
room [ruːm] Raum, Zimmer 5
°**route** [ruːt] Route, Weg
rubber ['rʌbə] Radiergummi 5
rubbish ['rʌbɪʃ]:
1. Müll, Abfall 6
2. Unsinn, dummes Zeug 7: 2 (46)
rubbish bin ['rʌbɪʃ bɪn] Mülleimer 6
rucksack ['rʌksæk] Rucksack 6
rugby ['rʌɡbi] Rugby (Ballsportart) 6
ruin ['ruːɪn] Ruine 7: 3 (59)
rule [ruːl] Regel, Vorschrift 6
ruler ['ruːlə] Lineal 5
run [rʌn], **ran, run** rennen 6

°**rung** [rʌŋ] siehe **ring**
runner ['rʌnə] Läufer/in 7: 1 (22)

S

sad [sæd] traurig 6
safe [seɪf] sicher (gefahrlos); in Sicherheit 6
said [sed] siehe **say**
salad ['sæləd] Salat (als Gericht oder Beilage) 5
sale [seɪl] Verkauf; Schlussverkauf 5
sales assistant ['seɪlz əsɪstənt] Verkäufer/in 7: 1 (18)
salt [sɔːlt] Salz 7: 3 (63)
same [seɪm]: **the same (as)** dasselbe / das gleiche (wie); gleich 6
sandwich ['sænwɪtʃ] Sandwich 5
sang [sæŋ] siehe **sing**
sat [sæt] siehe **sit**
Saturday ['sætədeɪ], ['sætədi] Samstag 5
sausage ['sɒsɪdʒ] Wurst, Würstchen 5
save [seɪv] retten 7: 2 (34)
saw [sɔː] siehe **see**
say [seɪ], **said, said** sagen 5
scared [skeəd]: **be scared (of)** Angst haben (vor) 6
scary ['skeəri] unheimlich, gruselig 6
°**scenario**, pl **scenarios** [səˈnɑːriəʊ] Szenario
scene [siːn] Szene 5
school [skuːl] Schule 5
science ['saɪəns] Naturwissenschaft 6
scone [skɒn] Milchbrötchen, leicht süß, oft mit Rosinen 5
score [skɔː]:
1. Spiel-/Punktestand; Punkt (Spiel/Sport) 7: 4 (85)
2. einen Punkt / ein Tor erzielen 7: 4 (85)
Scotland ['skɒtlənd] Schottland 7: 3 (52)
Scottish ['skɒtɪʃ] schottisch, aus Schottland 7: 1 (10)
scream [skriːm] schreien 6
°**screen** [skriːn] Leinwand (Kino)
°**script** [skrɪpt] Drehbuch
°**sculpture** ['skʌlptʃə] Bildhauerkunst, Bildhauerei; Skulptur
sea [siː] Meer 5
seaside ['siːsaɪd]: **at the seaside** am Meer 6
second ['sekənd] zweite(r, s) 5
second-hand shop [sekənd 'hænd ʃɒp] Second-Hand-Laden 6

184 one hundred and eighty-four

security [sɪˈkjʊərəti] Sicherheit 7: 1 (15)
see [siː], **saw, seen** sehen 5 **See you.** Bis dann. / Tschüs. 5
seen [siːn] *siehe* **see**
sell [sel], **sold, sold** verkaufen 7: 4 (78)
send (to) [send], **sent, sent** schicken, senden (an) 5
sent [sent] *siehe* **send**
sentence [ˈsentəns] Satz 6
September [sepˈtembə] September 5
°**serve** [sɜːv] servieren **breakfast is served** (das) Frühstück wird serviert
°**service** [ˈsɜːvɪs] Service; Dienst **bus service** Busverbindung
°**setting** [ˈsetɪŋ] Umgebung; Schauplatz
seven [ˈsevn] sieben 5
Shall we …? [ʃæl], [ʃəl] Sollen wir …? 7: 2 (43)
share [ʃeə] teilen; austauschen 6
sharpener [ˈʃɑːpnə] Anspitzer 5
she [ʃiː] sie *(weibliche Person)* 5 **she's (= she is)** sie ist 5
sheep, *pl* **sheep** [ʃiːp] Schaf 5
ship [ʃɪp] Schiff 5
shirt [ʃɜːt] Hemd 5
shoe [ʃuː] Schuh 5
shop [ʃɒp]:
1. Geschäft, Laden 5 **be at the shops** Einkäufe erledigen 5
2. **shop for sth.** etwas kaufen (gehen) 5
shopping [ˈʃɒpɪŋ]: **go shopping** einkaufen gehen 5
shopping centre [ˈʃɒpɪŋ sentə] Einkaufszentrum 7: 1 (10)
shopping list [ˈʃɒpɪŋ lɪst] Einkaufsliste 6
short [ʃɔːt] kurz; klein *(Person)* 6
°**shortly** [ˈʃɔːtli] bald, kurz *(Adv.)*
should [ʃʊd]: **you should** du solltest 6
shoulder [ˈʃəʊldə] Schulter 5
shout [ʃaʊt] rufen 5
show [ʃəʊ]:
1. Show, Vorführung, Aufführung 5
2. **show, showed, shown** zeigen 6
shower [ˈʃaʊə] Dusche; Schauer 7: 4 (91)
°**shown** [ʃəʊn] *siehe* **show**
Shut up! [ʃʌt ˈʌp] Halt den Mund! 5
side [saɪd] Seite 6
sign [saɪn] Schild; Zeichen 5
signal [ˈsɪɡnəl] Signal 7: 3 (59)

signature [ˈsɪɡnətʃə] Unterschrift 7: 3 (65)
silly [ˈsɪli] albern, dumm, blöd 5
sincerely [sɪnˈsɪəli]: **Yours sincerely** Mit freundlichen Grüßen *(Briefschluss)* 7: 4 (79)
sing [sɪŋ], **sang, sung** singen 5
singer [ˈsɪŋə] Sänger/in 5
single [ˈsɪŋɡl] einzeln, Einzel- 7: 3 (56) **single (ticket)** einfache Fahrkarte *(nur Hinfahrt)* 7: 1 (23)
single room [sɪŋɡl ˈruːm] Einzelzimmer 7: 3 (56)
sir [sɜː]: **Dear Sir/Madam** Sehr geehrte Damen und Herren 7: 4 (91)
sister [ˈsɪstə] Schwester 5
sit [sɪt], **sat, sat** sitzen; sich (hin)setzen 5
°**site** [saɪt]: **on-site (camping)** (Camping) vor Ort, an Ort und Stelle
six [sɪks] sechs 5
size [saɪz] Größe 7: 1 (18) **What size do you take?** Welche Größe hast du? 7: 1 (18)
skate park [ˈskeɪt pɑːk] Skatepark 7: 1 (21)
skateboard [ˈskeɪtbɔːd]:
1. Skateboard 6
2. Skateboard fahren 6
skateboarding [ˈskeɪtbɔːdɪŋ] *(das)* Skateboardfahren 5
skating [ˈskeɪtɪŋ]: **go skating** (Inline-)Skaten gehen 6
skiing [ˈskiːɪŋ] *(das)* Skilaufen *(Sport)* 6
skill [skɪl] Fähigkeit, Fertigkeit 7: 4 (84)
°**skills file** [ˈskɪlz faɪl] Anhang mit Lern- und Arbeitstechniken
skim a text [skɪm] einen Text überfliegen *(um den Inhalt grob zu erfassen)* 7: 3 (67)
skirt [skɜːt] Rock 6
skive [skaɪv] *(infml)* schwänzen *(Schule)* 6
sky [skaɪ] Himmel 7: 4 (77)
sleep [sliːp]:
1. Schlaf 7: 1 (22)
2. **sleep, slept, slept** schlafen 5
sleeping bag [ˈsliːpɪŋ bæɡ] Schlafsack 6
sleepover [ˈsliːpəʊvə] Übernachtungsparty 5
sleepy [ˈsliːpi] verschlafen, müde 7: 1 (22)
°**slept** [slept] *siehe* **sleep**
°**slice** [slaɪs] Scheibe *(z.B. Brot)*; Stück *(z.B. Kuchen)*

°**slide** [slaɪd] Dia(-); Folie *(bei Präsentation m. Computerprogramm)*
slow [sləʊ] langsam 6
small [smɔːl] klein 5
smart [smɑːt] schick, smart; schlau, clever 7: 4 (92)
smile [smaɪl]:
1. lächeln 6
smile at sb. jn. anlächeln 6
2. *(ein/das)* Lächeln 6
smoothie [ˈsmuːði] Smoothie *(Getränk aus Fruchtpüree, evtl. mit Milchprodukten)* 7: 1 (24)
smuggler [ˈsmʌɡlə] Schmuggler/in 5
snack [snæk] Snack, kleine Mahlzeit 5
snake [sneɪk] Schlange 5
so [səʊ]:
1. so 5
so cute so niedlich 5 °**so far** bis jetzt, bis hierher
2. also 5
3. **so (that)** sodass 7: 2 (37)
4. **I don't think so.** Das glaube/denke ich nicht. 7: 4 (87)
I think so. Ich glaube/denke ja. 7: 4 (87)
soap [səʊp] Seife; *(infml auch:)* Seifenoper 6
°**social media** *(pl)* [səʊʃl ˈmiːdiə] soziale Medien
sock [sɒk] Socke 7: 1 (20)
sofa [ˈsəʊfə] Sofa 5
°**soft drink** [ˈsɒft drɪŋk] alkoholfreies Getränk
sold [səʊld] *siehe* **sell**
some [sʌm], [səm] einige, ein paar; etwas 5
somebody [ˈsʌmbədi] jemand 6
someone [ˈsʌmwʌn] jemand 6
something [ˈsʌmθɪŋ] etwas 5
sometimes [ˈsʌmtaɪmz] manchmal 5
son [sʌn] Sohn 7: 4 (76)
song [sɒŋ] Lied 5
soon [suːn] bald 5
sore [sɔː] schmerzhaft 6 **a sore throat** Halsschmerzen 6 **Her leg was sore.** Ihr Bein tat weh. 6
sorry [ˈsɒri]: **Sorry. / I'm sorry.** Tut mir leid. / Entschuldigung. 5 **be/feel sorry for sb.** Mitleid mit jm. haben 6
sort [sɔːt]: **What sort of …?** Welche Art/Sorte (von) …? 7: 3 (57)
sound [saʊnd]:
1. Geräusch; Klang; Laut 5
2. klingen, sich anhören 5

DICTIONARY — English – German

Sounds fun. Hört sich gut an. / Klingt, als ob es Spaß macht. 5
soup [suːp] Suppe 5
south [saʊθ] Süden; südlich; Süd- 6
south-east [saʊθˈiːst] Südosten, südöstlich 6
southern [ˈsʌðən] südlich, Süd- 7: 2 (30)
south-west [saʊθˈwest] Südwesten, südwestlich 6
space [speɪs] Platz, Raum 6
Spain [speɪn] Spanien 6
Spanish [ˈspænɪʃ] spanisch; Spanisch 7: 4 (90)
speak, spoke, spoken [spiːk]: **speak (to)** sprechen (mit) 5 **speaking to friends** mit Freunden/Freundinnen sprechen 5 **Who's speaking?** Wer spricht (da)? *(am Telefon)* 7: 2 (35)
°**speaker** [ˈspiːkə] Sprecher/in
special [ˈspeʃl] besondere(r, s) 6
spell [spel] buchstabieren 5
°**spend (time/a week)** [spend] (Zeit/eine Woche) verbringen
spoke [spəʊk] *siehe* **speak**
spoken [ˈspəʊkən] *siehe* **speak**
spoon [spuːn] Löffel 6
sport [spɔːt] Sport; Sportart 5 **do sport** Sport treiben 5
sports hall [ˈspɔːts hɔːl] Sporthalle 6
sports shop [ˈspɔːts ʃɒp] Sportgeschäft 5
sporty [ˈspɔːti] sportlich 6
spot [spɒt] Tupfen *(Leopard)*; Pickel 6
stadium [ˈsteɪdiəm] Stadion 6
stand [stænd], **stood, stood** stehen 6 **stand up** aufstehen 6
°**standard-class ticket** [ˈstændəd klɑːs tɪkɪt] Normalticket, Ticket für die 2. Klasse
star [stɑː] Star 7: 1 (8)
start [stɑːt]:
1. anfangen 5
°2. Anfang, Start 7: 4 (79)
state [steɪt] (Bundes-)Staat 7: (74)
station [ˈsteɪʃn] Bahnhof 6
stay [steɪ]:
1. bleiben 5
°2. Aufenthalt
steak [steɪk] Steak 6
°**steam** [stiːm] Dampf
°**step** [step] Schritt; Stufe
stepbrother [ˈstepbrʌðə] Stiefbruder 5
stepdad [ˈstepdæd] Stiefvater 5

stepfather [ˈstepfɑːðə] Stiefvater 5
stepmother [ˈstepmʌðə] Stiefmutter 5
stepmum [ˈstepmʌm] Stiefmutter 5
stepsister [ˈstepsɪstə] Stiefschwester 5
still [stɪl]:
1. (immer) noch; trotzdem 6
°2. Standbild *(Film)*
stone [stəʊn] Stein 6
stood [stʊd] *siehe* **stand**
stop [stɒp]:
1. anhalten; stehen bleiben; aufhören (mit) 5
2. **(bus) stop** (Bus-)Haltestelle 6
story [ˈstɔːri] Geschichte 5
straight [streɪt]: **Go straight on.** Geh geradeaus (weiter). 6
street [striːt] Straße *(in Ortschaften)* 5
street surfing [ˈstriːt sɜːfɪŋ] Waveboarden 6
strict [strɪkt] streng, strikt 6
student [ˈstjuːdnt] Schüler/in; Student/in 5
studio [ˈstjuːdiəʊ] Studio 7: (75)
°**study** [ˈstʌdi] studieren, genau durchlesen
stuff [stʌf] *(infml)* Zeug, Kram 6
stupid [ˈstjuːpɪd] dumm, blöd; albern 5
°**subject** [ˈsʌbdʒɪkt] (Schul-)Fach
successful [səkˈsesfl] erfolgreich 7: 4 (81)
°**suck** [sʌk]: **It sucks!** *(infml)* Es nervt / Es ist Mist!
suddenly [ˈsʌdənli] plötzlich 7: 2 (36)
sugar [ˈʃʊɡə] Zucker 7: 3 (63)
sugary [ˈʃʊɡəri] süß(lich), zuckerhaltig
summer [ˈsʌmə] Sommer 5
sun [sʌn] Sonne 7: 1 (22)
suncream [ˈsʌnkriːm] Sonnencreme 5
Sunday [ˈsʌndeɪ], [ˈsʌndi] Sonntag 5
°**sung** [sʌŋ] *siehe* **sing**
sunglasses *(pl)* [ˈsʌnɡlɑːsɪz] Sonnenbrille 5
sunny [ˈsʌni] sonnig 6
°**super** [ˈsuːpə] super
°**superb** [suːˈpɜːb] ausgezeichnet
supermarket [ˈsuːpəmɑːkɪt] Supermarkt 6
sure [ʃʊə] sicher 5
surprise [səˈpraɪz] Überraschung 5
surprised [səˈpraɪzd] überrascht 6

°**suspension railway** [səˈspenʃn ˈreɪlweɪ] Schwebebahn
swam [swæm] *siehe* **swim**
°**swap** [swɒp] tauschen
Sweden [ˈswiːdn] Schweden 6
sweets *(pl)* [swiːts] Bonbons, Süßigkeiten 5
swim [swɪm], **swam, swum** schwimmen 5
°**swimmer** [ˈswɪmə] Schwimmer/in
swimming [ˈswɪmɪŋ] *(das)* Schwimmen 5 **go swimming** schwimmen gehen 5
swimming pool [ˈswɪmɪŋ puːl] Schwimmbad 5
swimming trunks *(pl)* [ˈswɪmɪŋ trʌŋks] Badehose 5
swimsuit [ˈswɪmsuːt] Badeanzug 5
°**swum** [swʌm] *siehe* **swim**
°**symbol (of)** [ˈsɪmbl] Symbol (für)
°**system** [ˈsɪstəm] System

T

table [ˈteɪbl]:
1. Tisch 5
°2. Tabelle
table tennis [ˈteɪbl tenɪs] Tischtennis 6
tae kwon do [taɪ kwɒn ˈdəʊ] Taekwondo 6
tail [teɪl] Schwanz 6
take [teɪk], **took, taken**:
1. bringen 6
2. nehmen, mitnehmen 5
take a message etwas ausrichten 7: 2 (35) **take a photo** ein Foto machen 6 **take part (in)** teilnehmen (an), mitmachen (bei) 7: 4 (81)
°**take a test** eine Prüfung machen
°**take notes** (sich) Notizen machen *(beim Lesen oder Zuhören)*
taken [ˈteɪkən] *siehe* **take**
talk [tɔːk]:
1. **talk (to)** sprechen (mit) 5
2. Vortrag, Rede; Gespräch 6
give a talk einen Vortrag halten 6
talk show [ˈtɔːk ʃəʊ] Talkshow 6
talker [ˈtɔːkə] Redner/in 7: 1 (22)
tall [tɔːl] groß *(Person)*; hoch *(Gebäude)* 6
°**tartan** [ˈtɑːtn] Schottenmuster/ -karo
°**task** [tɑːsk] Aufgabe
taught [tɔːt] *siehe* **teach**
taxi [ˈtæksi] Taxi 7: 1 (9)
tea [tiː] Tee 5
teach [tiːtʃ], **taught, taught** unterrichten, lehren 7: 3 (55)

teacher ['tiːtʃə] Lehrer/in 5
team [tiːm] Team, Mannschaft 6
technology [tek'nɒlədʒi] Technik, Technologie 5
teen [tiːn] *(infml)* Teenager 6
teenage life ['tiːneɪdʒ] *(etwa:)* das Leben der Teenager 6
teenager ['tiːneɪdʒə] Teenager 5
tell [tel], **told, told** erzählen, sagen 5 **tell sb. the way** jm. den Weg beschreiben 6
temperature ['temprətʃə] Temperatur; Fieber 6 **I have a temperature.** Ich habe Fieber. 6
ten [ten] zehn 5
tennis ['tenɪs] Tennis 6
tent [tent] Zelt 5
terrible ['terəbl] schrecklich 5
test [test]:
1. Test; Klassenarbeit 6
°**take a test** eine Prüfung machen
°2. testen
text [tekst]: **Text** 7: 3 (67)
text (message) ['tekst mesɪdʒ]:
1. SMS 5
2. **text sb.** jm. eine SMS schicken 5
than [ðən]: **older than me** älter als ich 6 **It's cheaper than that.** So viel kostet das nicht. 6
thank you ['θæŋk juː] danke (schön) 5
thanks [θæŋks] danke 5
that [ðæt]:
1. das (da) 5
That's £ 5. Das macht 5 Pfund. 5
that's why deswegen 6 **Is that Mr Taylor?** Ist da Herr Taylor? *(am Telefon)* 7: 2 (35)
2. dass 5
she thinks that ... sie denkt, dass ... 5 **so that** sodass 7: 2 (37)
3. der, die, das *(Relativpronomen)* 7: 1 (22)
words that you know ... Wörter, die du kennst ... 7: 1 (22)
the [ðə] der, die, das 5
theatre ['θɪətə] Theater 6
their [ðeə] ihr/e *(Plural)* 5
theirs [ðeəz] ihre/r, ihrs *(zu „they")* 7: 3 (55)
them [ðem], [ðəm] sie, ihnen *(Plural)* 5 °**all of them** sie alle
°**theme** [θiːm] Thema
themselves [ðəm'selvz] sie/sich selbst (Plural) 7: 3 (55)
then [ðen] dann 5
there [ðeə] da, dort; dahin, dorthin 5 **there are ...** es sind ... /

es gibt ... 5 **there's** es ist ... / es gibt ... 5
these kids [ðiːz] diese Kinder (hier) 6
they [ðeɪ] sie *(Plural)* 5 **they're (= they are)** sie sind 5
thing [θɪŋ] Ding, Sache 5
think [θɪŋk], **thought, thought** denken, meinen, glauben 5 **think of/about** halten von, denken über 6 **What do you think?** Was meinst du? / Was denkst du? 5 °**think about** nachdenken über °**think of sth.** sich etwas überlegen, ausdenken
third [θɜːd]:
1. dritte(r, s) 5
2. **one third** ein Drittel 7: 2 (30)
this [ðɪs] diese(r, s) 5 **This is Rob Blake.** Hier spricht Rob Blake. *(am Telefon)* 7: 2 (35) **This is ...** Dies ist ... / Das ist ... 5 **this morning/afternoon/evening** heute Morgen/Nachmittag/Abend 6
those CDs [ðəʊz] die CDs dort, jene CDs 6
thought [θɔːt] *siehe* **think**
thousand ['θaʊznd] tausend 7: 3 (64)
three [θriː] drei 5 **3-D** 3-D 7: 2 (40)
throat [θrəʊt] Hals 6 **a sore throat** Halsschmerzen 6
through [θruː] durch 5
Thursday ['θɜːzdeɪ], ['θɜːzdi] Donnerstag 5
°**tick** [tɪk]:
1. Häkchen
2. mit einem Häkchen versehen, ankreuzen
ticket ['tɪkɪt] Eintrittskarte, Fahrkarte 5
tidy ['taɪdi]:
1. aufräumen 6
2. ordentlich 6
tie [taɪ] Krawatte 5
tiger ['taɪgə] Tiger 5
time [taɪm]:
1. Zeit; Uhrzeit 5
have a great time viel Spaß haben 5 **on time** pünktlich 6 **What's the time?** Wie spät ist es? 5
2. Mal 6
next time nächstes Mal 6
timetable ['taɪmteɪbl] Stundenplan 5
°**tip** [tɪp] Tipp
tired ['taɪəd] müde 5

title ['taɪtl] Titel, Überschrift 7: 1 (11)
to [tu], [tə]:
1. zu, nach, in 5
to the country aufs Land 5 **go to bed** ins Bett gehen, schlafen gehen 5 **go to dad's flat** in Papas Wohnung gehen 5 **Have you ever been to London?** Warst du schon mal in London? 6 **talk to** sprechen mit 5 **write to a friend** an einen Freund/eine Freundin schreiben 5
2. bis 5
from Monday to Friday von Montag bis Freitag 5
3. (um) zu 5
time to go home Zeit, nach Hause zu gehen 5
toast [təʊst] Toast(brot) 6
today [tə'deɪ] heute 5
together [tə'geðə] zusammen 5
toilet ['tɔɪlət] Toilette 5
told [təʊld] *siehe* **tell**
tomato, *pl* **tomatoes** [tə'mɑːtəʊ] Tomate 7: 3 (63)
tomorrow [tə'mɒrəʊ] morgen 5
°**tone** [təʊn] Ton
too [tuː]:
1. auch 5
Me too. Ich auch. 5
2. **too small** zu klein 5
took [tʊk] *siehe* **take**
top [tɒp] Top *(ärmelloses Oberteil)* 7: 1 (18) **at the top (of)** oben, am oberen Ende (von); an der Spitze (von) 6
°**topic** ['tɒpɪk] Thema
°**total** ['təʊtl] Gesamtbetrag, Summe
tour [tʊə]:
1. Tour; Rundfahrt 7: 1 (8)
2. **tour (of)** Rundgang (durch) 5
a tour of the school ein Rundgang durch die Schule 5
°**tour guide** ['tʊə gaɪd] Reiseleiter/in, Fremdenführer/in
tourist ['tʊərɪst] Tourist/in 6
towel ['taʊəl] Handtuch 5
tower ['taʊə] Turm 7: 1 (8)
town [taʊn] Stadt 5 **in town** in der Stadt 5
toy [tɔɪ] Spielzeug 6
track [træk] Pfad, (Feld-)Weg 6
°**tractor** ['træktə] Traktor
traffic lights *(pl)* ['træfɪk laɪts] Verkehrsampel 6
train [treɪn] Zug, Eisenbahn 6
train station ['treɪn steɪʃn] Bahnhof 6

DICTIONARY — English – German

trainers *(pl)* ['treɪnəz] Sportschuhe 5
°**training** ['treɪnɪŋ] Training
transport ['trænspɔːt] Verkehrsmittel; Transport(wesen) 7: 1 (17)
travel ['trævl] reisen; fahren, sich fortbewegen 7: 1 (9)
tree [triː] Baum 5
trick [trɪk] Trick, Kunststück 7: 2 (37)
trip [trɪp] Fahrt, Ausflug 5 **do a trip** einen Ausflug machen 6 **go on a trip** einen Ausflug machen 5
trouble ['trʌbl] Ärger, Schwierigkeit(en) 5
trousers *(pl)* ['traʊzəz] Hose 5
true [truː] wahr 6
try [traɪ] versuchen, (aus)probieren 6 **try sth. on** etwas anprobieren *(Kleidung)* 7: 1 (17)
T-shirt ['tiːʃɜːt] T-Shirt 5
Tube [tjuːb] U-Bahn *(London)* 7: 1 (9)
Tuesday ['tjuːzdeɪ], ['tjuːzdi] Dienstag 5
°**tunnel** ['tʌnl] Tunnel
Turkey ['tɜːki] die Türkei 6
turn right/left [tɜːn] (nach) rechts/links abbiegen 6
TV [tiːˈviː] Fernseher 5
twelve [twelv] zwölf 5
twice [twaɪs] zweimal 6
twin(s) [twɪn] Zwilling(e) 7: 3 (56)
twin room [twɪn 'ruːm] Zweibettzimmer 7: 3 (56)
two [tuː] zwei 5
°**typical (of)** ['tɪpɪkl] typisch (für)

U

ugly ['ʌgli] hässlich 6
°**uncle** ['ʌŋkl] Onkel
uncool [ʌnˈkuːl] uncool 6
under ['ʌndə] unter 5
°**underground** ['ʌndəgraʊnd] U-Bahn
understand [ʌndəˈstænd], **understood, understood** verstehen 6
understood [ʌndəˈstʊd] *siehe* **understand**
unemployed [ʌnɪmˈplɔɪd] arbeitslos 7: 3 (54)
unfit [ʌnˈfɪt] nicht fit 7: 1 (22)
unfriendly [ʌnˈfrendli] unfreundlich 6
unhappy [ʌnˈhæpi] unglücklich 5
unhealthy [ʌnˈhelθi] ungesund 6
uniform ['juːnɪfɔːm] (Schul-)Uniform 5

uninteresting [ʌnˈɪntrəstɪŋ] uninteressant 6
unit ['juːnɪt] Unit *(Lerneinheit)* 5
United Kingdom (UK) [juːnaɪtɪd ˈkɪŋdəm] Vereinigtes Königreich 7: 2 (30)
United States [juːnaɪtɪd ˈsteɪts] Vereinigte Staaten 6
unpopular [ʌnˈpɒpjələ] unbeliebt 6
unreal [ʌnˈrɪəl] unwirklich 6
unsure [ʌnˈʃʊə] unsicher 6
untidy [ʌnˈtaɪdi] unordentlich, unaufgeräumt 7: 1 (22)
until [ənˈtɪl] bis *(zeitlich)* 6 **not (...) until I'm 13** erst, wenn ich 13 bin 6
°**unwell** [ʌnˈwel] unwohl, krank
up [ʌp] hinauf, hoch 6
upstairs [ʌpˈsteəz] oben; nach oben 5
US [juː 'es]: **the US** die USA 6
us [ʌs], [əs] uns 5
use [juːz] benutzen 5 °**it was used by ...** es wurde benutzt von ...
°**useful** ['juːsfl] nützlich
usually ['juːʒʊəli] meistens, normalerweise 5

V

van [væn] Transporter, Lieferwagen 7: 2 (32)
°**variety (of)** [vəˈraɪəti] Auswahl (an)
vegetables *(pl)* ['vedʒtəblz] Gemüse 5
vegetarian, *infml auch* **veggie** [vedʒəˈteərɪən], ['vedʒi] vegetarisch; Vegetarier/in 6
°**version** ['vɜːʃn] Version
very ['veri] sehr 5 **Thanks very much.** Vielen Dank. 6
video ['vɪdiəʊ] Video(-) 6
video chat ['vɪdiəʊ tʃæt] Videochat 6
°**viewer** ['vjuːə] Zuschauer/in
°**viewing** ['vjuːɪŋ] *(das)* Fernsehen, *(das)* Betrachten *(z.B. von Filmen)*
village ['vɪlɪdʒ] Dorf 5
violence ['vaɪələns] Gewalt; Gewalttätigkeit 7: 4 (90)
violent ['vaɪələnt] gewalttätig 7: 4 (90)
visit ['vɪzɪt]:
1. besuchen 6
2. Besuch 7: 2 (46)
visitor ['vɪzɪtə] Besucher/in, Gast 5
voice [vɔɪs] Stimme 7: 3 (66)

volleyball ['vɒlɪbɔːl] Volleyball 6
vote for [vəʊt] stimmen für 6

W

wait (for) [weɪt] warten (auf) 6 **Wait for this.** *(infml)* Stell dir nur vor!/Du wirst es kaum glauben! 6
waiter ['weɪtə] Kellner 7: 4 (88)
waitress ['weɪtrəs] Kellnerin 7: 4 (88)
wake [weɪk], **woke, woken** wecken 5
walk [wɔːk] (zu Fuß) gehen, wandern 5 **walk around** umhergehen (in) 5
walker ['wɔːkə] Wanderer/Wanderin, Fußgänger/in 7: 1 (22)
wall [wɔːl] Wand; Mauer 6
want [wɒnt] wollen 5 **want to do** tun/machen wollen 5
wardrobe ['wɔːdrəʊb] Kleiderschrank 5
warm [wɔːm] warm 6
was [wɒz], [wəz] *siehe* **be**
wash [wɒʃ] waschen 6
wash up [wɒʃ 'ʌp] abwaschen 5
waste [weɪst] Verschwendung 7: 4 (84)
watch [wɒtʃ] *(sich etwas)* anschauen; beobachten 5 **watching TV** Fernsehen 5
water ['wɔːtə] Wasser 5
way [weɪ] Weg 6 **ask sb. the way** jn. nach dem Weg fragen 6 **tell sb. the way** jm. den Weg beschreiben 6
we [wiː] wir 5 **we're (= we are)** wir sind 5
wear [weə], **wore, worn** tragen, anhaben *(Kleidung)* 6
weather ['weðə] Wetter 6
weather forecast ['fɔːkɑːst] Wettervorhersage 6
weather report ['weðə rɪpɔːt] Wetterbericht 7: 4 (89)
webcode ['webkəʊd] Webcode 6
website ['websaɪt] Website 7: 3 (56)
Wednesday ['wenzdeɪ], ['wenzdi] Mittwoch 5
°**wee** [wiː] klein *(schottisches Englisch)*
week [wiːk] Woche 5
weekend [wiːkˈend] Wochenende 5 **at the weekend** am Wochenende 5
welcome ['welkəm]:
1. **welcome sb. (to)** jn. begrüßen (in), jn. willkommen heißen (in)

7: 3 (64) **Welcome to Plymouth.** Willkommen in Plymouth! 5
2. You're welcome. Bitte, gern geschehen. / Nichts zu danken. 5
well [wel] gut *(Adverb)* 6
Well, … Nun, … / Also, … 5 **Well done.** Gut gemacht! 5 **do well** es gut machen; gut abschneiden, erfolgreich sein 7: 2 (34) **she can't walk well** sie kann nicht gut gehen/laufen 6 **She isn't feeling well.** Es geht ihr nicht gut. 6
went [went] *siehe* **go**
were [wɜː], [wə] *siehe* **be**
west [west] Westen; westlich; West- 6
western [ˈwestən] westlich, West- 7: 2 (30)
wet [wet] nass 5
what [wɒt]:
1. was 5
What about you? Und du? / Was ist mit dir? 5 **What do you think?** Was meinst du? / Was denkst du? 5 **What's the time?** Wie spät ist es? 5 **What's your name?** Wie heißt du? 5
2. welche(r, s) 5
wheelchair [ˈwiːltʃeə] Rollstuhl 5
when [wen]:
1. wann 5
When's (= when is) your birthday? Wann hast du Geburtstag? 5
2. wenn 5
3. als 5
where [weə] wo(hin) 5
which [wɪtʃ]:
1. welche(r, s) 6
Which club? Welcher Klub? 6
2. der, die, das; die *(Relativpronomen)* 7: 3 (52)
whistle [ˈwɪsl] (Triller-)Pfeife 6
white [waɪt] weiß 5
who [huː]:
1. wer 5
Who are you? Wer bist du? / Wer seid ihr? 5
2. wem; wen 5
3. der, die *(Relativpronomen, Person)* 7: 1 (19)
somebody who can help jemand, der helfen kann 7: 1 (19)
°**whole** [həʊl] ganze(r, s)
why [waɪ] warum 5 **that's why** deswegen 6
°**wide** [waɪd] breit, weit
Wi-Fi [ˈwaɪ faɪ] WLAN, kabellose Datenübertragung 7: 3 (56)
wild [waɪld] wild; wild lebend 5

will [wɪl]: **I'll (= I will) find him.** Ich werde ihn finden. 6 **50p will do** 50 Pence reichen (auch) 6
win [wɪn], **won, won** gewinnen 6
wind [wɪnd] Wind 6
window [ˈwɪndəʊ] Fenster 6
windy [ˈwɪndi] windig 6
winner [ˈwɪnə] Gewinner/in 5
winter [ˈwɪntə] Winter 6
wish [wɪʃ] Wunsch 5 **Best wishes** Viele Grüße, … *(Briefschluss)* 5
with [wɪð] mit 5 **with Ellie** bei Ellie 5 **He puts it with the other things.** Er legt sie zu den anderen Dingen. 6
without [wɪˈðaʊt] ohne 6
°**woke** [wəʊk] *siehe* **wake**
°**woken** [ˈwəʊkən] *siehe* **wake**
woman, *pl* **women** [ˈwʊmən], [ˈwɪmɪn] Frau 5
won [wʌn] *siehe* **win**
won't [wəʊnt]: **it won't rain** es wird nicht regnen 6
wood [wʊd]:
1. Holz 7: 3 (59)
2. Wald 7: 3 (59)
word [wɜːd] Wort 5 **words (of a song)** (Song-)Text 7: 3 (66)
°**wordweb** [ˈwɜːdweb] Wortnetz
wore [wɔː] *siehe* **wear**
work [wɜːk]:
1. Arbeit 5
at work bei der Arbeit, am Arbeitsplatz 5
2. arbeiten; funktionieren 5
work of art [wɜːk əv ˈɑːt] Kunstwerk 7: 4 (77)
worker [ˈwɜːkə] Arbeiter/in; Arbeitskraft 7: 1 (22)
°**workshop** [ˈwɜːkʃɒp] Workshop *(Kurs)*
world [wɜːld] Welt 7: 3 (64) **in the world** auf der Welt 7: 3 (64)
°**worn** [wɔːn] *siehe* **wear**
worry [ˈwʌri]:
1. **worry (about)** sich Sorgen machen (wegen, um) 6
2. **No worries.** *(infml)* Kein Problem. 7: 1 (13)
worse [wɜːs] schlechter, schlimmer 6
worst [wɜːst] der/die/das schlechteste, schlimmste; am schlechtesten, am schlimmsten 6
would [wʊd]: **I'd (= I would) like** ich hätte gern, ich möchte (…) haben 5 **I'd (= I would) love to come.** Ich komme sehr gern. /

Ich würde sehr gern kommen. 5 **I'd (= I would) like to join** ich würde/möchte gern mitmachen 6
write [raɪt], **wrote, written** schreiben 5 **write to sb.** an jn. schreiben 5 °**write down** aufschreiben
writer [ˈraɪtə] Autor/in, Verfasser/in 7: 1 (22)
°**written** [ˈrɪtn] *siehe* **write**
wrong [rɒŋ] falsch 5 **that's wrong** das stimmt nicht, das ist falsch 5 **What's wrong with …?** Was stimmt nicht mit …? 6
wrote [rəʊt] *siehe* **write**

X

X-ray [ˈeksreɪ] Röntgen(strahlen) 7: 2 (39)
°**X-ray fish** [ˈeksreɪ fɪʃ] Wasserstieglitz, Sternflecksalmler

Y

yeah [jeə] *(infml)* ja 6
year [jɪə] Jahr(gang) 5
yellow [ˈjeləʊ] gelb 5
yes [jes] ja 5
yesterday [ˈjestədeɪ] gestern 5
yet [jet]: **not … yet** noch nicht 7: 2 (32)
yogurt [ˈjɒgət] Joghurt 6
you [juː]:
1. du; ihr; Sie 5
you're (= you are) du bist, ihr seid, Sie sind 5
2. dich; dir; euch; Sie; Ihnen 5
young [jʌŋ] jung 6
your [jɔː] dein/e, euer/eure 5
yours [jɔːz] deine/r; deins; eure/r, eures 7: 3 (54)
yourself [jəˈself] du/dir/dich selbst 7: 3 (55)
yourselves [jɔːˈselvz] ihr/euch selbst; Sie/sich selbst 7: 3 (55)
°**youth** [juːθ] Jugend
°**youth club** [ˈjuːθ klʌb] Jugendklub
°**Yuck!** [jʌk] Igitt!
yum! [jʌm] lecker! 6

Z

zebra [ˈzebrə] Zebra 7: 2 (39)
zone [zəʊn] Zone 7: (74)
zoo [zuː] Zoo 5

DICTIONARY   German – English

Das **German–English dictionary** enthält den **Lernwortschatz** von *Highlight 7*.
Es kann dir eine erste Hilfe sein, wenn du vergessen hast, wie etwas auf Englisch heißt.

Wenn du wissen möchtest, wo das englische Wort zum ersten Mal in *Highlight 7* vorkommt,
dann kannst du im **English–German dictionary** (Seiten 172–189) nachschlagen.

A

abbiegen: (nach) rechts/links abbiegen turn right/left [tɜːn]
Abend evening [ˈiːvnɪŋ] **am Abend** in the evening **(zu) Abend essen** have dinner [ˈdɪnə]
Abendessen dinner [ˈdɪnə]
abends in the evening(s) **6 Uhr abends** 6 pm [piː ˈem]
Abenteuer adventure [ədˈventʃə]
aber but [bʌt]
abfahren leave [liːv]
Abfall rubbish [ˈrʌbɪʃ]
abgehen: von der Schule abgehen leave school [liːv ˈskuːl]
Abgemacht! It's a deal! [diːl]
abholen: jn. abholen meet sb. [miːt]
abschließend final [ˈfaɪnl]
abschneiden: besser abschneiden do better [ˈbetə] **gut abschneiden** do well [wel]
Abteilung department [dɪˈpɑːtmənt]
abwaschen wash up [wɒʃ ˈʌp]
acht eight [eɪt]
achten: auf etwas achten *(beim Zuhören)* listen for sth. [ˈlɪsn fə]
Adresse address [əˈdres]
Aerobic aerobics [eəˈrəʊbɪks]
Affe monkey [ˈmʌŋki]
Aktivität activity [ækˈtɪvəti]
albern silly [ˈsɪli]; stupid [ˈstjuːpɪd]
alle *(jeder)* everybody [ˈevribɒdi]; everyone [ˈevriwʌn] **alle(s)** all [ɔːl]
allein(e) alone [əˈləʊn]
allergisch (gegen) allergic (to) [əˈlɜːdʒɪk]
Alles Gute *(Briefschluss)* All the best [ɔːl ðə ˈbest]
alphabetisches Wörterverzeichnis dictionary [ˈdɪkʃənri]
als *(zeitlich)* when [wen] **älter als ich** older than me [ðən]
also so [səʊ] **Also, ...** Well, ... [wel]
alt old [əʊld]
Alter age [eɪdʒ] **Kinder im Alter von 7 Jahren** children aged 7 [eɪdʒd]

am: am Abend in the evening **am Arbeitsplatz** at work [æt], [ət] **am besten** best [best] **am Freitagmorgen** on Friday morning [ɒn] **am Montag** on Monday **am Morgen** in the morning **am Nachmittag** in the afternoon **am Strand** on the beach **immer am Montag** on Mondays
amerikanisch; Amerikaner/in American [əˈmerəkən]
an: an dieser Schule at this school [æt], [ət] **an einen Freund/eine Freundin schreiben** write to a friend [tuː], [tə] **an seinem Geburtstag** on his birthday [ɒn]
anbringen: etwas anbringen put sth. up [pʊt ˈʌp]
andere(r, s) other [ˈʌðə] **ein/e andere(r, s)** another [əˈnʌðə]
ändern; sich ändern change [tʃeɪndʒ]
anders different [ˈdɪfrənt]
Anfang start [stɑːt] **am Anfang** at first [ət ˈfɜːst]
anfangen start [stɑːt]; begin [bɪˈɡɪn]
Anfänger/in beginner [bɪˈɡɪnə]
anfeuern *(Sportler/innen)* cheer [tʃɪə]
Anführer/in leader [ˈliːdə]
Angst haben (vor) be scared (of) [skeəd]
anhaben *(Kleidung)* wear [weə]
anhalten stop [stɒp]
anhören: sich etwas anhören listen to sth. [ˈlɪsn] **sich (gut/schlecht) anhören** sound (good/bad) [saʊnd] **Hört sich gut an.** Sounds fun.
ankommen (in/an/bei) arrive (at) [əˈraɪv]
anlächeln: jn. anlächeln smile at sb. [ˈsmaɪl ət]
Anprobe *(Umkleidekabine)* changing room [ˈtʃeɪndʒɪŋ ruː]
anprobieren *(Kleidung)* try on [traɪ ˈɒn]
Anruf *(Telefon)* (phone) call [ˈfəʊn kɔːl]
anrufen phone [fəʊn]; call [kɔːl]

Ansage *(Durchsage)* announcement [əˈnaʊnsmənt]
anschauen look at [ˈlʊk ət] **sich etwas anschauen** *(beobachten)* watch [wɒtʃ]
Anspitzer sharpener [ˈʃɑːpnə]
Antwort answer [ˈɑːnsə]
antworten answer [ˈɑːnsə]
Anzahl number [ˈnʌmbə]
Anzeige advert [ˈædvɜːt]
anziehen: etwas anziehen *(Kleidung)* put sth. on [pʊt ˈɒn]
Apfel apple [ˈæpl]
April April [ˈeɪprəl]
Arbeit work [wɜːk] **Arbeiten erledigen** *(im Haus)* do chores [tʃɔːz]
arbeiten work [wɜːk]
Arbeiter/in worker [ˈwɜːkə]
Arbeitskraft worker [ˈwɜːkə]
arbeitslos unemployed [ˌʌnɪmˈplɔɪd]
Arbeitsplatz: am Arbeitsplatz at work [wɜːk]
Ärger trouble [ˈtrʌbl]
ärgerlich angry [ˈæŋɡri]
Arm arm [ɑːm]
arm poor [pʊə] **(die) arme Mrs Trent** poor Mrs Trent **Du Arme/r!** Poor you!
Art: Art (von) kind (of) [kaɪnd] **auf diese Art** like this [laɪk ˈðɪs] **Welche Art (von) ...?** What sort of ...? [sɔːt]
Artikel article [ˈɑːtɪkl]
Arzneimittel drug [drʌɡ]
Arzt/Ärztin doctor [ˈdɒktə]
Assistent/in assistant [əˈsɪstənt]
auch also [ˈɔːlsəʊ]; too [tuː] **Ich auch.** Me too.
auf on [ɒn] **auf dem Feld/der Weide** in the field [ɪn] **auf dem Foto** in the photo **auf dem Land** in the country **auf der Eggbuckland-Schule** at Eggbuckland [æt], [ət] **auf der Straße** in the street **auf dieser Schule** at this school **auf Englisch** in English **aufs Land** to the country [tuː], [tə] **Auf Wiedersehen.** Goodbye. [ɡʊdˈbaɪ]
aufführen act [ækt]

Aufführung performance [pə'fɔːməns]; show [ʃəʊ]
Aufgabe exercise ['eksəsaɪz]
aufgeben give up [gɪv 'ʌp]
aufgehen *(sich öffnen)* open ['əʊpən]
aufgeregt *(gespannt)* excited [ɪk'saɪtɪd]; *(nervös)* nervous ['nɜːvəs]
aufhängen put up [pʊt 'ʌp]
aufhören (mit) give up [gɪv 'ʌp]; stop [stɒp]
aufmachen open ['əʊpən]
aufpassen auf look after [lʊk 'ɑːftə]
aufräumen tidy ['taɪdi]
aufregend exciting [ɪk'saɪtɪŋ]
Aufseher/in *(in einem Nationalpark)* ranger ['reɪndʒə]
aufsetzen: etwas aufsetzen *(Hut, Brille)* put sth. on [pʊt 'ɒn]
aufstehen *(aus dem Bett)* get up [get 'ʌp]; *(sich hinstellen)* stand up [stænd 'ʌp]
Auge eye [aɪ]
August August ['ɔːgəst]
aus from [frɒm] **aus ... (heraus/hinaus)** out of ... ['aʊt əv]
Ausdruck phrase [freɪz]
Ausflug trip [trɪp]; *(Tagesausflug)* day out [deɪ 'aʊt] **einen Ausflug machen** do a trip; go on a trip
ausfüllen fill in [fɪl 'ɪn]
ausgehen go out [gəʊ 'aʊt]
ausleihen: sich etwas ausleihen borrow sth. ['bɒrəʊ]
ausmachen *(Termin)* arrange [ə'reɪndʒ] **etwas ausmachen** *(bewirken)* make a difference ['dɪfrəns] **Was macht ein perfektes Wochenende aus?** What makes a perfect weekend?
ausprobieren try [traɪ]
ausrichten: etwas ausrichten *(Nachricht)* take a message ['mesɪdʒ]
ausruhen: sich ausruhen chill [tʃɪl]
Ausrüstung equipment [ɪ'kwɪpmənt]
aussehen look **Wie sieht es (er sie) aus?** What's it like? [laɪk]
außerhalb (von) outside [aʊt'saɪd]
Ausstattung equipment [ɪ'kwɪpmənt]
aussteigen aus einem Bus get off a bus [get 'ɒf]
aussuchen pick [pɪk]
austauschen share [ʃeə]

austragen: Zeitungen austragen do a paper round ['peɪpə raʊnd]
auswählen pick [pɪk]
Auto car [kɑː]
Autokennzeichen car number ['kɑː nʌmbə]
Autor/in writer ['raɪtə]

B

Baby baby ['beɪbi]
Babysitter babysitter ['beɪbɪsɪtə]
Bad(ezimmer) bathroom ['bɑːθruːm]
Badeanzug swimsuit ['swɪmsuːt]
Badehose swimming trunks *(pl)* ['swɪmɪŋ trʌŋks]
Badminton badminton ['bædmɪntən]
Bahnhof (train) station ['treɪn steɪʃn]
Bahnsteig platform ['plætfɔːm]
bald soon [suːn]
Ball ball [bɔːl]
Banane banana [bə'nɑːnə]
Band *(Musikgruppe)* band [bænd]
Bank *(Geldinstitut)* bank [bæŋk]
Bär bear [beə]
Baseball baseball ['beɪsbɔːl]
Basketball basketball ['bɑːskɪtbɔːl]
Bauer, Bäuerin farmer ['fɑːmə]
Bauernhof farm [fɑːm]
Baum tree [triː]
Baumwolle cotton ['kɒtn]
bayerisch; Bayer/in Bavarian [bə'veərɪən]
Bayern Bavaria [bə'veərɪə]
beantworten answer ['ɑːnsə]
Beat *(Musik)* beat [biːt]
Bedient euch! *(Greift zu!)* Help yourselves. [jɔː'selvz]
beenden finish ['fɪnɪʃ]
beginnen begin [bɪ'gɪn]
begrüßen: jn. begrüßen (in) welcome sb. (to) ['welkəm]
behaart hairy ['heəri]
behalten keep [kiːp]
bei with [wɪð] **bei der Arbeit** at work [æt], [ət] **bei Ellie daheim/zu Hause** at Ellie's house **bei MARTINS** at MARTINS
Beifallsruf cheer [tʃɪə]
Bein leg [leg]
beinahe nearly ['nɪəli]
Beispiel example [ɪg'zɑːmpl] **zum Beispiel** for example
beitreten *(einem Klub)* join [dʒɔɪn]
bekommen get [get]
belebt busy ['bɪzi]

beliebt popular ['pɒpjələ]
Belohnung reward [rɪ'wɔːd]
benutzen use [juːz]
beobachten watch [wɒtʃ]
bequem comfortable ['kʌmftəbl]
Berg mountain ['maʊntən]
Bericht report [rɪ'pɔːt]
berichten (von/aus) report (from) [rɪ'pɔːt]
berichtigen correct [kə'rekt]
berühmt (für, wegen) famous (for) ['feɪməs]
beschäftigt sein be busy ['bɪzi]
Beschäftigung activity [æk'tɪvəti]
beschließen (etwas zu tun) decide (to do sth.) [dɪ'saɪd]
beschreiben describe [dɪ'skraɪb] **jm. den Weg beschreiben** tell sb. the way [tel]
beschweren: sich beschweren (über) complain (about/of) [kəm'pleɪn]
besondere(r, s) special ['speʃl] **Was ist das Besondere an ihm?** What's special about him?
besorgen: (sich) etwas besorgen get sth. [get]
besser better ['betə] **besser abschneiden** do better
beste(r, s); am besten best [best]
Besuch visit ['vɪzɪt]
besuchen visit ['vɪzɪt]
Besucher/in visitor ['vɪzɪtə]
Betrieb *(Geschäft)* business ['bɪznəs] **einen Betrieb gründen/eröffnen** start a business
Bett bed [bed] **ins Bett gehen** go to bed
bevor before [bɪ'fɔː]
bewirken: etwas bewirken make a difference ['dɪfrəns]
bewölkt cloudy ['klaʊdi]
bezahlen pay [peɪ]
Bikini bikini [bɪ'kiːni]
Bild picture ['pɪktʃə]
billig *(preiswert)* cheap [tʃiːp]
Binnensee lake [leɪk]
bis *(zeitlich)* until [ən'tɪl] **Bis dann.** See you. [siː juː] **von Montag bis Freitag** from Monday to Friday [tuː], [tə]
bisschen: ein bisschen a bit [bɪt]; a little [ə 'lɪtl]
bitte *(in Fragen und Aufforderungen)* please [pliːz] **Bitte schön. / Hier, bitte.** Here you are. [hɪə ju 'ɑː] **Bitte, gern geschehen.** *(Nichts zu danken.)* You're welcome. ['welkʌm]

DICTIONARY

German – English

blau blue [bluː]
bleiben stay [steɪ]
Bleistift pencil [ˈpensl]
Bleistiftanspitzer pencil sharpener [ˈpensl ʃɑːpnə]
Blick look [lʊk]
blöd silly [ˈsɪli]; stupid [ˈstjuːpɪd]
Blog blog [blɒg]
bloß just [dʒʌst]; (nur) only [ˈəʊnli]
Blues (Musikrichtung) blues [bluːz]
Bonbon sweet [swiːt]
Bonus- bonus [ˈbəʊnəs]
Boot boat [bəʊt]
borgen: sich etwas borgen borrow sth. [ˈbɒrəʊ]
Bowling spielen gehen go bowling [ˈbəʊlɪŋ]
Box box [bɒks]
Brathähnchen chicken [ˈtʃɪkɪn]
brauchen need [niːd]
braun brown [braʊn]
brechen break [breɪk]
Brief letter [ˈletə]
Brieffreund/in penfriend [ˈpenfrend]
Brille glasses (pl) [ˈglɑːsɪz]
bringen bring [brɪŋ]; take [teɪk]
 jn. dazu bringen, etwas zu tun make sb. do sth.
britisch British [ˈbrɪtɪʃ]
Broschüre brochure [ˈbrəʊʃə]
Brot bread [bred]
Brücke bridge [brɪdʒ]
Bruder brother [ˈbrʌðə]
Bub boy [bɔɪ]
Buch book [bʊk]
buchen book [bʊk]
Buchladen bookshop [ˈbʊkʃɒp]
Büchse can [kæn]
Buchseite page [peɪdʒ]
buchstabieren spell [spel]
Bundesstaat state [steɪt]
bunt colourful [ˈkʌləfl]
Burg castle [ˈkɑːsl]
Bürgerrechte civil rights (pl) [sɪvl ˈraɪts]
Büro office [ˈɒfɪs]
Bus bus [bʌs] **im Bus** on the bus
Busch bush [bʊʃ]
Bushaltestelle bus stop [ˈbʌs stɒp]
Butter butter [ˈbʌtə]

C

Café cafe [ˈkæfeɪ]
Camping camping [ˈkæmpɪŋ]
Campingplatz campsite [ˈkæmpsaɪt]
CD CD [siːˈdiː]
CD-Spieler CD player [siːˈdiː pleɪə]
Chat chat [tʃæt]
chatten (mit) chat (with) [tʃæt]
chillen chill [tʃɪl]
China China [ˈtʃaɪnə]
Chips crisps [krɪsps]; (potato) chips (AE) [pəˈteɪtəʊ tʃɪps]
clever smart [smɑːt]
Comedyshow comedy [ˈkɒmədi]
Comic cartoon [kɑːˈtuːn]
Comic(heft) comic [ˈkɒmɪk]
Computer computer [kəmˈpjuːtə]
cool cool [kuːl]
Cupcake (kleiner runder Kuchen) cupcake [ˈkʌpkeɪk]

D

da (dort) there [ðeə] **Ist da Herr Taylor?** (am Telefon) Is that Mr Taylor?
daheim: bei Ellie daheim at Ellie's house
dahin there [ðeə]
Damen: Sehr geehrte Damen und Herren Dear Sir/Madam [sɜː], [ˈmædəm]
danach: Mir ist nicht danach. I don't feel like it.
Dänemark Denmark [ˈdenmɑːk]
Dank: Vielen Dank. Thanks very much.
danke thanks [θæŋks] **danke (schön)** thank you [ˈθæŋk juː]
danken: Nichts zu danken. (Gern geschehen.) You're welcome. [ˈwelkʌm]
dann then [ðen]
darstellende Kunst drama [ˈdrɑːmə]
das (da) that [ðæt] **Das ist ...** This is ... [ˈðɪs ɪz]
das (Artikel) the [ðə]
das (Relativpronomen) that [ðæt]; which [wɪtʃ] **ein Ding, das ...** a thing that ...
dass that [ðæt]
dasselbe (wie) the same (as) [seɪm]
Datum date [deɪt]
dein/e (vor Nomen) your [jɔː]
deine/r; deins yours [jɔːz]
denken think [θɪŋk] **denken an** think of **denken über** think about **daran denken** remember [rɪˈmembə] **Das denke ich nicht.** I don't think so. [səʊ] **Ich denke ja.** I think so. **Was denkst/meinst du?** What do you think?
der (Artikel) the [ðə]
der (Relativpronomen) that [ðæt]; which [wɪtʃ]; (Person) who [huː]
deswegen that's why [ˈðæts waɪ]
Detektiv/in detective [dɪˈtektɪv]
deuten (auf) point (at/to) [pɔɪnt]
deutlich clear [klɪə]; (Adv.) clearly [ˈklɪəli]
Deutsch; deutsch German [ˈdʒɜːmən]
Deutsche/r German [ˈdʒɜːmən]
Deutschland Germany [ˈdʒɜːməni]
Dezember December [dɪˈsembə]
dich you [juː] **dich selbst** yourself [jɔːˈself], [jəˈself]
die (Artikel) the [ðə]
die (Relativpronomen) that [ðæt]; which [wɪtʃ]; (Person) who [huː]
Dienstag Tuesday [ˈtjuːzdeɪ], [ˈtjuːzdi]
diese(r, s) this [ðɪs] **diese Kinder (hier)** these kids [ðiːz]; **Dies ist ...** This is ...
Ding thing [θɪŋ]
Dinosaurier dinosaur [ˈdaɪnəsɔː]
dir you [juː] **dir selbst** yourself [jɔːˈself], [jəˈself]
direkt direct [dəˈrekt]
DJ (Discjockey) DJ [ˈdiː dʒeɪ]
Doktor/in doctor [ˈdɒktə]
Dollar dollar ($) [ˈdɒlə]
Donnerstag Thursday [ˈθɜːzdeɪ], [ˈθɜːzdi]
doppelt, Doppel- double [ˈdʌbl]
Doppelzimmer double room [dʌbl ˈruːm]
Dorf village [ˈvɪlɪdʒ]
dort there [ðeə] **die (CDs) dort** those (CDs) [ðəʊz]
dorthin there [ðeə]
Dose can [kæn]
Drachenfliegen hang-gliding [ˈhæŋ glaɪdɪŋ]
draußen; nach draußen outside [aʊtˈsaɪd]
drei three [θriː]; **3-D** 3-D [θriː ˈdiː]
drinnen; nach drinnen inside [ɪnˈsaɪd]
dritte(r, s) third [θɜːd]
Drittel third [θɜːd]
Droge drug [drʌg]
drüben: da drüben over there [əʊvə ˈðeə] **hier drüben** over here [əʊvə ˈhɪə]
du you [juː] **du bist** you're (= you are) [jʊə], [ju ˈɑː] **du selbst** yourself [jɔːˈself], [jəˈself]
Dudelsack bagpipes (pl) [ˈbægpaɪps]

dumm silly ['sɪli]; stupid ['stjuːpɪd]
dunkel dark [dɑːk]
durch through [θruː]
Durchsage announcement [ə'naʊnsmənt]
dürfen: etwas tun dürfen be allowed to do sth. [ə'laʊd] **nicht tun dürfen** mustn't do ['mʌsnt]
Dusche shower ['ʃaʊə]
DVD DVD [diːviː'diː]

E

E-Book-Reader e-reader ['iː riːdə]
echt real [rɪəl]
eifersüchtig (auf) jealous (of) ['dʒeləs]
eigene(r, s): seine eigene Mannschaft its own team [əʊn]
ein/e a [ə], (vor Vokalen) an [ən]
Einband (Buch) cover ['kʌvə]
einfach just [dʒʌst]; (nicht schwierig) easy ['iːzi]
einfangen catch [kætʃ]
einhundert a hundred, one hundred ['hʌndrəd]
einige a few [ə 'fjuː]; some [sʌm], [səm]
Einkäufe erledigen be at the shops [ʃɒps]
einkaufen gehen go shopping ['ʃɒpɪŋ]
Einkaufsliste shopping list ['ʃɒpɪŋ lɪst]
Einkaufszentrum shopping centre ['ʃɒpɪŋ sentə]
einladen invite [ɪn'vaɪt]
Einladung (zu, nach) invitation (to) [ɪnvɪ'teɪʃn]
Einleitung introduction [ɪntrə'dʌkʃn]
einmal once [wʌns]
einpacken pack [pæk]
eins one [wʌn]
einsam lonely ['ləʊnli]
einsetzen fill in [fɪl 'ɪn]; put in [pʊt 'ɪn]
einst once [wʌns]
einsteigen in einen Bus get on a bus [get 'ɒn]
Eintrittskarte ticket ['tɪkɪt]
einzeln, Einzel- single ['sɪŋgl]
Einzelzimmer single room [sɪŋgl 'ruːm]
einzige(r, s) only ['əʊnli]
Eis (Speiseeis) ice cream [aɪs 'kriːm]
Eisenbahn train [treɪn]
Eishockey ice hockey ['aɪs hɒki]

electronic elektronisch [ɪlek'trɒnɪk]
Elefant elephant ['elɪfənt]
elf eleven [ɪ'levən]
Eltern parents ['peərənts]
E-Mail email ['iːmeɪl]
Empfang (auch beim Telefon) reception [rɪ'sepʃn]
Ende end [end]; (Text, Geschichte) ending ['endɪŋ] **am Ende (von ...)** at the end (of ...) **am oberen Ende (von)** at the top (of) [tɒp]
enden finish ['fɪnɪʃ]
Endung ending ['endɪŋ]
Energie energy ['enədʒi]
eng narrow ['nærəʊ]
England England ['ɪŋglənd]
Englisch; englisch English ['ɪŋglɪʃ]
Ente duck [dʌk]
entlang: die Straße entlang along the street [ə'lɒŋ]
entscheiden: (sich) entscheiden (etwas zu tun) decide (to do sth.) [dɪ'saɪd]
Entschuldigung.: (Darf ich mal stören?) Excuse me, ... [ɪks'kjuːz miː]; (Tut mir leid.) Sorry. / I'm sorry. ['sɒri]
entspannen: sich entspannen relax [rɪ'læks]
enttäuscht disappointed (with sb./sth.) [dɪsə'pɔɪntɪd]
er he [hiː]; (bei Dingen und Tieren) it [ɪt] **er/sich selbst** himself [hɪm'self] **er ist** he's (= he is)
Erdbeben earthquake ['ɜːθkweɪk]
Erde (Erdboden) ground [graʊnd]
Erdkunde geography [dʒi'ɒgrəfi]
erfolgreich successful [sək'sesfl] **erfolgreich sein** do well [wel]
Erholungspark entertainment park [entə'teɪnmənt pɑːk]
erinnern: sich erinnern an remember [rɪ'membə]
erkundigen: sich bei jm. nach etwas erkundigen ask sb. about sth. [ɑːsk]
erlaubt sein be allowed [ə'laʊd]
erst only ['əʊnli] **erst, wenn sie 13 sind** not (...) until they're 13 [ən'tɪl]
erstaunlich amazing [ə'meɪzɪŋ]
erste(r, s) first (= 1st) [fɜːst]
Erste Hilfe first aid [fɜːst 'eɪd]
Erste-Hilfe-Set first-aid kit [fɜːst 'eɪd kɪt]
Erwachsene/r adult ['ædʌlt]
erwarten expect [ɪk'spekt]

erwischen (Bus/Zug/...) catch [kætʃ]
erzählen tell [tel]
erzielen: einen Punkt / ein Tor erzielen score [skɔː]
es it [ɪt] **es/sich selbst** itself [ɪt'self] **es ist** it's (= it is)
Esel donkey ['dɒŋki]
Essen food [fuːd]; (Mahlzeit) meal [miːl]
essen eat [iːt]
etwas something ['sʌmθɪŋ]; (ein bisschen) some [sʌm], [səm] **Sonst noch etwas?** Anything else? [eniθɪŋ 'els]
euch you [juː] **euch selbst** yourselves [jɔː'selvz]
euer/eure (vor Nomen) your [jɔː]
eure/r, eures yours [jɔːz]
Europa Europe ['jʊərəp]
europäisch; Europäer/in European [jʊərə'piːən]
existieren exist [ɪg'zɪst]

F

Fabrik factory ['fæktri]
Fähigkeit skill [skɪl]
Fahne flag [flæg]
Fähre ferry ['feri]
fahren go [gəʊ]; (mit dem Auto) drive [draɪv]; (reisen) travel ['trævl] **mit dem Bus fahren** go by bus **Rad fahren** cycle ['saɪkl]; ride a bike [raɪd]
Fahrer/in driver ['draɪvə]
Fahrkarte ticket ['tɪkɪt] **einfache Fahrkarte** (nur Hinfahrt) single (ticket) ['sɪŋgl]
Fahrrad bike [baɪk]
Fahrt trip [trɪp]
fallen fall [fɔːl]
falls if [ɪf]
falsch wrong [rɒŋ]; false [fɔːls] **das ist falsch** that's wrong
Familie family ['fæməli]
familienfreundlich family-friendly [fæməli 'frendli]
Familienstammbaum family tree [fæməli 'triː]
Fan fan [fæn]
fangen catch [kætʃ]
fantastisch fantastic [fæn'tæstɪk]; like a million dollars [ə mɪljən 'dɒləz]
Farbe colour ['kʌlə]
farbenfroh colourful ['kʌləfl]
fast nearly ['nɪəli]
Februar February ['februəri]

DICTIONARY

German – English

Federball badminton ['bædmɪntən]
Federmäppchen pencil case ['pensl keɪs]
fehlen be missing ['mɪsɪŋ] **die fehlenden Taschen** the missing bags
feiern celebrate ['selɪbreɪt] **eine Party feiern** have a party
Feiertag: (gesetzlicher) Feiertag public holiday [pʌblɪk 'hɒlədeɪ]
Feld field [fiːld] **auf dem Feld** in the field
Fenster window ['wɪndəʊ]
Ferien holidays ['hɒlədeɪz]
Fernsehen (Tätigkeit) watching TV [wɒtʃɪŋ tiː'viː]
Fernseher TV [tiː'viː]
Fernsehsendung programme ['prəʊɡræm]
Fertigkeit skill [skɪl]
Fest festival ['festɪvl]
Feuer fire ['faɪə]; (Freudenfeuer) bonfire ['bɒnfaɪə]
Feuerwehrmann/-frau firefighter ['faɪəfaɪtə]
Feuerwerk fireworks (pl) ['faɪəwɜːks]
Feuerwerkskörper firework ['faɪəwɜːk]
Fieber temperature ['temprətʃə] **Ich habe Fieber.** I have a temperature.
fies mean [miːn]
Film film [fɪlm]
filmen film [fɪlm]
Filmstar film star ['fɪlm stɑː]
finden find [faɪnd] **Freunde finden** make friends [meɪk]
Fisch fish, pl fish [fɪʃ]
fit fit [fɪt] **nicht fit** unfit [ʌn'fɪt]
Fitness fitness ['fɪtnəs]
Flagge flag [flæɡ]
Flasche bottle ['bɒtl]
Flaschenpost message in a bottle [mesɪdʒ ɪn ə 'bɒtl]
Fleisch meat [miːt]
Fliege (Krawatte) bow tie [bəʊ 'taɪ]
Flughafen airport ['eəpɔːt]
Flugzeug plane [pleɪn]
Fluss river ['rɪvə]
Föhn hairdryer ['heədraɪə]
formell formal ['fɔːml]
Formular form [fɔːm]
fort away [ə'weɪ]
fortbewegen: sich fortbewegen travel ['trævl]

Foto photo ['fəʊtəʊ] **auf dem Foto** in the photo **ein Foto machen** take a photo
Fotoapparat camera ['kæmərə]
Frage (an jn.) question (to sb.) ['kwestʃən]
Fragebogen questionnaire [kwestʃə'neə]
fragen ask [ɑːsk] **jn. nach dem Weg fragen** ask sb. the way **jn. nach etwas fragen** ask sb. about sth.
Französisch; französisch French [frentʃ]
Frau woman, pl women ['wʊmən], ['wɪmɪn]; (allgemeine Anrede f. Frauen) Ms ... [mɪz], [məz]; (Anrede f. verheiratete Frauen) Mrs ... ['mɪsɪz]
frei free [friː]
Freitag Friday ['fraɪdeɪ], ['fraɪdi]
freitagmorgens, am Freitagmorgen on Friday morning(s)
fressen eat [iːt]
Freund/in friend [frend]; (feste Freundin) girlfriend ['ɡɜːlfrend]; (fester Freund) boyfriend ['bɔɪfrend]
freundlich friendly ['frendli]; kind [kaɪnd] **Mit freundlichen Grüßen** (Briefschluss) Yours sincerely [jɔːz sɪn'sɪəli]
Frisör/in hairdresser ['heədresə]
froh happy ['hæpi] **Ich bin froh.** I'm glad. [ɡlæd]
Frucht; Früchte fruit [fruːt]
früh early ['ɜːli]
Frühstück breakfast ['brekfəst]
frühstücken have breakfast ['brekfəst]
Frühstückspension bed and breakfast (B&B)
Fuchs fox [fɒks]
fühlen; sich fühlen feel [fiːl]
Führerschein driving licence ['draɪvɪŋ laɪsns]
füllen fill [fɪl]
Füller pen [pen]
fünf five [faɪv]
funktionieren work [wɜːk]
für for [fɔː], [fə]
Fußball football ['fʊtbɔːl]; **Fußballspielen** playing football
Fußballspieler/in footballer ['fʊtbɔːlə]
Fußgänger/in walker ['wɔːkə]
Futter food [fuːd]
füttern feed [fiːd]

G

Galerie gallery ['ɡæləri]
Gang (Bande) gang [ɡæŋ]
ganz: den ganzen Tag (lang) all day [ɔːl 'deɪ]
Garage garage ['ɡærɑːʒ]
Garagenflohmarkt (privater Flohmarkt) garage sale ['ɡærɑːʒ seɪl]
Garten garden ['ɡɑːdn]
Gast guest [ɡest]; visitor ['vɪzɪtə]
Gebäude building ['bɪldɪŋ]
geben give [ɡɪv] **es gibt** there are ... ['ðeər ɑː]; there's [ðeəz]
geboren: sie wurden geboren they were born [bɔːn]
gebrochen (kaputt) broken ['brəʊkən]
Geburt birth [bɜːθ]
Geburtsdatum date of birth [deɪt əv 'bɜːθ]
Geburtsort place of birth [pleɪs əv 'bɜːθ]
Geburtstag birthday ['bɜːθdeɪ] **Herzlichen Glückwunsch zum Geburtstag!** Happy birthday! **Sie hat Geburtstag.** It's her birthday. **Wann hast du Geburtstag?** When's (= when is) your birthday?
Gedicht poem ['pəʊɪm]
geehrte: Sehr geehrte Damen und Herren Dear Sir/Madam [sɜː], ['mædəm]
gefährlich dangerous ['deɪndʒərəs]
gegen against [ə'ɡenst]
Gegend neighbourhood ['neɪbəhʊd]
Gegenteil opposite ['ɒpəzɪt]
gehen go [ɡəʊ] **Wie geht's? / Wie geht es dir/euch?** How are you? **(zu Fuß) gehen** walk [wɔːk]
geizig mean [miːn] **die geizigsten Eltern** the meanest parents ['miːnəst]
gelangen (nach) get (to) [ɡet]
gelb yellow ['jeləʊ]
Geld money ['mʌni] **Geld verdienen** make money
gelegentlich occasionally [ə'keɪʒənəli]
gemein mean [miːn]
Gemüse vegetables (pl) ['vedʒtəblz]
gemütlich comfortable ['kʌmftəbl]
genau: genau wie Berry just like Berry ['dʒʌst laɪk] **ganz genau zuhören** listen carefully ['keəfəli]
genervt sein feel fed up [fed 'ʌp]
genial brilliant ['brɪljənt]
genießen enjoy [ɪn'dʒɔɪ]

genug enough [ɪ'nʌf]
geöffnet open ['əʊpən]
Geografie geography [dʒɪ'ɒgrəfi]
geradeaus: Geh geradeaus (weiter). Go straight on. [streɪt]
Geräusch sound [saʊnd]; *(unangenehm, laut)* noise [nɔɪz]
gern: gern(e) etwas tun be happy to do sth. ['hæpi] **ich hätte gern** I'd like (= I would like) [laɪk] **ich würde gern mitmachen** I'd like to (= I would like to) join **Ich würde sehr gern kommen.** I'd love to come. [lʌv]
Geschäft shop [ʃɒp]; *(Betrieb)* business ['bɪznəs]; *(Vereinbarung)* deal [diːl]; *(verkauft gespendete Waren für wohltätige Zwecke)* charity shop ['tʃærəti ʃɒp] **ein Geschäft abschließen/vereinbaren** make a deal **ein Geschäft aufmachen** start a business
Geschäftsführer/in manager ['mænɪdʒə]
geschehen happen ['hæpən] **Bitte, gern geschehen.** You're welcome. ['welkʌm]
Geschenk present ['preznt]
Geschichte *(Erzählung)* story ['stɔːri]; *(vergangene Zeiten)* history ['hɪstri]
Geschirrspülmaschine dishwasher ['dɪʃwɒʃə]
geschlossen sein be closed [kləʊzd]
gespannt excited [ɪk'saɪtɪd]
Gespenst ghost [gəʊst]
Gespräch talk [tɔːk]; *(Unterhaltung)* chat [tʃæt]
gestern yesterday ['jestədeɪ]
gesund healthy ['helθi]
Gesundheit health [helθ]
Getränk drink [drɪŋk]
Gewalt(tätigkeit) violence ['vaɪələns]
gewalttätig violent ['vaɪələnt]
Gewinn *(Profit)* profit ['prɒfɪt]
gewinnen win [wɪn]
Gewinner/in winner ['wɪnə]
Gitarre guitar [gɪ'tɑː]
Glas glass [glɑːs]
glauben think [θɪŋk] **Das glaube ich nicht.** I don't think so. [səʊ] **Du wirst es kaum glauben!** Wait for this. *(infml)* ['weɪt] **Ich glaube ja.** I think so.
gleich the same [seɪm] **das gleiche (wie)** the same (as)

Glocke bell [bel]
Glück: du hast Glück you're lucky ['lʌki]
glücklich happy ['hæpi] **Du Glückliche/r!** Lucky you! ['lʌki]
Glückwunsch: Herzlichen Glückwunsch zum Geburtstag! Happy birthday! [hæpi 'bɜːθdeɪ]
GPS GPS [dʒi: piː 'es]
Grad degree [dɪ'griː]
Gras grass [grɑːs]
grau grey [greɪ]
Grieche/Griechin Greek [griːk]
griechisch; Griechisch Greek [griːk]
groß big [bɪg]; *(Person)* tall [tɔːl]
großartig great [greɪt]
Großbritannien (Great) Britain ['brɪtn]
Größe size [saɪz] **Welche Größe hast du?** What size do you take?
Großeltern grandparents ['grænpeərənts]
Großmutter grandmother ['grænmʌðə]
Großstadt city ['sɪti]
Großvater grandfather ['grænfɑːðə]
grün green [griːn]
Gruppe group [gruːp]
gruselig scary ['skeəri]
Grüße: Mit besten Grüßen *(Briefschluss)* All the best [ɔːl ðə 'best] **Mit freundlichen Grüßen** Yours sincerely [jɔːz sɪn'sɪəli] **Viele Grüße, ...** Best wishes [best 'wɪʃɪz]
gut good [gʊd]; fine [faɪn]; *(Adverb)* well [wel] **gut abschneiden** do well **Gute Nacht.** Good night. **Guten Morgen.** Good morning. **Gut gemacht!** Well done. [wel 'dʌn] **gut sein in etwas** be good at sth. **Alles Gute** *(Briefschluss)* All the best [ɔːl ðə 'best] **Es geht ihr nicht gut.** She isn't feeling well. **Es geht mir gut.** I'm fine.; I'm OK. **es gut machen** do well **Hört sich gut an.** Sounds fun. [saʊndz 'fʌn]
Gymnastik gymnastics [dʒɪm'næstɪks]

H

Haar(e) hair [heə]
haarig hairy ['heəri]
Haartrockner hairdryer ['heədraɪə]
haben have [hæv]
Hafen harbour ['hɑːbə]

Hähnchen chicken ['tʃɪkɪn]
halbe(r, s), Halb- half [hɑːf] **zum halben Preis** half price [hɑːf 'praɪs]
Hälfte half [hɑːf]
Hallo. Hi! [haɪ]; Hello. [hə'ləʊ]
Hals throat [θrəʊt] **Mir tut der Hals weh.** I have a sore throat. [sɔː 'θrəʊt]
Halsschmerzen a sore throat [sɔː 'θrəʊt]
halten keep [kiːp] **halten von** think of/about [θɪŋk] **Halt den Mund!** Shut up! [ʃʌt 'ʌp]
Hamburger *(Frikadelle)* burger ['bɜːgə]
Hamster hamster ['hæmstə]
Hand hand [hænd]
Handschuh glove [glʌv]
Handtuch towel ['taʊəl]
Handy mobile (phone) [məʊbaɪl 'fəʊn]
Happy End *(glückliches Ende)* happy ending [hæpi 'endɪŋ]
hart hard [hɑːd] **hart arbeiten** work hard
hässlich ugly ['ʌgli]
Hauptstadt capital (city) ['kæpɪtl]
Haus house [haʊs] **ich bin zu Hause** I'm home [həʊm] **nach Hause** home
Hausarbeiten chores [tʃɔːz] **Hausarbeiten erledigen** *(Haushalt)* do chores
Hausaufgabe/n homework ['həʊmwɜːk] **ich mache (meine) Hausaufgaben** I do my homework
Hausboot houseboat ['haʊsbəʊt]
Häuschen cottage ['kɒtɪdʒ]
Haustier pet [pet]
Heftseite page [peɪdʒ]
Heim *(Zuhause)* home [həʊm]
heiß hot [hɒt]
heißen be called [kɔːld] **Wie heißt du?** What's your name? [wɒts jɔː 'neɪm]
helfen help [help]
Helfer/in helper ['helpə]; assistant [ə'sɪstənt]
Helm helmet ['helmɪt]
Hemd shirt [ʃɜːt]
heraus out [aʊt]
herausfinden find out [faɪnd 'aʊt]
herauskommen get out [get 'aʊt]
herein in [ɪn]
hereinkommen come in [kʌm 'ɪn]
Herr Lee Mr Lee ['mɪstə]

DICTIONARY

German – English

Herren: Sehr geehrte Damen und Herren Dear Sir/Madam [sɜː], ['mædəm]
herrisch bossy ['bɒsi]
herstellen make [meɪk]
herüber: hier herüber over here [əʊvə 'hɪə]
herumlaufen run around [ə'raʊnd]
herunter von ... off ... [ɒf]
herunterfallen von etwas *(Fahrrad, Pferd)* fall off sth. [fɔːl ɒf]
Herz heart [hɑːt]
Herzlichen Glückwunsch zum Geburtstag! Happy birthday! [hæpi 'bɜːθdeɪ]
heute today [tə'deɪ] **heute Morgen/Nachmittag/Abend** this morning/afternoon/evening
hier here [hɪə] **Hier, bitte.** Here you are. **Hier spricht Rob Blake.** *(am Telefon)* This is Rob Blake.
hierher here [hɪə]
Hilfe help [help]
Himmel sky [skaɪ]
hinauf up [ʌp]
hinaus out [aʊt]
hinausgehen go out [gəʊ 'aʊt]
hinein in [ɪn]
hinfallen fall [fɔːl]
hinsetzen: sich hinsetzen sit [sɪt]
hinter behind [bɪ'haɪnd]
hinüber: da hinüber over there [əʊvə 'ðeə]
hinunter: hinunter von ... off ... [ɒf] **den Hügel hinunter** down the hill [daʊn]
Hobby hobby ['hɒbi]
hoch high [haɪ]; *(z.B. große Gebäude)* tall [tɔːl]; *(nach oben)* up [ʌp]
Hockey hockey ['hɒki]
hoffen hope [həʊp]
holen: (sich) etwas holen get sth. [get]
Holz wood [wʊd]
horchen auf listen for ['lɪsn fə]
hören hear [hɪə]
Hose trousers *(pl)* ['traʊzəz]
Hot Dog *(heißes Würstchen in einem Brötchen)* hot dog ['hɒt dɒg]
Hotel hotel [həʊ'tel]
Hügel hill [hɪl]
hügelig hilly ['hɪli]
Huhn chicken ['tʃɪkɪn]
Hülle *(DVD, CD)* cover ['kʌvə]
Hund dog [dɒg]
Hundeheim dogs' home [dɒgz 'həʊm]
hundert a hundred, one hundred ['hʌndrəd]
Hunger haben be hungry ['hʌŋgri]
Hurra(geschrei) cheer [tʃɪə]
Hut hat [hæt]
Hütte cottage ['kɒtɪdʒ]

I

ich I [aɪ] **Ich auch.** Me too. **ich bin** I'm (= I am) **Ich bin's.** It's me. **ich (selbst)** myself [maɪ'self]
Idee idea [aɪ'dɪə]
Idiot/in idiot ['ɪdiət]
ihm him [hɪm]
ihn him [hɪm]
Ihnen *(höfliche Anrede)* you [juː]
ihnen them [ðem], [ðəm]
ihr *(Plural von „du")* you [juː] **ihr seid** you're (= you are) [jʊə], [juˈɑː] **ihr selbst** yourselves [jɔː'selvz]
ihr *(weibliche Person)* her [hɜː] **mit ihr** with her
Ihr/e *(vor Nomen; besitzanzeigend)* your [jɔː]
ihr/e *(vor Nomen; besitzanzeigend): (zu „she")* her [hɜː]; *(zu „they")* their [ðeə]
ihrer, ihre, ihrs: *(zu „she")* hers [hɜːz]; *(zu „they")* theirs [ðeəz]
im: im Bus on the bus [ɒn] **im Kino** at the cinema [æt], [ət]
Imbissstube diner *(AE)* ['daɪnə]
immer always ['ɔːlweɪz]
immer noch still [stɪl]
in in [ɪn] **in der Nacht** at night [æt], [ət] **in der Schule** at school **in der Stadt** in town **in einem Restaurant** at a restaurant **in England** in England **in Papas Wohnung gehen** go to dad's flat [tu], [tə] **ins Klassenzimmer (hinein)** into the classroom ['ɪntu], ['ɪntə] **Warst du schon mal in London?** Have you ever been to London?
Information(en) (über) information (about) [ɪnfə'meɪʃn]
Informations- und Kommunikationstechnologie ICT (information and communication technology) [aɪ siː 'tiː], [ɪnfəmeɪʃn ənd kəmjuːnɪkeɪʃn tek'nɒlədʒi]
Informationsblatt newsletter ['njuːzletə]
informell informal [ɪn'fɔːml]
Ingwer ginger ['dʒɪndʒə]
Inlineskaten gehen go skating ['skeɪtɪŋ]
insbesondere especially [ɪ'speʃəli]
Insel island ['aɪlənd]
Instrument instrument ['ɪnstrəmənt]
interessant interesting ['ɪntrəstɪŋ]
Interesse interest ['ɪntrəst]
interessieren: sich interessieren für be interested in ['ɪntrəstɪd]
interessiert: interessiert sein an be interested in **daran interessiert, etwas zu tun** interested in doing sth. ['ɪntrəstɪd]
Internet internet ['ɪntənet]
Interview interview ['ɪntəvjuː]
irgendjemand: Spricht (irgend)jemand ...? Does anybody speak ...? ['enibɒdi]
irgendwelche: Hast du/Habt ihr irgendwelche Fragen? Do you have any questions? ['eni]
irisch Irish ['aɪrɪʃ]
Irland Ireland ['aɪələnd] **aus Irland** Irish ['aɪrɪʃ]
Italien Italy ['ɪtəli]

J

ja yes [jes]; yeah *(infml)* [jeə]
Jacke coat [kəʊt]; jacket ['dʒækɪt]
Jackett jacket ['dʒækɪt]
Jahr(gang) year [jɪə]
jammern complain [kəm'pleɪn]
Januar January ['dʒænjuəri]
je(mals) ever ['evə]
Jeans jeans *(pl)* [dʒiːnz]
jede(r, s) *(einzelne)* each [iːtʃ]; *(vor Nomen)* every ['evri] **jeder** *(alle)* everybody ['evribɒdi] everyone ['evriwʌn]
jemand somebody ['sʌmbədi]; someone ['sʌmwʌn] **Spricht (irgend)jemand ...?** Does anybody speak ...? ['enibɒdi]
jene (CDs) those (CDs) [ðəʊz]
jetzt now [naʊ]
jeweils: jeweils 50 pence 50 p each [iːtʃ]
Job job [dʒɒb]
Jogging jogging ['dʒɒgɪŋ]
Joghurt yogurt ['jɒgət]
jubeln cheer [tʃɪə]
Judo judo ['dʒuːdəʊ]
Jugendliche/r kid [kɪd]
Juli July [dʒu'laɪ]
jung young [jʌŋ]
Junge boy [bɔɪ]
Juni June [dʒuːn]
Junkfood *(ungesundes Essen)* junk food ['dʒʌŋk fuːd]

K

Kaffee coffee [ˈkɒfi]
Käfig cage [keɪdʒ]
Kakao hot chocolate [hɒt ˈtʃɒklət]
Kalender calendar [ˈkælɪndə]; diary [ˈdaɪəri]
kalt cold [kəʊld]
Kamera camera [ˈkæmərə]
Kaninchen rabbit [ˈræbɪt]
Kantine canteen [kænˈtiːn]
Kanu canoe [kəˈnuː]
kaputt broken [ˈbrəʊkən]
kaputtgehen break [breɪk]
kaputtmachen break [breɪk]
Kapuzenpullover hoodie [ˈhʊdi]
Karotte carrot [ˈkærət]
Karte card [kɑːd]
Kartoffel potato [pəˈteɪtəʊ]
Kartoffelchips crisps [krɪsps]; (potato) chips *(AE)* [pəˈteɪtəʊ tʃɪps]
Käse cheese [tʃiːz]
Kasten box [bɒks]
Katastrophe disaster [dɪˈzɑːstə]
Kategorie category [ˈkætəgəri]
Kätzchen kitten [ˈkɪtn]
Katze cat [kæt] **junge Katze** kitten [ˈkɪtn]
kaufen buy [baɪ] **etwas kaufen (gehen)** shop for sth. [ˈʃɒp fə]
Kaufhaus department store [dɪˈpɑːtmənt stɔː]
Kaufpreis price [praɪs]
kein/e no [nəʊ] **Ich bin kein Junge.** I'm not a boy. [nɒt] **Wir haben keine (Haus-)Tiere.** We don't have any pets. [ˈeni]
Keks biscuit [ˈbɪskɪt]
Kellner waiter [ˈweɪtə]
Kellnerin waitress [ˈweɪtrəs]
kennen know [nəʊ]
kennenlernen meet [miːt] **Schön, dich/euch/Sie kennenzulernen.** Nice to meet you.
Kilometer kilometre (km) [ˈkɪləmiːtə]
Kilt *(Schottenrock)* kilt [kɪlt]
Kind child, *pl* children [tʃaɪld], [ˈtʃɪldrən]; kid [kɪd]
Kino cinema [ˈsɪnəmə]
Kissen cushion [ˈkʊʃn]
Klang sound [saʊnd]
klar clear [klɪə]
Klasse class [klɑːs]
Klassenarbeit test [test]
Klassenlehrer/in class teacher [ˈklɑːs tiːtʃə]
Klassenzimmer classroom [ˈklɑːsruːm]
Klavier piano [piˈænəʊ]
Kleid dress [dres]
Kleiderschrank wardrobe [ˈwɔːdrəʊb]
Kleidung clothes *(pl)* [kləʊðz]
klein small [smɔːl]; *(Person)* short [ʃɔːt]
Klettern *(Sport)* climbing
klettern (auf) climb [klaɪm]
Klingel bell [bel]
klingeln ring [rɪŋ]
Klingelton *(Handy)* ringtone [ˈrɪŋtəʊn]
klingen sound [saʊnd] **Klingt, als ob es Spaß macht.** Sounds fun.
Klub club [klʌb]
klug clever [ˈklevə]
Kneipe pub [pʌb]
kochen cook [kʊk]
kommen come [kʌm] **kommen (nach)** get (to) [get] **Ich würde sehr gern kommen.** I'd love to come. **Komm(t) (schon)!** Come on!
Kommentar comment [ˈkɒment] **einen Kommentar abgeben** make a comment
Komödie comedy [ˈkɒmədi]
König king [kɪŋ]
Königin queen [kwiːn]
Königreich: das Vereinigte Königreich the United Kingdom (UK) [juːnaɪtɪd ˈkɪŋdəm]
können can [kæn], [kən] **nicht können** can't (= cannot) [kɑːnt], [ˈkænɒt] **etwas gut können** be good at sth. [ˈgʊd ət] **wir könnten** we could [kʊd] **sie konnte** she could
Kontrolle check [tʃek]
kontrollieren check [tʃek]
Konzert concert [ˈkɒnsət]
Kopfschmerzen haben have a headache [ˈhedeɪk]
Kopfsprung: einen Kopfsprung machen dive [daɪv]
korrekt correct [kəˈrekt]
korrigieren correct [kəˈrekt]
kosten cost [kɒst] **Es kostet 31 Pfund.** It's £ 31. **Sie kosten 90 Pfund.** They're £ 90. **Was (Wie viel) kosten …?** How much are …? **Was (Wie viel) kostet …?** How much is …?
kostenlos (for) free [friː]
Kram *(Zeug)* stuff [stʌf]
krank ill [ɪl]
Krankenhaus hospital [ˈhɒspɪtl]
Krawatte tie [taɪ]
Krebs *(Tier)* crab [kræb]
Kreuz cross [krɒs]
Kricket *(Mannschaftssportart)* cricket [ˈkrɪkɪt]
kriegen get [get]
Krimiserie crime series [ˈkraɪm sɪəriːz]
Küche kitchen [ˈkɪtʃɪn]
Kuchen cake [keɪk]
Kugelschreiber pen [pen]
Kuh cow [kaʊ]
kühl cool [kuːl]
Kultur culture [ˈkʌltʃə]
kümmern: sich kümmern um look after [lʊk ˈɑːftə]
Kunde, Kundin customer [ˈkʌstəmə]
Kunst art [ɑːt]
Künstler/in artist [ˈɑːtɪst]
Kunstspringer/in diver [ˈdaɪvə]
Kunststoff plastic [ˈplæstɪk]
Kunststück trick [trɪk]
Kunstwerk work of art [wɜːk əv ˈɑːt]
kurz short [ʃɔːt]

L

lächeln; *(das)* **Lächeln** smile [smaɪl]
lachen laugh [lɑːf]
Laden shop [ʃɒp]
Lampe lamp [læmp]; light [laɪt]
Land land [lænd]; country [ˈkʌntri] **auf dem Land** in the country **aufs Land** to the country
landen land [lænd]
Landkarte map [mæp]
Landwirt/in farmer [ˈfɑːmə]
lang; lange long [lɒŋ]
langsam slow [sləʊ]
langweilig boring [ˈbɔːrɪŋ]
Laptop laptop [ˈlæptɒp]
Lärm noise [nɔɪz]
Lasagne lasagne [ləˈzænjə]
lassen let [let] **lass(t) uns** let's (= let us) **Lass(t) uns (mal) sehen.** Let's see.
Laterne lantern [ˈlæntən]
Läufer/in runner [ˈrʌnə]
Laut sound [saʊnd]
laut loud [laʊd]; *(voller Lärm)* noisy [ˈnɔɪzi]
läuten ring [rɪŋ]
Leben life, *pl* lives [laɪf], [laɪvz]
leben live [lɪv]
Lebensmittel food [fuːd]
Lebensstil lifestyle [ˈlaɪfstaɪl]
lecker! yum! [jʌm]
leer empty [ˈempti]

DICTIONARY — German – English

leeren empty ['empti]
legen *(hin-, ablegen)* put [pʊt]
lehren teach [tiːtʃ]
Lehrer/in teacher ['tiːtʃə]
leicht *(einfach)* easy ['iːzi]
leidtun: Tut mir leid. Sorry. / I'm sorry. ['sɒri]
leihen hire ['haɪə] **sich etwas leihen** borrow sth. ['bɒrəʊ]
leise quiet ['kwaɪət]
Leiter/in leader ['liːdə]
lernen learn [lɜːn]
lesen read [riːd] *(das)* **Lesen** reading
Leser/in reader ['riːdə]
letzte(r, s) final ['faɪnl]; last [lɑːst] **letzte Woche** last week
Leute people ['piːpl]; *(als Anrede verwendet)* guys [gaɪz]
Licht light [laɪt]
Liebe/r ... Dear ... [dɪə]
lieben love [lʌv]
lieber: etwas lieber mögen like sth. better ['betə] **etwas lieber mögen als etwas** prefer sth. to sth. [prɪ'fɜː]
Liebling love [lʌv]
Lieblings- favourite ['feɪvərɪt] **Lieblingssache** favourite thing
Lied song [sɒŋ]
Lieferwagen van [væn]
Limonade lemonade [lemə'neɪd]
Lineal ruler ['ruːlə]
Linie line [laɪn]
links; nach links left [left] **auf der linken Seite** on the left
Liste list [lɪst]
live live [laɪv]
locker *(informell)* informal [ɪn'fɔːml]
Löffel spoon [spuːn]
Lokal diner *(AE)* ['daɪnə]
Londoner/in Londoner ['lʌndənə]
los: Na los! Come on! [kʌm 'ɒn]
lustig funny ['fʌni]

M

machen do [duː]; make [meɪk] **Das macht 5 Pfund.** That's £ 5. **ein Foto machen** take a photo [teɪk] **Gut gemacht!** Well done. [wel 'dʌn] **ich mache (meine) Hausaufgaben** I do my homework
Mädchen girl [gɜːl]
Magazin magazine [mægə'ziːn]
mähen *(Rasen)* cut [kʌt]
Mahlzeit meal [miːl] **kleine Mahlzeit** snack [snæk] **warme Mahlzeit** hot meal
Mai May [meɪ]
Make-up make-up ['meɪkʌp]
Mal time [taɪm] **nächstes Mal** next time
Mama mum [mʌm]; *(AE)* mom [mɒm]
Manager/in manager ['mænɪdʒə]
manchmal sometimes ['sʌmtaɪmz]
Mann man, *pl* men [mæn], [men]
Mannschaft team [tiːm]
Mantel coat [kəʊt]
Markt market ['mɑːkɪt]
Marmelade jam [dʒæm]
Marsch march [mɑːtʃ]
marschieren march [mɑːtʃ]
März March [mɑːtʃ]
Maske mask [mɑːsk]
Mathematik maths [mæθs]
Matsch mud [mʌd]
Mauer wall [wɔːl]
Maus mouse [maʊs]
Meer sea [siː] **am Meer** at the seaside ['siːsaɪd]
mehr more [mɔː]
Meile *(ca. 1,6 km)* mile [maɪl]
mein/e *(vor Nomen)* my [maɪ]
meine/r; meins mine [maɪn]
meinen *(denken, glauben)* think [θɪŋk]; *(sagen wollen)* mean [miːn] **Was denkst/meinst du?** What do you think?
meisten: die meisten Leute most people [məʊst]
meistens usually ['juːʒʊəli]
Mensa canteen [kæn'tiːn]
Menschen people ['piːpl]
Messer knife [naɪf]
Meter metre ['miːtə]
mich me [mi] **mich (selbst)** myself [maɪ'self]
mieten hire ['haɪə]
Milch milk [mɪlk]
Milchbrötchen *(leicht süß, oft mit Rosinen)* scone [skɒn]
Milchshake milkshake ['mɪlkʃeɪk]
Million million ['mɪljən]
mindestens at least [ət 'liːst]
Mineralwasser mineral water ['mɪnərəl wɔːtə]
Minute minute ['mɪnɪt]
mir me [mi] **Mir ist nicht danach.** I don't feel like it. **mir (selbst)** myself [maɪ'self]
mit with [wɪð] **mit dem Bus fahren** go by bus [baɪ] **sprechen mit** talk to ['tɔːk tu]
mitbringen bring [brɪŋ]
mitkommen come [kʌm]
Mitleid mit jm. haben be/feel sorry for sb. ['sɒri]
mitmachen (bei) join [dʒɔɪn]; take part (in) [teɪk 'pɑːt]
mitnehmen take [teɪk]
Mittag: (zu) Mittag essen have lunch [lʌntʃ]
Mittagessen lunch [lʌntʃ]
mittags at lunchtime ['lʌntʃtaɪm]
Mittagszeit: zur Mittagszeit at lunchtime ['lʌntʃtaɪm]
Mitte centre ['sentə]; middle ['mɪdl] **in der Mitte** in the middle
Mitteilung message ['mesɪdʒ]
Mitteilungsblatt newsletter ['njuːzletə]
Mittwoch Wednesday ['wenzdeɪ], ['wenzdi]
möchte: ich möchte (...) haben I'd like (= I would like) [laɪk] **ich möchte gern mitmachen** I'd like to (= I would like to) join
Mode(trend) fashion ['fæʃn]
mögen like [laɪk] **etwas am liebsten mögen** like sth. best **etwas lieber mögen** like sth. better **etwas lieber mögen als etwas** prefer sth. to sth. [prɪ'fɜː] **sehr mögen** love [lʌv]
Möhre carrot ['kærət]
Monat month [mʌnθ]
Monitor monitor ['mɒnɪtə]
Monster monster ['mɒnstə]
Montag Monday ['mʌndeɪ], ['mʌndi]
montags on Mondays [ɒn 'mʌndeɪz]
Morgen morning ['mɔːnɪŋ] **am Morgen** in the morning
morgen tomorrow [tə'mɒrəʊ]
morgens in the morning(s) **11 Uhr morgens** 11 am [eɪ 'em]
müde tired ['taɪəd]; sleepy ['sliːpi]
Müll rubbish ['rʌbɪʃ]
Mülleimer rubbish bin ['rʌbɪʃ bɪn]
München Munich ['mjuːnɪk]
Mund: Halt den Mund! Shut up! [ʃʌt 'ʌp]
Museum museum [mjuː'ziːəm]
Musik music ['mjuːzɪk]
Musiker/in musician [mjuː'zɪʃn]
Musikgruppe band [bænd]
müssen must [mʌst] **etwas tun müssen** have to do sth. ['hæv tə]
mutig brave [breɪv]

Mutter mother [ˈmʌðə]
Mutti mum [mʌm]; *(AE)* mom [mɒm]
Mütze hat [hæt]

N

nach: *(örtlich)* to [tu], [tə]; *(zeitlich)* after [ˈɑːftə] **nach Hause** home [həʊm] **Züge nach ...** trains for ...
Nachbar/in neighbour [ˈneɪbə]
Nachbarschaft neighbourhood [ˈneɪbəhʊd]
Nachmittag afternoon [ɑːftəˈnuːn] **am Nachmittag** in the afternoon
nachmittags in the afternoon(s)
Nachricht: *(Mitteilung)* message [ˈmesɪdʒ] **Nachrichten** *(Neuigkeiten)* news [njuːz] **Nachrichten (an jn.) schicken, (mit jm.) austauschen** message (sb.)
nächste(r, s), als Nächstes next **am nächsten Tag** the next day
Nacht night [naɪt] **Gute Nacht.** Good night. **in der Nacht** at night
nachts at night [ət ˈnaɪt]
nahe (bei) near [nɪə]
Nähe: in der Nähe von near [nɪə]
Name name [neɪm]
Nase: die Nase voll haben feel fed up [fed ˈʌp]
nass wet [wet]
national national [ˈnæʃnəl]
Nationalfeiertag national day [næʃnəl ˈdeɪ]
Nationalität nationality [næʃəˈnæləti]
Nationalpark national park [næʃnəl ˈpɑːk]
natürlich of course [əv ˈkɔːs]
Naturwissenschaft science [ˈsaɪəns]
nebelig foggy [ˈfɒgi]
neben next to [ˈnekst tə]
nehmen take [teɪk]; *(Bus/Zug/...)* catch [kætʃ]
neidisch (auf) jealous (of) [ˈdʒeləs]
nein no [nəʊ]
nennen call [kɔːl] **genannt werden** be called [kɔːld]
nervös nervous [ˈnɜːvəs]
nett nice [naɪs]; *(freundlich)* friendly [ˈfrendli]; kind [kaɪnd]
neu new [njuː]
Neuigkeiten news [njuːz]
neun nine [naɪn]
Neunzigerjahre 90s [ˈnaɪntiz]

nicht not [nɒt] **noch nicht** not ... yet [jet]
nichts not (...) anything [ˈeniθɪŋ]; nothing [ˈnʌθɪŋ]
nie(mals) never [ˈnevə]
niedlich cute [kjuːt]
niedrig low [ləʊ]
niemand nobody [ˈnəʊbədi]; not ... anybody [ˈenibɒdi]
noch still [stɪl] **noch ein/e another** [əˈnʌðə] **noch eine Sache** one more thing [mɔː] **noch einmal** again [əˈgen] **noch nicht** not ... yet [jet]
Norden, Nord- north [nɔːθ]
nördlich north [nɔːθ]
nördliche(r, s), Nord- northern [ˈnɔːðən]
Nordosten; nordöstlich north-east [nɔːθˈiːst]
Nordwesten; nordwestlich north-west [nɔːθˈwest]
normal normal [ˈnɔːml]
normalerweise usually [ˈjuːʒʊəli]
November November [nəʊˈvembə]
Null *(im gesprochenen Englisch)* oh [əʊ]
Nummer number [ˈnʌmbə]
nun now [naʊ] **Nun, ...** Well, ... [wel]
nur just [dʒʌst]; only [ˈəʊnli]
Nuss nut [nʌt]

O

oben *(am oberen Ende)* at the top [tɒp]
oben; nach oben *(im Haus)* upstairs [ʌpˈsteəz]
Obst fruit [fruːt]
oder or [ɔː]
offen open [ˈəʊpən]
öffnen, sich öffnen open [ˈəʊpən]
oft often [ˈɒfn], [ˈɒftən]
ohne without [wɪˈðaʊt]
Ohr ear [ɪə]
Oje! Oh dear. [dɪə]
Oktober October [ɒkˈtəʊbə]
Oma grandma [ˈgrænmɑː]
online, Online- online [ɒnˈlaɪn]
Opa grandad [ˈgrændæd]; grandpa [ˈgrænpɑː]
Orange orange [ˈɒrɪndʒ]
orange(farben) orange [ˈɒrɪndʒ]
ordentlich tidy [ˈtaɪdi]
Original original [əˈrɪdʒənl]
originell original [əˈrɪdʒənl]
Ort place [pleɪs]
Osten, Ost- east [iːst]
östlich east [iːst]

östliche(r, s), Ost- eastern [ˈiːstən]

P

Paar pair [peə]
paar: ein paar a few [ə ˈfjuː]; *(einige)* some [sʌm], [səm] **in den letzten paar Wochen** in the last few weeks
packen pack [pæk]
Paddelboot canoe [kəˈnuː]
Palast palace [ˈpæləs]
Panda panda [ˈpændə]
Panik: Panik bekommen panic [ˈpænɪk] **Keine Panik.** Don't panic.
Papa dad [dæd]
Parade parade [pəˈreɪd]
Park park [pɑːk]
parken park (a car) [pɑːk]
Parkplatz car park [ˈkɑː pɑːk]
Parlament parliament [ˈpɑːləmənt]
Partner/in partner [ˈpɑːtnə] **Partnerarbeit** partner work
Party party [ˈpɑːti] **eine Party feiern** have a party
passieren *(geschehen)* happen [ˈhæpən]
Pastete *(mit Fleisch-/Gemüsefüllung)* pasty [ˈpæsti]
Pause break [breɪk]
Pence: 50 Pence 50p [piː]
Penny *(kleinste britische Münze)* penny, *pl* pence [ˈpeni], [pens]
perfekt perfect [ˈpɜːfɪkt]
Person person [ˈpɜːsn]
Pfad track [træk]
Pfeffer pepper [ˈpepə]
Pfeife *(Trillerpfeife)* whistle [ˈwɪsl]
Pfund *(britische Währung)* pound (£) [paʊnd]
Pickel spot [spɒt]
Picknick picnic [ˈpɪknɪk] **ein Picknick machen** have a picnic
Pizza pizza [ˈpiːtsə]
Plan plan [plæn]
planen plan [plæn]
Plastik plastic [ˈplæstɪk]
Plastiktüte plastic bag [plæstɪk ˈbæg]
Platz: *(Stelle, Ort)* place [pleɪs]; *(freier Raum)* space [speɪs]
Plätzchen *(Keks)* biscuit [ˈbɪskɪt]
plaudern (mit) chat (with) [tʃæt]
plötzlich suddenly [ˈsʌdnli]
Polizei police *(pl)* [pəˈliːs]
Polizeibeamter/-beamtin police officer [pəˈliːs ɒfɪsə]
Pommes frites chips [tʃɪps]; French fries *(AE)* [frentʃ ˈfraɪz]

DICTIONARY

German – English

Pony pony ['pəʊni]
populär popular ['pɒpjələ]
Post *(Teil eines Blogs)* post [pəʊst]
Post(amt) post office ['pəʊst ɒfɪs]
posten *(im Internet veröffentlichen)*: **gepostet von** posted by ['pəʊstɪd baɪ]
Poster poster ['pəʊstə]
Postkarte postcard ['pəʊstkɑːd]
Praline chocolate ['tʃɒklət]
Präsident/in president ['prezɪdənt]
Preis: *(Gewinn)* prize [praɪz]; *(Kaufpreis)* price [praɪs] **zum halben Preis** half price
preiswert cheap [tʃiːp]
Prinz prince [prɪns]
pro: pro Person per person [pɜː] **einmal pro Woche** once a week
probieren try [traɪ]
Problem problem ['prɒbləm] **Kein Problem.** *(infml)* No worries. [nəʊ 'wʌriz]
Produkt product ['prɒdʌkt]
Profit profit ['prɒfɪt]
Prospekt brochure ['brəʊʃə]
Protest*(demonstration)* protest ['prəʊtest]
protestieren protest [prə'test]
prüfen check [tʃek]
Prüfung *(Überprüfung)* check [tʃek]
Pullover pullover ['pʊləʊvə]
Punkt *(im Sport erzielt)* score [skɔː]
Punktestand score [skɔː]
pünktlich on time [ɒn 'taɪm]
putzen clean [kliːn]
Pyramide ['pɪrəmɪd] pyramid

Q
Quiz quiz [kwɪz]

R
Rad *(Fahrrad)* bike [baɪk] **Rad fahren** cycle ['saɪkl]; ride a bike
Radfahren cycling ['saɪklɪŋ]
Radiergummi rubber ['rʌbə]
Radweg cycle track ['saɪkl træk]
Rap rap [ræp]
rappen rap [ræp]
Rapper/in rapper ['ræpə]
Ratte rat [ræt]
Raum *(Zimmer)* room [ruːm]; *(freier Raum)* space [speɪs]
raus out [aʊt]
Rauschgift drug [drʌg]
Realität reality [ri'ælɪti]
Rechte rights *(pl)* [raɪts]

rechts; nach rechts right [raɪt] **auf der rechten Seite** on the right
Rede talk [tɔːk]
reden *(sich unterhalten)* have a chat [tʃæt]
Redewendung phrase [freɪz]
Redner/in talker ['tɔːkə]
Regel rule [ruːl]
Regen rain [reɪn]
Regenhose rain trousers *(pl)* ['reɪn traʊzəz]
Regenjacke rain jacket
regnen rain [reɪn]
regnerisch rainy ['reɪni]
reichen: 50 Pence reichen (auch) 50p will do
Reihe line [laɪn]
reisen travel ['trævl]
reiten ride [raɪd] **auf einem Pony / ein Pony reiten** ride a pony
relaxen chill [tʃɪl]
rennen run [rʌn]
Reporter/in reporter [rɪ'pɔːtə]
reservieren book [bʊk]
Restaurant restaurant ['restrɒnt] **in einem Restaurant** at a restaurant
retten save [seɪv]
Rezeption reception [rɪ'sepʃn] **an der Rezeption** in reception
Rhythmus *(Musik)* beat [biːt]
richtig right [raɪt] **das ist richtig** that's right
Rock skirt [skɜːt]
Rock(musik) rock (music) ['rɒk mjuːzɪk]
Rock and Roll *(Musikrichtung)* rock and roll [rɒk ənd 'rəʊl]
Rollstuhl wheelchair ['wiːltʃeə]
Röntgen(strahlen) X-ray ['eksreɪ]
rosa pink [pɪŋk]
rot red [red]
rotblond ginger ['dʒɪndʒə]
Rückfahrkarte return (ticket) [rɪ'tɜːn]
Rucksack rucksack ['rʌksæk]
rufen shout [ʃaʊt]; call [kɔːl]
Rugby *(Ballsportart)* rugby ['rʌgbi]
Ruhe: Immer mit der Ruhe. Don't panic. ['pænɪk]
ruhig quiet ['kwaɪət]
Ruine ruin ['ruːɪn]
Rundfahrt tour [tʊə]
Rundgang (durch) tour (of) [tʊə]
runter: den Hügel runter down the hill [daʊn]

S
Sache thing [θɪŋ]
Saft juice [dʒuːs]
sagen say [seɪ]; tell [tel] **sagen wollen** *(meinen)* mean [miːn]
Sahne cream [kriːm]
Salat *(Gericht/Beilage)* salad ['sæləd]
Salz salt [sɔːlt]
sammeln collect [kə'lekt]
Samstag Saturday ['sætədeɪ], ['sætədi]
Sandwich sandwich ['sænwɪtʃ]
Sänger/in singer ['sɪŋə]
Satz sentence ['sentəns]
sauber clean [kliːn]
sauber machen clean [kliːn]
sauer sein feel fed up [fed 'ʌp]
schade: Das ist schade. That's a pity. ['pɪti]
Schaf sheep, *pl* sheep [ʃiːp]
Schatz love [lʌv]
schauen look [lʊk]
Schauer shower ['ʃaʊə]
Schauspiel drama ['drɑːmə]
schauspielern act [ækt]
Scherz joke [dʒəʊk]
schick smart [smɑːt]
schicken (an) send (to) [send] **eine SMS schicken** text [tekst]
schießen *(mit dem Fuß)* kick [kɪk]
Schiff ship [ʃɪp]; boat [bəʊt]
Schild sign [saɪn]
Schinken *(gekocht)* ham [hæm]
Schlaf sleep [sliːp]
schlafen sleep [sliːp] **schlafen gehen** go to bed [gəʊ tə 'bed]
Schlafsack sleeping bag ['sliːpɪŋ bæg]
Schlafzimmer bedroom ['bedruːm]
Schlagzeug drums *(pl)* [drʌmz]
Schlamm mud [mʌd]
Schlange snake [sneɪk]
schlau clever ['klevə]; smart [smɑːt]
schlecht bad [bæd] **schlechter** worse [wɜːs] **am schlechtesten** worst [wɜːst]
Schleife bow [bəʊ]
schließen close [kləʊz]
schließlich in the end [ɪn ði 'end]
schlimm bad [bæd] **schlimmer** worse [wɜːs] **am schlimmsten** worst [wɜːst]
Schlittschuhlaufen ice skating ['aɪs skeɪtɪŋ]
Schluss end [end] **zum Schluss** in the end
Schlussverkauf sale [seɪl]

schmal narrow [ˈnærəʊ]
schmerzhaft sore [sɔː]
Schmuggler/in smuggler [ˈsmʌɡlə]
schneiden cut [kʌt]
schnell fast [fɑːst]; quick [kwɪk]
Schokolade chocolate [ˈtʃɒklət] **heiße (Trink-)Schokolade** hot chocolate
Schokoriegel chocolate bar [ˈtʃɒklət bɑː]
schon already [ɔːlˈredi] **Warst du schon mal …?** Have you ever been …? [ˈevə]
schön beautiful [ˈbjuːtɪfl]; fine [faɪn]; nice [naɪs] **Schön, dich/euch/Sie kennenzulernen.** Nice to meet you. **Schön, wieder zusammen zu sein.** Nice to be together again. **Ich wünsche dir einen schönen Tag. / Schönen Tag noch.** Have a good day. [ɡʊd]
schottisch *(aus Schottland)* Scottish [ˈskɒtɪʃ]
Schottland Scotland [ˈskɒtlənd] **aus Schottland** Scottish [ˈskɒtɪʃ]
schrecklich terrible [ˈterəbl]
schreiben write [raɪt]
Schreibtisch desk [desk]
schreien scream [skriːm]
Schuh shoe [ʃuː]
Schule school [skuːl] **auf/an dieser Schule** at this school
Schüler/in student [ˈstjuːdnt]
Schulheft exercise book [ˈeksəsaɪz bʊk]
Schulklasse class [klɑːs]
Schulleiter/in principal [ˈprɪnsəpl]
Schulmensa canteen [kænˈtiːn]
Schulsport PE (physical education) [piː ˈiː], [fɪzɪkl edʒuˈkeɪʃn]
Schulter shoulder [ˈʃəʊldə]
Schuluniform uniform [ˈjuːnɪfɔːm]
Schwanz tail [teɪl]
schwänzen skive [skaɪv]
schwarz black [blæk]
Schweden Sweden [ˈswiːdn]
Schwein pig [pɪɡ]
schwer *(schwierig)* difficult [ˈdɪfɪkəlt]; hard [hɑːd]
Schwester sister [ˈsɪstə]
schwierig difficult [ˈdɪfɪkəlt]; hard [hɑːd]
Schwierigkeiten trouble [ˈtrʌbl]
Schwimmbad swimming pool [ˈswɪmɪŋ puːl]
schwimmen swim [swɪm] **schwimmen gehen** go swimming *(das)* **Schwimmen** swimming

sechs six [sɪks]
Second-Hand-Laden second-hand shop [sekənd ˈhænd ʃɒp]
See *(Binnensee)* lake [leɪk]; *(die See, das Meer)* sea [siː]
sehen look [lʊk]; see [siː] **Lass(t) uns (mal) sehen.** Let's see. **Sieh mal, Adam.** Look, Adam.
sehr very [ˈveri] **jn. so sehr vermissen/mögen/lieben** miss/like/love sb. so much [səʊ ˈmʌtʃ]
Seife soap [səʊp]
Seifenoper soap [səʊp]
sein be [biː]
sein/e *(besitzanzeigend)*: *(zu „he")* his [hɪz]; *(zu „it")* its [ɪts]
Seite side [saɪd]; page [peɪdʒ]
selbst *(sogar)* even [ˈiːvn]
selbstverständlich of course [əv ˈkɔːs]
seltsam funny [ˈfʌni]
senden (an) send (to) [send]
Sendung programme [ˈprəʊɡræm]
September September [sepˈtembə]
Servus.: *(Begrüßung)* Hello. [həˈləʊ]; *(Abschied)* Bye. [baɪ]
setzen: sich setzen sit [sɪt]
Show show [ʃəʊ]
sicher sure [ʃʊə]; *(gefahrlos)* safe [seɪf] **Bei … bin ich mir nicht (so) sicher.** I don't know about …
Sicherheit security [sɪˈkjʊərəti] **in Sicherheit** safe [seɪf]
Sie *(höfliche Anrede)* you [juː] **Sie/sich selbst** yourselves [jɔːˈselvz] **Sie sind** you're (= you are)
sie *(bei Dingen und Tieren)* it [ɪt]
sie *(Plural)* they [ðeɪ] **sie/sich selbst** themselves [ðəmˈselvz] **für sie** for them [ðem], [ðəm] **sie sind** they're (= they are)
sie *(weibliche Person)* she [ʃiː] **sie/sich selbst** herself [həˈself] **sie ist** she's (= she is) **für sie** for her [həː]
sieben seven [ˈsevn]
Signal signal [ˈsɪɡnəl]
singen sing [sɪŋ]
sitzen sit [sɪt]
Skateboard; Skateboard fahren skateboard [ˈskeɪtbɔːd]
Skateboardfahren skateboarding [ˈskeɪtbɔːdɪŋ]
Skaten gehen *(Inlineskaten)* go skating [ˈskeɪtɪŋ]
Skatepark skate park [ˈskeɪt pɑːk]
Skilaufen *(Sport)* skiing [ˈskiːɪŋ]
smart smart [smɑːt]

Smoothie *(Getränk aus Fruchtpüree, evtl. mit Milchprodukten)* smoothie [ˈsmuːði]
SMS text (message) [ˈtekst mesɪdʒ] **eine SMS schicken** text [tekst]
Snack snack [snæk]
so so [səʊ]; *(auf diese Art)* like this [laɪk ˈðɪs] **so eine Mütze** a hat like that **so ein Unfall** an accident like this [laɪk] **So viel kostet das nicht.** It's cheaper than that.
Socke sock [sɒk]
sodass so (that) [səʊ], [ˈsəʊ ðət]
Sofa sofa [ˈsəʊfə]
sogar even [ˈiːvn]
Sohn son [sʌn]
solche/r: eine solche Mütze a hat like that **ein solcher Unfall** an accident like this [laɪk] **solche Unfälle** accidents like this
sollen: sollen wir …? Shall we …? [ʃæl], [ʃəl] **du solltest** you should [ʃʊd]
Sommer summer [ˈsʌmə]
Sonne sun [sʌn]
Sonnenbrille sunglasses *(pl)* [ˈsʌnɡlɑːsɪz]
Sonnencreme suncream [ˈsʌnkriːm]
sonnig sunny [ˈsʌni]
Sonntag Sunday [ˈsʌndeɪ], [ˈsʌndi]
Sonst noch etwas? Anything else? [eniθɪŋ ˈels]
Sorgen: sich Sorgen machen (wegen, um) worry (about) [ˈwʌri]
sorgfältig careful [ˈkeəfl]
Sorte: Sorte (von) kind (of) [kaɪnd] **Welche Sorte (von) …?** What sort of …? [sɔːt]
Spanien Spain [speɪn]
spanisch; Spanisch Spanish [ˈspænɪʃ]
Spaß fun [fʌn] **… macht Spaß.** … is fun. **es macht Spaß, mit ihnen zusammenzusein** they're fun **Klingt, als ob es Spaß macht.** Sounds fun. **viel Spaß haben** have a great time
spät late [leɪt] **Wie spät ist es?** What's the time? [wɒts ðə ˈtaɪm]
später later [ˈleɪtə]
Speck bacon [ˈbeɪkən]
Speiseeis ice cream [aɪs ˈkriːm]
Spiel game [ɡeɪm]
spielen act [ækt]; play [pleɪ]
Spieler/in player [ˈpleɪə]

DICTIONARY — German – English

Spielstand score [skɔ:]
Spielzeug toy [tɔɪ]
Spitze: an der Spitze (von) at the top (of) [tɒp]
Sport(art) sport [spɔ:t] **Sport treiben** do sport **Sport(unterricht)** *(in der Schule)* PE (physical education) [pi: 'i:], [fɪzɪkl edʒu'keɪʃn]
Sportgeschäft sports shop ['spɔ:ts ʃɒp]
Sporthalle sports hall ['spɔ:ts hɔ:l]
sportlich sporty ['spɔ:tɪ]
Sportschuhe trainers ['treɪnəz]
Sprache language ['læŋgwɪdʒ]
sprechen (mit) speak (to) [spi:k]; talk (to) ['tɔ:k tu] **mit Freunden/Freundinnen sprechen** speaking to friends **Wer spricht (da)?** *(am Telefon)* Who's speaking?
Staat state [steɪt]
Staatsangehörigkeit nationality [næʃə'nælətɪ]
Stadion stadium ['steɪdɪəm]
Stadt *(Großstadt)* city ['sɪtɪ]; *(Kleinstadt)* town [taʊn]
Stadtmitte centre ['sentə] **London Stadtmitte** Central London ['sentrəl]
Stadtplan map [mæp]
Stammbaum *(der Familie)* family tree [fæməli 'tri:]
Star star [stɑ:]
Start start [stɑ:t]
Startseite *(Internet)* home [həʊm]
stattfinden *(Kino, Theater)* be on [ɒn]
staubsaugen hoover ['hu:və]
Steak steak [steɪk]
stehen stand [stænd]
stehen bleiben stop [stɒp]
Stein stone [stəʊn]
Stelle: *(Job)* job [dʒɒb]; *(Ort)* place [pleɪs]
stellen *(hin-, abstellen)* put [pʊt] **eine Frage stellen** ask a question [ɑ:sk ə 'kwestʃən]
sterben die [daɪ]
Stiefbruder stepbrother ['stepbrʌðə]
Stiefel boot [bu:t]
Stiefmutter stepmum ['stepmʌm]; stepmother ['stepmʌðə]
Stiefschwester stepsister ['stepsɪstə]
Stiefvater stepdad ['stepdæd]; stepfather ['stepfɑ:ðə]
Stift pen [pen]

still quiet ['kwaɪət]
Stimme voice [vɔɪs]
stimmen: das stimmt that's right [raɪt] **das stimmt nicht** that's wrong [rɒŋ] **Was stimmt nicht mit ...?** What's wrong with ...?
stimmen für jn. vote for sb. [vəʊt]
stolz (auf) proud (of) [praʊd]
Strand beach ['bi:tʃ] **am Strand** on the beach
Straße *(in Ortschaften)* street [stri:t]; *(Landstraße zwischen Orten / Straße in Orten)* road [rəʊd] **auf der Straße** in the street
Strauch bush [bʊʃ]
streng strict [strɪkt]
strikt strict [strɪkt]
Student/in student ['stju:dnt]
Studio studio ['stju:dɪəʊ]
Stuhl chair [tʃeə]
Stunde hour [aʊə]; *(Unterrichtsstunde)* lesson ['lesn]
stundenlang for hours and hours ['aʊəz]
Stundenplan timetable ['taɪmteɪbl]
suchen look for ['lʊk fə]
Süden, Süd- south [saʊθ]
südlich south [saʊθ]
südliche(r, s), Süd- southern ['sʌðən]
Südosten; südöstlich south-east [saʊθ'i:st]
Südwesten; südwestlich south-west [saʊθ'west]
Supermarkt supermarket ['su:pəmɑ:kɪt]
Suppe soup [su:p]
süß *(niedlich)* cute [kju:t]
   süß(lich) sugary ['ʃʊgərɪ]
Süßigkeiten sweets [swi:ts]
Szene scene [si:n]

T

Taekwondo tae kwon do [taɪ kwɒn 'dəʊ]
Tag day [deɪ]
Tagebuch diary ['daɪərɪ] **Tagebuch führen** keep a diary [ki:p]
Tagesausflug day out [deɪ 'aʊt]
Tageslicht daylight ['deɪlaɪt]
Tageszeitung newspaper ['nju:zpeɪpə]
Talkshow talk show ['tɔ:k ʃəʊ]
Tante aunt [ɑ:nt]
tanzen dance [dɑ:ns] *(das)* **Tanzen** dancing
Tänzer/in dancer ['dɑ:nsə]

Tasche bag [bæg]; *(an Kleidungsstücken)* pocket ['pɒkɪt]
Taschengeld pocket money ['pɒkɪt mʌnɪ]
Taschenrechner calculator ['kælkjʊleɪtə]
Tauchen *(Sport)* diving ['daɪvɪŋ]
tausend thousand ['θaʊznd]
Taxi taxi ['tæksɪ]
Team team [ti:m]
Technik technology [tek'nɒlədʒɪ]
Technologie technology [tek'nɒlədʒɪ]
Tee tea [ti:]
Teenager teenager ['ti:neɪdʒə]; teen [ti:n] **das Leben der Teenager** teenage life ['ti:neɪdʒ]
Teil part [pɑ:t]
teilen share [ʃeə]
teilnehmen (an) take part (in) [teɪk 'pɑ:t]
Telefon phone [fəʊn]
Telefonanruf (phone) call [kɔ:l]
Telefonnummer phone number ['fəʊn nʌmbə]
Temperatur temperature ['temprətʃə]
Tennis tennis ['tenɪs]
Test test [test]
teuer expensive [ɪk'spensɪv]
Text text [tekst]; *(eines Songs)* words (of a song) [wɜ:dz]
Theater theatre ['θɪətə] **Theater spielen** act [ækt]
Theaterstück play [pleɪ]
tief deep [di:p]; low [ləʊ]
Tier animal ['ænɪml]
Tierhandlung pet shop ['pet ʃɒp]
Tiger tiger ['taɪgə]
Tisch table ['teɪbl]
Tischtennis table tennis ['teɪbl tenɪs]
Titel title ['taɪtl]
Toast(brot) toast [təʊst]
Tochter daughter ['dɔ:tə]
Toilette toilet ['tɔɪlət]
toll great [greɪt]
Tomate tomato [tə'mɑ:təʊ]
Top *(ärmelloses Oberteil)* top [tɒp]
Tor gate [geɪt]
Tour tour [tʊə]
Tourist/in tourist ['tʊərɪst]
tragen *(Kleidung)* wear [weə]
Transport(wesen) transport ['trænspɔ:t]
Transporter *(Lieferwagen)* van [væn]
Traum dream [dri:m]
traurig sad [sæd]

Treffen meeting ['miːtɪŋ]
treffen; sich treffen meet [miːt]
treiben: Sport treiben do sport [duː 'spɔːt]
treten kick [kɪk]
Trick trick [trɪk]
trinken drink [drɪŋk]
Trommel drum [drʌm]
trotzdem still [stɪl]
Tschüs. Bye. [baɪ]; See you. ['siː juː]
T-Shirt T-shirt ['tiːʃɜːt]
tun do [duː]; *(etwas wohin)* **tun** put [pʊt] **(viel) zu tun haben** be busy ['bɪzi]
Tupfen *(Leopard)* spot [spɒt]
Tür door [dɔː]
Türkei Turkey ['tɜːki]
Turm tower ['taʊə]
Turmspringer/in diver ['daɪvə]
Turnen gymnastics [dʒɪm'næstɪks]

U

U-Bahn *(in London)* the Tube [tjuːb]
U-Bahn-Linie line [laɪn]
über about [ə'baʊt] **über 18** over 18 ['əʊvə] **schreiben über** write about
überfliegen *(Text)* skim [skɪm]
überhaupt nicht ... not ... at all [nɒt ət 'ɔːl]
Übernachtungsparty sleepover ['sliːpəʊvə]
überprüfen check [tʃek]
Überprüfung check [tʃek]
überqueren cross [krɒs]
überrascht surprised [sə'praɪzd]
Überraschung surprise [sə'praɪz]
Überschrift title ['taɪtl]
Überwachungskamera CCTV camera [siː siː tiː 'viː 'kæmərə]
Überwachungssystem CCTV [siː siː tiː 'viː]
Übung exercise ['eksəsaɪz]
Übungsheft exercise book ['eksəsaɪz bʊk]
Uhr clock [klɒk] **11 Uhr morgens** 11 am [eɪ 'em] **6 Uhr abends, 18 Uhr** 6 pm [piː 'em] **um 1 Uhr / um 13 Uhr** at one o'clock [ə'klɒk]
Uhrzeit time [taɪm]
um 1 Uhr at 1 o'clock [æt], [ət]
umher- around [ə'raʊnd]
umhergehen (in) walk around [wɔːk ə'raʊnd]
umherrennen run around [rʌn ə'raʊnd]

Umkleide(kabine) changing room ['tʃeɪndʒɪŋ ruːm]
Umschlag *(Buch)* cover ['kʌvə]
umsteigen *(Zug)* change (trains) [tʃeɪndʒ]
umziehen (nach) move (to) [muːv]
Umzug *(Parade)* parade [pə'reɪd]
Unabhängigkeit (von) independence (from) [ɪndɪ'pendəns]
Unabhängigkeitstag Independence Day [ɪndɪ'pendəns deɪ]
unaufgeräumt untidy [ʌn'taɪdi]
unbeliebt unpopular [ʌn'pɒpjələ]
uncool uncool [ʌn'kuːl]
und and [ænd], [ənd] **Und du?** What about you? [wɒt əbaʊt 'juː]
Unfall accident ['æksɪdənt]
unfreundlich unfriendly [ʌn'frendli]
ungefähr about [ə'baʊt]
ungesund unhealthy [ʌn'helθi]
Unglück *(Katastrophe)* disaster [dɪ'zɑːstə]
unglücklich unhappy [ʌn'hæpi]
unheimlich: *(beängstigend)* scary ['skeəri] **unheimlich viel/e ...** lots and lots of ... [lɒts]
Uniform uniform ['juːnɪfɔːm]
uninteressant uninteresting [ʌn'ɪntrəstɪŋ]
Unit *(Lerneinheit)* unit ['juːnɪt]
unordentlich messy ['mesi]; untidy [ʌn'taɪdi]
unrichtig false [fɔːls]
uns us [ʌs], [əs] **uns selbst** ourselves [aʊə'selvz]
unser/e *(vor Nomen)* our ['aʊə], [ɑː]
unserer, unsere, unseres ours [ɑːz], ['aʊəz]
unsicher unsure [ʌn'ʃʊə]
Unsinn rubbish ['rʌbɪʃ]
unten below [bɪ'ləʊ]
unter under ['ʌndə]; below [bɪ'ləʊ]
unterhalb (von) below [bɪ'ləʊ]
unterhalten: sich unterhalten *(reden)* have a chat [tʃæt]
Unterhaltung *(Gespräch)* chat [tʃæt]
Unterricht: im Unterricht in class [ɪn 'klɑːs]
unterrichten teach [tiːtʃ]
Unterrichtsstunde lesson ['lesn]
Unterschied difference ['dɪfrəns]
unterschiedlich different ['dɪfrənt]
Unterschrift signature ['sɪgnətʃə]
unterwegs sein be out [aʊt]
unwirklich unreal [ʌn'rɪəl]

Urlaub holiday ['hɒlədeɪ]
USA (= Vereinigte Staaten von Amerika) US (= the United States) [juːnaɪtɪd 'steɪts]; USA
usw. (und so weiter) etc. [et'setərə]

V

Vater father ['fɑːðə]
Vati dad [dæd]
Vegetarier/in; vegetarisch vegetarian, *infml auch* veggie [vedʒə'teəriən], ['vedʒi]
verändern; sich verändern change [tʃeɪndʒ]
Verbandkasten first-aid kit [fɜːst 'eɪd kɪt]
verdienen: Geld verdienen make money
Verein club [klʌb]
vereinbaren arrange [ə'reɪndʒ]
Vereinbarung deal [diːl]
Vereinigte Staaten (von Amerika) USA; US (United States) [juːnaɪtɪd 'steɪts]
Vereinigtes Königreich United Kingdom (UK) [juːnaɪtɪd 'kɪŋdəm]
Verfasser/in writer ['raɪtə]
Vergangenheit past [pɑːst]
vergessen forget (about) [fə'get] **nicht vergessen** remember [rɪ'membə]
Vergnügungspark entertainment park [entə'teɪnmənt pɑːk]
Verkauf sale [seɪl]
verkaufen sell [sel]
Verkäufer/in (sales) assistant ['seɪlz əsɪstənt]
Verkehrsampel traffic lights *(pl)* ['træfɪk laɪts]
Verkehrsmittel transport ['trænspɔːt]
verkehrsreich busy ['bɪzi]
verlassen leave [liːv]
verlieren lose [luːz]
vermissen miss [mɪs]
vermisst missing ['mɪsɪŋ]
verrückt crazy ['kreɪzi]
verschieden different ['dɪfrənt]
verschlafen *(müde)* sleepy ['sliːpi]
Verschwendung waste [weɪst]
Verspätung: mein Bus hat Verspätung my bus is late [leɪt]
verstehen understand [ʌndə'stænd]
versuchen try [traɪ]
verwirrt puzzled ['pʌzld]
verwundert puzzled ['pʌzld]
Video(-) video ['vɪdiəʊ]

DICTIONARY — German – English

Videochat video chat ['vɪdiəʊ tʃæt]
viel much [mʌtʃ]; a lot (of) [ə 'lɒt]; lots (of) [lɒts] **viele** a lot (of); lots (of); many ['mæni] **unheimlich viel(e) ...** lots and lots of ... **So viel kostet das nicht.** It's cheaper than that. **Viele Grüße, ...** (Briefschluss) Best wishes [best 'wɪʃɪz] **Wie viele ...?** How many ...?
vielleicht maybe ['meɪbi]; perhaps [pə'hæps]
vier four [fɔː]
Viertel quarter ['kwɔːtə]; (Nachbarschaft) neighbourhood ['neɪbəhʊd]
Vogel bird [bɜːd]
voll full [fʊl] **voller ...** full of ...
Volleyball volleyball ['vɒlibɔːl]
von from [frɒm]; (von ... herunter/hinunter) off [ɒf] **eine SMS von Mama** a text from mum (geschrieben) **von Berry Donovan** by Berry Donovan [baɪ] **von Montag bis Freitag** from Monday to Friday **herunterfallen von etwas** (Fahrrad, Pferd) fall off sth. **von den Ferien** of the holidays
vor: (räumlich) in front of [ɪn 'frʌnt əv]; outside [aʊt'saɪd]; (zeitlich) before [bɪ'fɔː] **vor zwei Jahren** two years ago [ə'gəʊ]
vorbei over ['əʊvə] **am Geschäft vorbei** past the shop [pɑːst]
Vorführung show [ʃəʊ]
vorher before [bɪ'fɔː]
Vorhersage forecast ['fɔːkɑːst]
vorige Woche last week [lɑːst 'wiːk]
vormittags: 11 Uhr vormittags 11 am [eɪ 'em]
Vorschrift rule [ruːl]
vorsichtig careful ['keəfl]
vorstellen: Stell dir nur vor! Wait for this. (infml) ['weɪt]
Vorstellung (Aufführung) performance [pə'fɔːməns]
Vortrag talk [tɔːk] **einen Vortrag halten** give a talk
vorziehen: etwas einer Sache vorziehen prefer sth. to sth. [prɪ'fɜː]

W

wählen pick [pɪk]
wahr true [truː]
Wald wood [wʊd]
Wand wall [wɔːl]
Wanderer/Wanderin walker ['wɔːkə]
wandern walk [wɔːk] (das) **Wandern** hiking ['haɪkɪŋ]
Wandgemälde mural ['mjʊərəl]
wann? when? [wen] **Wann hast du Geburtstag?** When's your birthday?
war: es war it was [wɒz], [wəz]
waren: sie waren they were [wɜː], [wə]
warm warm [wɔːm]; hot [hɒt]
warten (auf) wait (for) [weɪt]
warum? why? [waɪ]
was? what? [wɒt] **Was ist mit dir?** What about you?
waschen wash [wɒʃ]
Wasser water ['wɔːtə]
Wasserkocher (elektrisch) kettle ['ketl]
Waveboarden street surfing ['striːt sɜːfɪŋ]
Webcode webcode ['webkəʊd]
Website website ['websaɪt]
wecken wake, woke, woken [weɪk]
Weg way [weɪ]; (Feldweg) track [træk] **jm. den Weg beschreiben** tell sb. the way **jn. nach dem Weg fragen** ask sb. the way
weg away [ə'weɪ]
weggehen go away [gəʊ ə'weɪ]
wehtun: Ihr Bein tat weh. Her leg was sore. [sɔː] **Mir tut der Hals weh.** I have a sore throat. [sɔː 'θrəʊt]
Weide field [fiːld] **auf der Weide** in the field
Weihnachten Christmas ['krɪsməs]
Weihnachtstag: 1. Weihnachtstag (25. 12.) Christmas Day [krɪsməs 'deɪ]
weil because [bɪ'kɒz]
weinen cry [kraɪ]
weiß white [waɪt]
weit far [fɑː] **100 Meter weit** for 100 metres
weitere more [mɔː]
welche(r, s)? which? [wɪtʃ]; what? [wɒt] **welcher Klub?** which club? **Welche(s) sind ...?** What are ...?
Welt world [wɜːld] **auf der Welt** in the world
wem? who? [huː]
wen? who? [huː]
wenig little ['lɪtl] **weniger** less [les] **am wenigsten** least [liːst] **ein wenig** a little [ə 'lɪtl]
wenigstens at least [ət 'liːst]
wenn (falls) if [ɪf]; (zeitlich) when [wen] **erst, wenn sie 13 sind** not (...) until they're 13 [ən'tɪl]
wer? who? [huː]
Werbung advert ['ædvɜːt]
werden (Veränderung) become [bɪ'kʌm] **Erste/r werden** (Rennen, Wettkampf) come (in) first **verrückt werden** go crazy [gəʊ]
werden (Zukunft) be going to ['gəʊɪŋ tə]; will [wɪl] **es wird nicht regnen** it won't (= will not) rain [weʊnt] **ich werde helfen** I'm going to help **Wir werden ihn finden.** We'll (= we will) find him. [wiːl], [wɪl]
Westen, West- west [west]
westlich west [west]
westliche(r, s), West- western ['westən]
Wettbewerb competition [kɒmpə'tɪʃn]
Wetter weather ['weðə]
Wetterbericht weather report ['weðə rɪpɔːt]
Wettervorhersage weather forecast ['fɔːkɑːst]
wichtig important [ɪm'pɔːtənt]
widersprechen disagree [dɪsə'griː]
wie as [æz], [əz]; (so wie) like [laɪk] **wie in ...** as in ... **genau wie Berry** just like Berry
wie? how? [haʊ] **Wie alt bist du?** How old are you? **Wie geht's?** How are you? **Wie ist es (er, sie)? / Wie sieht es (er sie) aus?** What's it like? [laɪk] **Wie spät ist es?** What's the time?
wieder again [ə'gen]
wiederholen repeat [rɪ'piːt]
Wiedersehen: Auf Wiedersehen. Goodbye. [gʊd'baɪ]
wild (lebend) wild [waɪld]
willkommen: Willkommen in Plymouth! Welcome to Plymouth. **jn. willkommen heißen (in)** welcome sb. (to) ['welkəm]
Wind wind [wɪnd]
windig windy ['wɪndi]
Winter winter ['wɪntə]
wir we [wiː] **wir selbst** ourselves [aʊə'selvz] **wir sind** we're (= we are)
wirklich real [rɪəl] **wirklich nett** really nice ['rɪəli]
Wirklichkeit reality [rɪ'æləti]
Wirtschaft(slehre) business (studies) ['bɪznəs]
wissen know [nəʊ]

Witz joke [dʒəʊk]
WLAN *(kabellose Datenübertragung)* Wi-Fi [ˈwaɪ faɪ]
wo? where? [weə]
Woche week [wiːk] **eine Woche / sechs Wochen Urlaub** a week's / six weeks' holiday
Wochenende weekend [wiːkˈend] **am Wochenende** at the weekend
wohin? where? [weə]
wohltätige Organisation charity [ˈtʃærəti]
wohnen live [lɪv]
Wohnung flat [flæt]
Wohnzimmer living room [ˈlɪvɪŋ ruːm]
Wolke cloud [klaʊd]
wolkig cloudy [ˈklaʊdi]
wollen want [wɒnt] **tun/machen wollen** want to do
Wort word [wɜːd]
Wörterbuch dictionary [ˈdɪkʃənri]
Wörterverzeichnis: alphabetisches Wörterverzeichnis dictionary [ˈdɪkʃənri]
wunderschön beautiful [ˈbjuːtɪfl]
Wunsch wish [wɪʃ]
Wurst sausage [ˈsɒsɪdʒ]
Würstchen sausage [ˈsɒsɪdʒ]
wütend angry [ˈæŋgri]

Z

Zahl number [ˈnʌmbə]
zahlen pay [peɪ]
Zebra zebra [ˈzebrə]
zehn ten [ten]
Zeichen sign [saɪn]
Zeichentrickfilm cartoon [kɑːˈtuːn]
zeigen show [ʃəʊ] **zeigen (auf)** point (at/to) [pɔɪnt] **gezeigt werden** *(Kino, Theater)* be on [ɒn]
Zeit time [taɪm] **Hast du um ein Uhr Zeit?** Are you free at one o'clock?
Zeitschrift magazine [mægəˈziːn]
Zeitung paper [ˈpeɪpə]; newspaper [ˈnjuːzpeɪpə] **Zeitungen austragen** do a paper round
Zelt tent [tent]
Zeltplatz campsite [ˈkæmpsaɪt]
zentral central [ˈsentrəl]
Zentrum centre [ˈsentə]
zerbrechen break [breɪk]
zerbrochen broken [ˈbrəʊkən]
Zeug *(Kram)* stuff [stʌf] **dummes Zeug** *(Unsinn)* rubbish [ˈrʌbɪʃ]
ziehen nach *(umziehen)* move to [muːv]

Ziffer number [ˈnʌmbə]
Zimmer room [ruːm] **Zimmer mit Frühstück** bed and breakfast (B&B)
Zirkus circus [ˈsɜːkəs]
Zone zone [zəʊn]
Zoo zoo [zuː]
Zoogeschäft pet shop [ˈpet ʃɒp]
zu *(örtlich)* to [tu], [tə] **zu Hause** at home **zu klein** too small [tuː] **zum Beispiel** for example **zum letzten Mal** for the last time **zu sein** *(geschlossen)* be closed [kləʊzd] **zu spät** late [leɪt] **bei Ellie zu Hause** at Ellie's house **Er legt sie zu den anderen Dingen.** He puts it with the other things. **Zeit, (um) nach Hause zu gehen** time to go home
Zucker sugar [ˈʃʊgə]
zuckerhaltig sugary [ˈʃʊgəri]
zuerst first [fɜːst]; at first [ət ˈfɜːst]
Zug train [treɪn]
zugreifen: Greift zu! *(z.B. beim Essen)* Help yourselves. [jɔːˈselvz]
Zuhause home [həʊm]
zuhören listen (to) [ˈlɪsn]
Zukunft future [ˈfjuːtʃə]
zumachen close [kləʊz]
zurück back [bæk]
zurücklassen leave [liːv]
zusammen together [təˈgeðə] **Schön, wieder zusammen zu sein.** Nice to be together again.
Zusammenkunft meeting [ˈmiːtɪŋ]
zustimmen agree (with) [əˈgriː] **nicht zustimmen** disagree [dɪsəˈgriː]
zuvor before [bɪˈfɔː]
zwei two [tuː]
Zweibettzimmer twin room [twɪn ˈruːm]
zweimal twice [twaɪs]
zweite(r, s) second [ˈsekənd]
Zwilling(e) twin(s) [twɪn]
zwischen between [bɪˈtwiːn]
zwölf twelve [twelv]

English sounds

[iː]	gr**ee**n, h**e**, t**ea**
[ɑː]	**a**sk, cl**a**ss, c**a**r, p**a**rk
[ɔː]	**or**, b**a**ll, f**our**, m**or**ning
[uː]	r**u**ler, bl**ue**, t**oo**, tw**o**, y**ou**
[ɜː]	**ear**ly, h**er**, g**ir**l, w**or**k, T-sh**ir**t
[ɪ]	**i**n, b**i**g, **e**xpensive
[e]	y**e**s, b**e**d, **a**gain, br**ea**kfast

[æ]	**a**nimal, **A**frica, bl**a**ck, c**a**t
[ʌ]	m**u**m, b**u**s, c**o**lour
[ɒ]	s**o**ng, **o**n, d**o**g, wh**a**t
[ʊ]	b**oo**k, g**oo**d, p**u**llover
[ə]	**a**gain, t**o**day, **a** sist**er**
[i]	happ**y**, monk**ey**
[u]	y**ou**, t**o**
[eɪ]	n**a**me, **eigh**t, pl**ay**, gr**ea**t
[aɪ]	**I**, t**i**me, r**igh**t, m**y**
[ɔɪ]	b**oy**, t**oi**let, n**oi**se
[əʊ]	**o**ld, n**o**, r**oa**d, yell**ow**
[aʊ]	n**ow**, h**ou**se
[eə]	wh**ere**, ch**air**, b**ear**
[ɪə]	h**ere**, d**ear**
[ʊə]	y**our**
[b]	**b**ike, ta**b**le, cra**b**
[p]	**p**en, stu**p**id, sho**p**
[d]	**d**ay, i**d**ea, goo**d**
[t]	**t**en, le**tt**er, a**t**
[g]	**g**o, a**g**ain, ba**g**
[k]	**k**itchen, **c**ar, bla**ck**
[m]	**m**an, re**m**ember, **m**u**m**
[n]	**n**o, o**n**e, te**n**
[ŋ]	wro**ng**, E**ng**land, tha**n**ks
[l]	**l**ike, o**l**d, sma**ll**
[r]	**r**uler, f**r**iend, so**rr**y
[w]	**w**e, **wh**ere, **o**ne
[j]	**y**es, **y**ou, **u**niform
[f]	**f**amily, a**f**ter, lau**gh**
[v]	**v**ery, se**v**en, ha**v**e
[s]	**s**ix, po**s**ter, ye**s**
[z]	**z**oo, qui**z**, hi**s**, mu**s**ic, plea**s**e
[ʃ]	**sh**e, bro**ch**ure, Engli**sh**
[ʒ]	gara**ge**
[tʃ]	**ch**ild, tea**ch**er, wa**tch**
[dʒ]	**G**erman, oran**ge**
[θ]	**th**ing, **th**ree, ba**th**room, mon**th**
[ð]	**th**e, bro**th**er, wi**th**
[h]	**h**ouse, **wh**o, be**h**ind

The English alphabet

a	[eɪ]	n	[en]
b	[biː]	o	[əʊ]
c	[siː]	p	[piː]
d	[diː]	q	[kjuː]
e	[iː]	r	[ɑː]
f	[ef]	s	[es]
g	[dʒiː]	t	[tiː]
h	[eɪtʃ]	u	[juː]
i	[aɪ]	v	[viː]
j	[dʒeɪ]	w	[ˈdʌbljuː]
k	[keɪ]	x	[eks]
l	[el]	y	[waɪ]
m	[em]	z	[zed]

GRAMMATICAL TERMS (Grammatische Fachbegriffe)

adjective	[ˈædʒɪktɪv]	Adjektiv (Eigenschaftswort)	good, red, new, boring, …
comparative	[kəmˈpærətɪv]	Komparativ	cheaper, more expensive
comparison	[kəmˈpærɪsn]	Vergleich, Steigerung	old – older – oldest
chunk	[tʃʌŋk]	zusammenhängende Wortgruppe	Would you like to …?
countable	[ˈkaʊntəbl]	zählbar	boy, girl, class, …
irregular verb	[ɪregjələ ˈvɜːb]	unregelmäßiges Verb	go – went – gone
form	[fɔːm]	Form	forms of "(to) be": am, is, are, was, …
grammar	[ˈgræmə]	Grammatik	
linking word	[ˈlɪŋkɪŋ wɜːd]	Bindewort (Konjunktion)	and, because, but, so
negative	[ˈnegətɪv]	negativ, verneint	I don't know …
(negative) statement	[negətɪv ˈsteɪtmənt]	(verneinter) Aussagesatz	I **don't** like pizza.
noun	[naʊn]	Nomen, Hauptwort	boy, mother, time, crab, …
numbers	[ˈnʌmbəz]	Zahlen	one, two, three, …
object	[ˈɒbdʒɪkt]	Objekt, Satzergänzung	Berry loves **animals**.
personal pronoun	[pɜːsənl ˈprəʊnaʊn]	Personalpronomen (persönliches Fürwort)	I, you, he, they, …
plural	[ˈplʊərəl]	Plural, Mehrzahl	apples, lessons, colours, …
positive	[ˈpɒzətɪv]	positiv, bejaht	I know …
(positive) statement	[pɒzətɪv ˈsteɪtmənt]	(bejahter) Aussagesatz	That was good. She's my friend.
possessive pronoun	[pəzesɪv ˈprəʊnaʊn]	Possessivpronomen	my, your, his/her …
preposition	[prepəˈzɪʃn]	Präposition	in, on, at, next to, under, …
present progressive	[preznt prəˈgresɪv]	Verlaufsform der Gegenwart	They**'re having** lunch.
pronoun	[ˈprəʊnaʊn]	Pronomen, Fürwort	I, you, he, it, …
question word	[ˈkwestʃən wɜːd]	Fragewort	what?, when?, where?, how?, …
regular verb	[regjələ ˈvɜːb]	regelmäßiges Verb	help – helped – helped
sentence	[ˈsentəns]	Satz	It's not new.
short answer	[ʃɔːt ˈɑːnsə]	Kurzantwort	Yes, I do. / No, I'm not.
simple past	[sɪmpl ˈpɑːst]	einfache Vergangenheit	Yesterday we **went** to school.
simple present	[sɪmpl ˈpreznt]	einfache Gegenwart	I always **go** to school by bike.
singular	[ˈsɪŋgjələ]	Singular, Einzahl	an apple, a lesson, a colour, …
subject	[ˈsʌbdʒɪkt]	Subjekt, Satzgegenstand	**Berry** loves animals.
superlative	[suˈpɜːlətɪv]	Superlativ	cheapest, most expensive
tense	[tens]	Zeit(form), Tempus	present tense, past tense
time phrase	[ˈtaɪm freɪz]	Zeitangabe, Zeitbestimmung	today, last week, …
uncountable	[ʌnˈkaʊntəbl]	unzählbar	sugar, weather, water, …
verb	[vɜːb]	Verb	go, see, like, …
word order	[ˈwɜːd ɔːdə]	Wortstellung	subject – verb – object (S-V-O)

LIST OF NAMES

First names (Vornamen)
Abi [ˈæbi]
Aidan [ˈeɪdən]
Albert [ˈælbət]
Alfie [ˈælfi]
Ali [ˈæli], [ˈɑːli]
Angelo [ˈændʒələʊ]
Anthony [ˈæntəni]
Ashling [ˈæʃlɪŋ]
Calvin [ˈkælvɪn]
Dave [deɪv]
Duncan [ˈdʌŋkən]
Elva [ˈelvə]
Elvis [ˈelvɪs]
Evie [ˈiːvi]
Hamish [ˈheɪmɪʃ]
Hana [ˈhænə]
Jamie [ˈdʒeɪmi]
Jeanie [ˈdʒiːni]
Jodie [ˈdʒəʊdi]
John [dʒɒn]
Jonas [ˈdʒəʊnəs]
Josh [dʒɒʃ]
Justin [ˈdʒʌstɪn]
Kara [ˈkɑːrə]
Lauren [ˈlɔːrən]
Leo [ˈliːəʊ]
Louis [ˈluːi]
Mara [ˈmɑːrə]
Mehdy [ˈmedi]
Michelle [mɪˈʃel]
Mo [məʊ]
Natasha [nəˈtæʃə]
Ninette [nɪˈnet]
Noah [ˈnəʊə]
Paddy [ˈpædi]
Patrick [ˈpætrɪk]
Rob [rɒb]
Roger [ˈrɒdʒə]
Roy [rɔɪ]
Ruby [ˈruːbi]
Sam [sæm]
Sarah [ˈseərə]
Sean [ʃɔːn]
Shelagh [ˈʃiːlə]
Sherlock [ˈʃɜːlɒk]
Tally [ˈtæli]

Family names / Surnames (Familiennamen)
Blake [bleɪk]
Burns [bɜːnz]
Butler [ˈbʌtlə]
Chung [tʃʌŋ]
Grant [ɡrɑːnt]
Harris [ˈhærɪs]
Holbek [ˈhɒlbek]
Holmes [həʊmz]
Johnson [ˈdʒɒnsn]
Johnston [ˈdʒɒnstən]
Jones [dʒəʊnz]
Kane [keɪn]
Malone [məˈləʊn]
O'Brien [əʊˈbraɪən]
O'Connor [əʊˈkɒnə]
Patel [pəˈtel]
Presley [ˈpresli]
Taylor [ˈteɪlə]
Timberlake [ˈtɪmbəleɪk]
Turner [ˈtɜːnə]
Wyles [waɪlz]

Place names (Ortsnamen)
Abbey Road [æbi ˈrəʊd]
Aberdeen [æbəˈdiːn]
Achill Island [ækɪl ˈaɪlənd]
Amazon River [æməzən ˈrɪvə]
Arizona [ærɪˈzəʊnə]
Atlantic Ocean [ətlæntɪk ˈəʊʃn]
Ballypatrick [bæliˈpætrɪk]
Beale Street [ˈbiːl striːt]
Belladrum [beləˈdrʌm]
Ben Nevis [ben ˈnevɪs]
Buckingham Palace [bʌkɪŋəm ˈpæləs]
Burkle [ˈbɜːkl]
California [kæləˈfɔːniə]
Camden [ˈkæmdən]
Canada [ˈkænədə]
Chelsea [ˈtʃelsi]
Clonmel [klɒnˈmel]
Derry [ˈderi]
Dores [dɔːz]
Dublin [ˈdʌblɪn]
Edinburgh [ˈedɪnbərə]
Egypt [ˈiːdʒɪpt]
Euston [ˈjuːstən]
Fort William [fɔːt ˈwɪljəm]
France [frɑːns]
Fulham Broadway [fʊləm ˈbrɔːdweɪ]
Glasgow [ˈɡlɑːzɡəʊ]
Glenfinnan [ɡlenˈfɪnən]
Graceland [ˈɡreɪslænd]
Grafton Street [ˈɡrɑːftən striːt]
Grand Canyon [ɡrænd ˈkænjən]
Hammersmith [ˈhæməsmɪθ]
Highbury [ˈhaɪbəri]
Hyde Park [haɪd ˈpɑːk]
Inverness [ɪnvəˈnes]
Islington [ˈɪzlɪŋtən]
Leaky Cauldron [liːki ˈkɔːldrən]
Leeds [liːdz]
Limerick [ˈlɪmərɪk]
Liverpool [ˈlɪvəpuːl]
Lochside [ˈlɒxsaɪd]
Los Angeles [lɒs ˈændʒəliːz]
Mallaig [ˈmæleɪɡ]
Manchester [ˈmæntʃɪstə]
Manhattan [mænˈhætn]
Memphis [ˈmemfɪs]
Moore Street [ˈmʊə striːt]
New Orleans [njuː ˈɔːliːənz]
Nuremberg [ˈnjʊərəmbɜːɡ]
Ormonde [ˈɔːmənd]
Oxford [ˈɒksfəd]
Paddington [ˈpædɪŋtən]
Piccadilly Circus [pɪkədɪli ˈsɜːkəs]
Queensway [ˈkwiːnzweɪ]
Rockies (Rocky Mountains) [ˈrɒkiz]
Rome [rəʊm]
San Francisco [sæn frənˈsɪskəʊ]
Shetland Islands [ʃetlənd ˈaɪləndz]
St James's Park [sənt dʒeɪmzɪz ˈpɑːk]
St Stephen's Green [sənt stiːvnz ˈɡriːn]
Stamford Bridge [stæmfəd ˈbrɪdʒ]
Temple Bar [templ ˈbɑː]
Tennessee [ˈtenəsi]
Tipperary [tɪpəˈreəri]
Tottenham Court Road [tɒtnəmkɔːt ˈrəʊd]
Union Chapel [juːniən ˈtʃæpl]
Victoria [vɪkˈtɔːriə]
Wales [weɪlz]
Warren Street [wɒrən striːt]
Washington DC [wɒʃɪŋtən diːˈsiː]
Waterford [ˈwɔːtəfəd]
Wembley [ˈwembli]
Westgate [ˈwestɡeɪt]
Westminster [ˈwestmɪnstə]
Wimbledon [ˈwɪmbldən]

Other names (Andere Namen)
Bakerloo Line [beɪkəˈluː laɪn]
buzz [bʌz]
Celsius [ˈselsiəs]
Condor Diner [ˈkɒndə daɪnə]
Cyberdog [ˈsaɪbədɔːɡ]
Darkuz [ˈdɑːkəs]
Eid al-Fitr [iːd ɔːl ˈfɪtrə]
Fahrenheit [ˈfærənhaɪt]
Garda [ˈɡɑːdə]
Gardai [ˈɡɑːdiː]
Gilmen [ˈɡɪlmən]
Golden Gate Bridge [ɡəʊldən ˈɡeɪt brɪdʒ]
Harrods [ˈhærədz]
Hogwarts Express [hɒɡwɔːts ɪkˈspres]
Jacobite [ˈdʒækəbaɪt]
Jubilee Line [ˈdʒuːbɪli laɪn]
Kelpies [ˈkelpiz]
Labor Day [ˈleɪbə deɪ]
Loch Ness [lɒx ˈnes]
Macbean's [məkˈbiːnz]
Marcellous Lovelace [mɑːˈseləs lʌvleɪs]
Mardi Gras [mɑːdi ˈɡrɑː]
Martin Luther King [mɑːtɪn ˈluːθə kɪŋ]
Memphis Echo [memfɪs ˈekəʊ]
Memorial Day [məˈmɔːriəl deɪ]
Mississippi [mɪsɪˈsɪpi]
Mona [ˈməʊnə]
Niagara Falls [naɪæɡərə ˈfɔːlz]
Oyster card [ˈɔɪstə kɑːd]
Tate Modern [teɪt ˈmɒdn]
Thames [temz]
Titanic [taɪˈtænɪk]
Urquhart Castle [ɜːkət ˈkɑːsl]
Wally [ˈwɒli]
Waterloo [wɔːtəˈluː]
Wiseguy [ˈwaɪzɡaɪ]

Answers to TEST AND CHECK!

Unit 1 → page 25

1 WORDS London words

1 Eye • minutes
2 Houses
3 Palace • King • Queen
4 dinosaurs • earthquake

4 points

2 SPEAKING On the Tube

Jonas   Excuse me, please. Which line should I take for Baker Street?
Woman   You need the Victoria Line.
Jonas   Do I have to change?
Woman   Yes, change at Green Park and take the Jubilee Line for Baker Street.
Jonas   Thanks very much.
Woman   No worries.

6 points

3 LANGUAGE Back home

1 anybody
2 anything
3 something
4 nothing
5 any
6 some

6 points

Tests 1 und 3: Für jedes korrekte Wort bekommst du einen halben Punkt.
Test 2: Für jeden korrekten Satz gibt es einen Punkt.

16–14 points	13–8 points	7–0 points
☺ Very good!	😐 OK, but you can do better.	☹ You should do more practice. Ask your teacher for help.

208   two hundred and eight

Answers to TEST AND CHECK!

Unit 2 → page 47

1 WORDS Town and country words

Lösungsbeispiel:
Town: department store, park, stadium, swimming pool, tall buildings, underground trains
Country: farm, farm gate, field, hill, sheep, track, village
Town and country: bridge, hairdresser's, post office, pub, river, shop, station

10 points

2 LANGUAGE A visit to a farm park

1 have
2 has
3 Have
4 have
5 have
6 have

3 points

3 WRITING A picture story

2 because
3 So
4 but
5 On Friday morning
6 and
7 That night
8 Suddenly

7 points

Tests 1 und 2: Für jedes korrekte Wort bekommst du einen halben Punkt.
Test 3: Für jedes richtige Wort gibt es einen Punkt.

20–17 points	**16–10 points**	**9–0 points**
☺ Very good!	😐 OK, but you can do better.	☹ You should do more practice. Ask your teacher for help.

Answers to TEST AND CHECK!

Unit 3 → page 69

1 LANGUAGE The phone on the beach

1. his
2. yours
3. theirs
4. ours
5. hers
6. mine

6 points

2 SPEAKING Booking a B&B

You	Hi. This is Simon Koch. I'd like to book two double rooms for tomorrow night.
B&B	Yes, no worries. The price is 110 pounds.
You	Is that with breakfast?
B&B	Yes, it is. What time will you arrive?
You	We'll arrive in the evening.
B&B	In the evening is fine.
You	Thank you very much.
B&B	No problem. Have a good journey! Bye.

4 points

3 READING A train trip in Scotland

1. true
2. true
3. true
4. false
5. true
6. false

6 points

Tests 1 und 3: Für jede richtige Lösung bekommst du einen Punkt.
Test 2: Für jeden korrekten Satz gibt es einen Punkt.

16–14 points ☺ Very good!

13–8 points 😐 OK, but you can do better.

7–0 points ☹ You should do more practice. Ask your teacher for help.

Answers to TEST AND CHECK!

Unit 4 → page 93

1 `WORDS` **Unhealthy food**

a candy/sweets, cookies/biscuits, French fries/chips, crisps, chocolate bars, cake, ice cream, sausages. *(3 points)*

b
1–F (to) win a competition
2–D (to) be good at business
3–E (to) catch a bus
4–C (to) go crazy
5–B (to) sell your bike to a friend
6–A (to) make money. *(6 points)*

2 `LANGUAGE` **Comparing**

Lösungsbeispiel:
AA is more expensive than BB. CC is the most expensive.
DD is more popular than EE. FF is the most popular.
GG is more exciting than HH. KK is the most exciting. *(6 points)*

3 `LISTENING` **The Memphis Music Bus Tour**

a 1 yes 2 yes 3 no *(3 points)*

b 1 They will talk and play music. 2 90 minutes. 3 28 dollars 4 lunch *(4 points)*

4 `WRITING` **A letter**

1 Sir/Madam
2 about
3 from
4 was
5 did
6 back
7 sincerely *(7 points)*

Test 1a: Für jedes korrekte Wort bekommst du einen halben Punkt.
Alle anderen Tests: Für jede richtige Lösung gibt es einen Punkt.

29–26 points
☺ Very good!

25–15 points
😐 OK, but you can do better.

14–0 points
☹ You should do more practice. Ask your teacher for help.

QUELLENVERZEICHNIS

Titelbild

Shutterstock/Lukasz Pajor

Illustrationen

Cornelsen/Roland Beier: U2 *computer icon.* **Cornelsen/Carlos Borrell Eiköter:** U2 *Karte,* U3 *Karte.* **Cornelsen/David Norman:** S.18 *unten;* S.19; S.22 *unten links, unten rechts;* S.33; S.34; S.35; S.36; S.37; S.38; S.40; S.43 *oben links;* S.47; S.48; S.49; S.61; S.80; S.81; S.82; S.83; S.84; S.85; **Cornelsen/Dorina Tessmann:** S.14; S.15; S.16; S.25; S.41; S.62; S.69; S.74; S.88; S.89 (Hintergrund Wetterkarten); S.93; S.94; S.104; S.111; S.112; S 113; S.115; S.128; S.131; S.133; S.134; S.135; S.136; S.137; S.138; S.139;151. **Cornelsen/Jeongsook Lee:** U2 a*lle icons außer computer;* S.126; S.154. **Cornelsen/Pete Smith:** S.43 *oben rechts;* S.55; S.57; S.58; S.59; S.60; S.121. **Cornelsen/finedesign Büro für Gestaltung:** *Rahmen:* S.20; S.44; S.56; S.70; S.91; S.134.

Fotos

akg-images GmbH: S.8 *(1):* De Agostini Picture Lib./W. Buss. **Belldrum/Tartan Heart Festival: S.67. Colourbox EU GmbH: S.63** *tomatoes:* Copyright by Birgit Korber – kb-photodesign, *bacon:* Viktor Lugovskoy; **S.75** *(3):* Enrico Mariotti. **dpa Picture-Alliance: S.9** *(7):* Andy Rain; **S.12** *(B):* NurPhoto/Kieran Galvin; **S.123** *oben re.:* PAL/United Archiv. **F1online digitale Bildagentur GmbH: S.125** *(3):* Naum Chayer. **Fotofinder.com: S.87** *(B):* hemis.fr/MAISANT **Glow Images GmbH: S.79** BlendRF/Blend Images LLC/Hill Street Studios. **imago stock&people GmbH: S.66** LNP/ZUMA Press; **S.70** blickwinkel; **S.75** *(5)* UPI Photo. **INTERFOTO: S.12** *(A):* LatitudeStock; **S.77** *(B);* (F): Friedrich. **laif: S.50:** hemis/Bertrand Rieger, **S.77** *(B):* Polaris/St Louis Post-Dispatch/Robert Cohen. **LOOK Die Bildagentur der Fotografen GmbH: S.76** age fotostock/Murray Lee. **mauritius images GmbH: S.9** (6): age fotostock/Charles Bowman, **S.12** *(C):* alamy/Ian Macpherson, *(D):* alamy/roger parkes, (F) alamy/Mark Richardson; **S.21** *rechts:* alamy/Peter Scholey; **S.25** *(4):* alamy/Mick Sinclair; **S.31** *(6):* alamy/Maurice Savage; **S.51** *(3):* alamy/Thornton Cohen, (6): alamy/David Hunter; **S.56** *house:* Senarb Commercial; **S.72** *oben:* alamy/Paula Solloway; **S.77** *(C):* alamy/Tim Graham; **S.97** alamy/Alex Segre; **S.119** *oben links:* alamy/A.P.S. (UK); **S.123** *Mitte li.:* alamy/Daniel Dempster Photography; **S.125** *(7):* JT Vintage; *(9):* alamy/Ninette Maumus. **Rockfinch Ltd./Claire Cunningham: S.4** *re. oben;* **S.10; S.24; S.46; S.68. Shutterstock GmbH: S.4** *oben li.:* Tom Stilwell, *Mitte li.:* Patryk Kosmider, *Mitte re.:* KateStone, *unten li.:* Rob van Esch, *unten re.:* travelview; **S.6** *oben li.:* f11photo, *oben re.:* East; **S.8** *(2):* Dan Breckwoldt, *(3):* Renata Sedmakova; **S.9** *(4):* McKerrell Photography, *(5):* QQ7; **S.17** *(1):* Mary Long, *(2):* Denis_M, *(3)*: art-sonik, *(4):* Greenclerk, *(5):* Vasilyeva Larisa, *(6):* Ivan_Nikulin; **S.18** *oben:* zhu difeng; **S.19** *chocolate cake:* jan_ta_r, *fish and chips:* Janet Faye Hastings, *salad:* DUSAN ZIDAR, *vegetables:* Robin Mackenzie, *soup:* MaraZe, *tea:* Africa Studio, *water:* Mariyana M; **S.20** *blue gloves:* SmileAon, *blue shirt:* mapichai, *blue socks:* Oleksandr Rybitskiy, *blue trousers:* mapichai, *green gloves:* Photo and Vector, *green helmet:* endeavor, *green trousers:* mapichai, *red helmet:* zawafoto, *red helmet:* NPavelN, *red shoes:* wk1003mike, *red trousers:* DESIGNER-XIXI, *white gloves:* BonD80, *white helmet:* pio3, *white shoes:* jocic, *white socks:* Bekshon, *yellow helmet:* wk1003mike, *yellow shirt:* mapichai; **S.21** *"thumbs up" symbol:* Holly graphic, *speech bubble:* Hollygraphic; **S.22** *(A):* Aleutie, *(B):* Millena, *(C):* Parinya Panyana, *(D):* bus109; **S.23** *map of London:* Art Berry, *train station symbol:* M-vector; **S.25** *(1):* Giovanni G, *(2):* Luciano Mortula – LGM, *(3):* Songquan Deng; **S.26** *oben links:* cycreation; **S.28** *oben:* Africa Studio, *unten:* Martin Rettenberger; **S.30** *(1):* Patryk Kosmider, *(3):* UTBP; **S.31** *(5):* Rolf G Wackenberg, *unten:* KateStone; *flag:* Maxx-Studio; **S.32** *(A):* Kekyalyaynen, *(B) rechts:* Phovoir, *(B) links:* **S**ally Wallis, *(C) links:* fiphoto, *(C) rechts:* oliveromg, *(D) links:* Deborah Kolb, *(D) rechts:* Maxx-Studio; **S.34** *flag:* Maxx-Studio; **S.39** *(A):* TTphoto, *(B):* Phonlamai Photo, *(D):* Pushish Images, *(F):* Rudmer Zwerver, *(G):* Master3D, *(H):* Golik Alexander, *(E):* Africa Studio, *(C):* Jim Cumming; **S.42** *(1):* Newman Studio, *(2):* Ralf Gosch, *(4):* Yulia_B, *unten:* Cultura Motion; **S.44** Deborah Kolb; **S.45** Africa Studio; **S.51** *(1):* Mick Harper, *(2):* Leonid Andronov, *(4):* jajaladdawan, *(5):* Richard Pinder, *unten:* Bobb Klissourski; **S.52** *(A):* Rob van Esch, *(B):* Simon Booth, *(C):* Targn Pleiades, *(D):* AridOcean; **S.53** *(F):* Dieter Hawlan, *(G):* Francois Loubser, *(H):* Jan Holm, *(E):* tony mills, *Beware of the Monster:* Jeff Morion; **S.54** *(A):* Anna Nahabed, *(B):* Mat Hayward, *(C):* travelview, *(D):* Tracy Whiteside, **S.55:** Gail Johnson; **S.56** *Hintergrund oben:* ags1973, *room:* ArchiVIZ; **S.62** *hat:* Bourbon-88; **S.64** DebsG; **S.65** 3RUS; **S.69** Milosz Maslanka; **S.71** *oben:* Iakov Filimonov, *Mitte:* antoniodiaz, *unten:* Syda Productions; **S.72** *unten:* Iakov Filimonov; **S.73** *oben* Fotokostic, *weather symbols:* En min Shen; **S.75** *(1):* TRphotos, *(6):* Tono Balaguer, *(4):* Galyna Andrushko; **S.77** *(D):* Natalia Bratslavsky; *(E):* Caron Badkin; **S.78** *Mitte links:* tishomir, *Mitte rechts:* Monkey Business Images, *Ben oben:* East, *unten links:* Monkey Business Images, *unten rechts:* SpeedKingz; **S.80** *(A):* Madlen, *(B):* Nata-Lia; *(C):* Rob Byron, *(D):* margouillat photo, *(E):* nito, *(F):* Ian 2010, *flag of England:* NirdalArt, *flag of USA:* Maximumvector; **S.86** *links:* NextMars, *Mitte:* BrunoGarridoMacias, *oben* Nearbirds; **S.87** *(A):* Leonard

QUELLENVERZEICHNIS

Zhukovsky, (C): Tala-Natali; **S.88** haveseen; **S.89** *weather symbols*: En min Shen, *flag of USA*: Maximumvector; **S.90** Olga Osadchaya; **S.91** *(A)*: Byjeng, *(B)*: Africa Studio, *(D)*: David Papazian, *(E)*: SpeedKingz; **S.95** Africa Studio; **S.99** Shutterstock/Room27; **S.101** *Wellen*: bus109; **S.105** *oben*: Semmick Photo; **S.107** *(A)*: Africa Studio, *(C)*: gopfaster, *(D)*: ElephantCastle, *(E)*: Hong Vo, *(F)*: gcpics, *(G)*: chuyuss, *(H)*: Jin young-in, *unten* Christopher Hall; **S.108** antoniodiaz; **S.109** *(A)*: Robert Adrian Hillman, *(B)*: Eviled, *(C)*: hxdbzxy, *(D)*: grocap, *(E)* DD Images, *(F)*: Jiffy Avril, *(G)*: Inspired By Maps, *(H)*: Marina Hannus, *(I)*: Halfpoint; **S.110** *oben links*: PavleMarjanovic, *oben Mitte*: VGstockstudio, *oben rechts*: SpeedKingz, *unten links*: Diego Cervo, *unten Mitte*: Mandy Godbehear, *unten rechts*: Tero Vesalainen; **S.118** *oben links*: Stefano Bellotti, *oben Mitte*: Samot, *oben rechts*: MagicBones, *unten links*: Tom Stilwell, *unten rechts*: Joan Connelly Manzo; **S.119** *oben rechts*: 470images, *unten links*: Alex Segre, *unten rechts*: Adrian Reynolds; **S.120** *oben*: Olga Sapegina, *unten links*: Michael Mantke, *unten rechts*: samritk; **S.121** Eskymaks; **S.122** *map*: leigh, *Mitte links*: Yvan, *Mitte rechts*: Robnroll, *(B) flag*: Maxx-Studio, *(B) money*: StockCube; **S.123** *unten li.*: DarkBird; **S.125** *(1)*: Sunny studio, *(2)*: Brent Hofacker, *(4)*: rozbyshaka, *(5)*: Tita77, *(6)*: Africa Studio, *(8)*: Ivan Marc; **S.126** *oben links*: Hong Vo, *oben rechts*: GreenTree, *unten*: Jacek Chabraszewski; **S.127** *oben*: Emilia Ennessy, *2. von oben*: Blend Images, *2. von unten*: Fresnel, *unten*: gpointstudio; **S.132** *links*: Shaiith, *ball*: The Cute Design Studio, *stick*: Tribalium; **S.139** *Mitte*: Roman Samborskyi; **S.139** *radio*: Nenov Brothers Images; **S.139** *sign*: Vitezslav Valka; **S.140; S.141; S.143; S.144; S.146; S.147; S.148; S.149** Ron Leishman; **S.150** *butcher's*: Arturo Limon, *chemist's*: Tyler Olson, *children's playground*: Againstar, *dry cleaner's*: sirtravelalot, *fast food stand*: oneinchpunch, *garage*: Dmitry Kalinovsky, *inline skate track*: Alexey Skumer, *petrol station*: Avesun, *skate park*: lzf; **S.152** *drums*: Milosz Aniol; *trumpet*: Vereshchagin Dmitry, *saxophone*: Mindscape studio, *oben rechts*: Alliance, *unten rechts*: karelnoppe; **S.153** *cereals*: mikute, *chocolate spread*: angelo gilardelli, *egg*: Karramba Production, *gherkins*: Andrey Starostin, *ham*: Viktor1, *honey*: DR-images, *jam*: Rafa Irusta, *pasta*: Aaron Amat, *rice*: showice, *trail mix*: Andre Bonn; **S.155** *oben links* Andy.M, *oben rechts*: Alexander Weingart, *unten*: budibubee; **S.156** *unten*: Hedzun Vasyl, *oben*: SLdesign; **S.157** Rvector; **S.158** *oben* saravector, *unten*: Brothers Good; **S.159** nullplus; **S.160** *oben*: Dim Dimich, *police officers*: CLICKMANIS, *dog*: fongleon356, *accident*: Kwangmoozaa; **S.161** *oben*: Sergey Peterman, *2. von oben*: MichalDobes, *2. von unten*: wavebreakmedia, *unten*: rainieC; **S.162** Peera_stock_foto; **S.163** *oben*: meunierd, *Mitte*: schab, *unten*: Alexander Raths; **S.164** *oben*: Vydrin, *unten*: Rvector; **S.165** *oben*: Evgeny Bakharev, *Mitte*: Peter Guess, *unten links*: koosen, *unten rechts*: artproem; **S.167** *oben*: lasha, *unten*: phive; **S.168** monticello; **S.169** *oben*: Bildagentur Zoonar GmbH, *unten*: worradirek; **S.170** *oben*: grmarc, *unten li.*: Aha-Soft, *unten re.*: LoopAll. **stock.adobe.com: S.17** *(D)* teracreonte; **S.30** *(4)*: Eric Carlson, *boy with green hat*: robyelo357; **S.39** *unten*: mikhailg; **S.42** *(3)*: Printemps; **S.54** *unten*: martincp; **S.75** *(2)*: TTstudio; **S.91** *(C)*: Prostock-studio; **S.107** *(B)*: Vladimir Konjushenko; **S.150** *baker's*: contrastwerkstatt, *ice rink*: zsv3207, *basketball court*: milanmarkovic78, *newsagent's*: contrastwerkstatt. **Cornelsen/Thomas Schulz, Teupitz**: **S.26** *oben rechts, unten*; **S.27; S.43** *unten*; **S.48; S.60; S.61; S.105** *unten*. **©Transport for London (TFL)**: **S.12** *(E)*; **S. 13**: Transport for London (TFL)/Registered User No 18/E/3283/P. **ZDF und Telekult Film- und Medienproduktion GmbH/interfilm Berlin Management GmbH**: **S.92** (Filmstills aus ‚Mo can tie a bow')

IRREGULAR VERBS (unregelmäßige Verben)

infinitive	simple past	past participle	
(to) be	he/she/it **was** you/we/you/they **were**	been	sein
(to) become	became	become	werden
(to) begin	began	begun	beginnen, anfangen
(to) break	broke	broken	(zer)brechen; kaputtgehen/-machen
(to) bring	brought	brought	bringen, mitbringen
(to) buy	bought	bought	kaufen
(to) catch	caught	caught	(ein)fangen; erwischen
(to) come	came	come	(mit)kommen
(to) cost	cost	cost	kosten
(to) cut	cut	cut	schneiden; *(Rasen)* mähen
(to) do	did	done [ʌ]	machen, tun
(to) drink	drank	drunk	trinken
(to) drive	drove	driven	fahren *(mit dem Auto)*
(to) eat	ate [et, eɪt]	eaten	essen; fressen
(to) fall	fell	fallen	fallen; hinfallen
(to) feed	fed	fed	füttern
(to) feel	felt	felt	sich fühlen; fühlen
(to) find	found	found	finden
(to) forget	forgot	forgotten	vergessen
(to) get	got	got	bekommen, kriegen
(to) give	gave	given	geben
(to) go	went	gone [ɒ]	gehen; fahren
(to) have	had	had	haben
(to) hear [ɪə]	heard [ɜː]	heard [ɜː]	hören
(to) keep	kept	kept	behalten
(to) know [nəʊ]	knew [njuː]	known [nəʊn]	wissen; kennen
(to) leave	left	left	verlassen; zurücklassen; abfahren
(to) lose	lost	lost	verlieren
(to) make	made	made	machen, herstellen
(to) mean	meant	meant	bedeuten; meinen, sagen wollen
(to) meet	met	met	kennenlernen; (sich) treffen; abholen
(to) pay	paid	paid	(be)zahlen
(to) put	put	put	stellen, legen, *(etwas wohin)* tun
(to) read [iː]	read [e]	read [e]	lesen
(to) ride [aɪ]	rode	ridden [ɪ]	reiten; (Rad) fahren
(to) ring	rang	rung	läuten, klingeln
(to) run	ran	run	rennen
(to) say [eɪ]	said [e]	said [e]	sagen
(to) see	saw	seen	sehen
(to) sell	sold	sold	verkaufen
(to) send	sent	sent	schicken, senden (an)
(to) show	showed	shown	zeigen
(to) sing	sang	sung	singen
(to) sink	sank	sunk	sinken
(to) sit	sat	sat	sitzen; sich (hin)setzen
(to) sleep	slept	slept	schlafen
(to) speak	spoke	spoken	sprechen (mit)
(to) stand	stood	stood	aufstehen
(to) swim	swam	swum	schwimmen
(to) take	took	taken	(mit)nehmen; bringen

IRREGULAR VERBS / ENGLISH NUMBERS

(to) teach	taught	taught	unterrichten; lehren
(to) tell	told	told	erzählen, sagen
(to) think	thought	thought	denken, meinen, glauben
(to) understand	understood	understood	verstehen
(to) wake	woke	woken	wecken
(to) wear [eə]	wore [ɔː]	worn [ɔː]	tragen, anhaben (Kleidung)
(to) win	won	won	gewinnen
(to) write [aɪ]	wrote	written [ɪ]	schreiben

English numbers

Cardinal numbers

- 0 oh, zero, nil [əʊ, ˈzɪərəʊ, nɪl]
- 1 one [wʌn]
- 2 two [tuː]
- 3 three [θriː]
- 4 four [fɔː]
- 5 five [faɪv]
- 6 six [sɪks]
- 7 seven [ˈsevn]
- 8 eight [eɪt]
- 9 nine [naɪn]
- 10 ten [ten]
- 11 eleven [ɪˈlevn]
- 12 twelve [twelv]
- 13 thirteen [θɜːˈtiːn]
- 14 fourteen [fɔːˈtiːn]
- 15 fifteen [fɪfˈtiːn]
- 16 sixteen [sɪksˈtiːn]
- 17 seventeen [sevnˈtiːn]
- 18 eighteen [eɪˈtiːn]
- 19 nineteen [naɪnˈtiːn]
- 20 twenty [ˈtwenti]
- 21 twenty-one [twentiˈwʌn]
- 22 twenty-two [twentiˈtuː]
- 23 twenty-three [twentiˈθriː]
- ...
- 30 thirty [ˈθɜːti]
- 40 forty [ˈfɔːti]
- 50 fifty [ˈfɪfti]
- 60 sixty [ˈsɪksti]
- 70 seventy [ˈsevnti]
- 80 eighty [ˈeɪti]
- 90 ninety [ˈnaɪnti]
- 100 a/one hundred [ə/wʌn ˈhʌndrəd]
- 101 one hundred and one
- ...
- 400 four hundred
- ...
- 1,000 one thousand
- 1,001 one thousand and one
- ...
- 5,169 five thousand one hundred and sixty-nine
- ...
- 100,000 one hundred thousand
- 1,000,000 one million
- 2,600,000 two million six hundred thousand

Ordinal numbers

- 1st first [fɜːst]
- 2nd second [ˈsekənd]
- 3rd third [θɜːd]
- 4th fourth [fɔːθ]
- 5th fifth [fɪfθ]
- 6th sixth [sɪksθ]
- 7th seventh [ˈsevnθ]
- 8th eighth [eɪtθ]
- 9th ninth [naɪnθ]
- 10th tenth [tenθ]
- 11th eleventh [ɪˈlevnθ]
- 12th twelfth [twelfθ]
- 13th thirteenth [θɜːˈtiːnθ]
- 14th fourteenth [fɔːˈtiːnθ]
- 15th fifteenth [fɪfˈtiːnθ]
- 16th sixteenth [sɪksˈtiːnθ]
- 17th seventeenth [sevnˈtiːnθ]
- 18th eighteenth [eɪˈtiːnθ]
- 19th nineteenth [naɪnˈtiːnθ]
- 20th twentieth [ˈtwentiəθ]
- 21st twenty-first [twentiˈfɜːst]
- 22nd twenty-second [twentiˈsekənd]
- 23rd twenty-third [twentiˈθɜːd]
- ...
- 30th thirtieth [ˈθɜːtiəθ]
- 40th fortieth [ˈfɔːtiəθ]
- 50th fiftieth [ˈfɪftiəθ]
- 60th sixtieth [ˈsɪkstiəθ]
- 70th seventieth [ˈsevntiəθ]
- 80th eightieth [ˈeɪtiəθ]
- 90th ninetieth [ˈnaɪntiəθ]
- 100th hundredth [ˈhʌndrədθ]
- 101th one hundred and first
- ...
- 400th four hundredth
- ...
- 1,000th one thousandth
- 1,001st one thousand and first
- ...
- 5,169th five thousand one hundred and sixty-ninth
- ...
- 100,000th one hundred thousandth
- 1,000,000th one millionth
- 2,600,000th two million six hundred thousandth

CLASSROOM ENGLISH

Du und dein Lehrer/deine Lehrerin
Guten Morgen, Herr/Frau …
Guten Tag, Herr/Frau …
Entschuldigung, dass ich zu spät komme.
Kann ich bitte das Fenster öffnen/zumachen?
Kann ich bitte zur Toilette gehen?
Auf Wiedersehen!/Bis morgen.

Hausaufgaben und Übungen
Es tut mir leid, ich habe mein Schulheft nicht dabei.
Ich verstehe die Übung nicht.
Ich kann Nummer 4 nicht lösen.
Entschuldigung, ich bin noch nicht fertig.
Ich habe … Ist das auch richtig?
Es tut mir leid, das weiß ich nicht.
Was haben wir (als Hausaufgabe) auf?
Entschuldigung, ich habe meine Hausaufgaben vergessen.

Du brauchst Hilfe
Können Sie mir bitte helfen?
Auf welcher Seite sind wir/steht das?
Was heißt … auf Englisch/Deutsch?
Können Sie das bitte an die Tafel schreiben?
Kann ich das auf Deutsch sagen?
Können Sie/Kannst du bitte lauter sprechen?
Können Sie das bitte noch einmal sagen/abspielen?

Partnerarbeit
Kann ich mit Julian arbeiten?
Wer ist dran?/Du bist/Ich bin dran.
Was machen wir zuerst?
Lass uns ein … machen/zeichnen.
Lass uns die Geschichte/den Dialog spielen.

Was dein Lehrer/deine Lehrerin sagt
Schlagt bitte Seite 8 auf.
Schreibt die Sätze ab und vervollständigt sie.
Korrigiert die Fehler.
Füllt die Tabelle aus.
Hört zu und macht euch Notizen.
Hört bitte zu./Ruhe bitte.
Ordnet den Sätzen die richtigen Fotos zu.
Wählt die richtige Antwort.
Arbeitet in verschiedenen Rollen.
Tauscht die Rollen.
Seid ihr fertig?
Macht bitte Übung … als Hausaufgabe.
Das ist alles für heute. Ihr könnt gehen.

You and your teacher
Good morning, Mr/Mrs … (bis 12 Uhr)
Good afternoon, Mr/Mrs… (ab 12 Uhr)
Sorry, I'm late.
Can I open/close the window, please?
Can I go to the toilet, please?
Goodbye./See you tomorrow.

Homework and exercises
Sorry, I have no exercise book.
I don't understand this exercise.
I can't do number 4.
Sorry, I haven't finished.
I have … Is that right too?
Sorry, I don't know.
What's for homework?
Sorry, I've forgotten to do my homework.

You need help
Can you help me, please?
What page is it, please?
What's … in English/German?
Can you write it on the board, please?
Can I say it in German?
Can you speak louder, please?
Can you say/play that again, please?

Work with a partner
Can I work with Julian?
Whose turn is it?/It's your/my turn.
What are we going to do first?
Let's make/draw a …
Let's act the story/dialogue.

What your teacher says
Open your books at page 8, please.
Copy and complete the sentences.
Correct the mistakes.
Fill in the table.
Listen and take notes.
Listen, please./Quiet, please.
Match the sentences with the right photos.
Pick the correct answer.
Take roles.
Swap roles.
Have you finished?
Do exercise … for homework, please.
That's all for today. You can go.